The Trial of Joan of Arc

The Trial of Joan of Arc

TRANSLATED AND INTRODUCED BY
Daniel Hobbins

Harvard University Press
Cambridge, Massachusetts
London, England
2005

Library of Congress Cataloging-in-Publication Data

Procès de condamnation de Jeanne d'Arc. English.
The trial of Joan of Arc / translated and introduced by Daniel Hobbins.
p. cm.
Includes bibliographical references and index.
ISBN 0-674-01894-X
1. Joan, of Arc, Saint, 1412–1431—Trials, litigation, etc.
2. Trials (Heresy)—France—Rouen.
I. Hobbins, Daniel, 1966–   II. Title.

KJV130.J625P76 2005
262.9'2—dc22   2005046382

To the memory of my uncle

Philip Trabue Woll

1952–2004

Acknowledgments

It is a pleasure to thank those who helped this idea become a reality. I wish to thank Elaine Scarry for taking an interest in the project and helping it on its way. Michael Bailey and James Mixson helped get the project off the ground, David Mengel generously created the map and helped with revisions, Christine Caldwell proved a valuable resource, as always, by reading a draft of the introduction and by offering helpful insights into inquisitorial theory, and John Van Engen carefully read the introduction and gave useful feedback. Rachel Koopmans in particular offered encouragement and support from the beginning, as well as a careful reading of the introduction at a critical stage. I would also like to thank my editors, Susan Abel, Kathleen McDermott, and Kathleen Drummy, for their assistance with the project, and the anonymous readers for Harvard University Press for their helpful comments and suggestions.

Contents

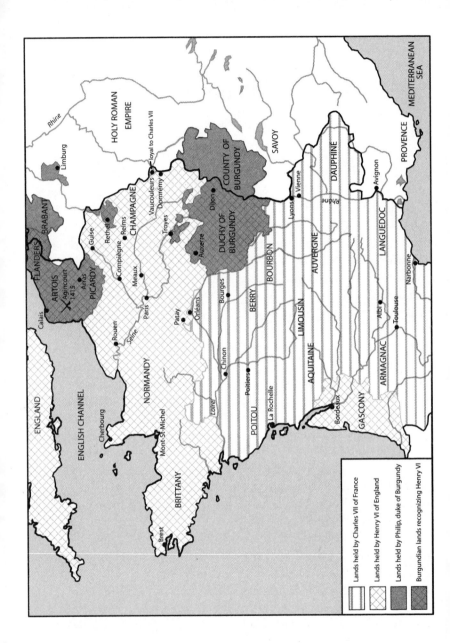

MEDITERRANEAN SEA

HOLY ROMAN EMPIRE

Rhine

Limburg

BRABANT

FLANDERS

Loyal to Charles VII

Calais

ARTOIS

Agincourt 1415

Arras

PICARDY

Guise

Rethel

Compiègne

Reims

CHAMPAGNE

Vaucouleurs

Domrémy

Troyes

Auxerre

Meaux

Paris

Seine

Rouen

ENGLAND

ENGLISH CHANNEL

Cherbourg

NORMANDY

Mont-St-Michel

Brest

BRITTANY

Patay

Orléans

Loire

Chinon

Poitiers

POITOU

La Rochelle

Bourges

BERRY

BOURBON

DUCHY OF BURGUNDY

Dijon

COUNTY OF BURGUNDY

SAVOY

DAUPHINE

Vienne

Lyons

Rhône

Avignon

PROVENCE

AUVERGNE

LIMOUSIN

AUQUITAINE

LANGUEDOC

Narbonne

Albi

Toulouse

ARMAGNAC

GASCONY

Bordeaux

Lands held by Charles VII of France

Lands held by Henry VI of England

Lands held by Philip, duke of Burgundy

Burgundian lands recognizing Henry VI

Note on the Translation

This translation is based on the Latin text of the trial found in the edition of Pierre Champion, *Procès de condamnation de Jeanne d'Arc* (Paris, 1920). I have also consulted the edition of Pierre Tisset, *Procès de condamnation de Jeanne d'Arc* (Paris, 1960).

The core of the Latin text is the so-called French minute of the proceedings. Following the trial, Pierre Cauchon had this French minute translated into Latin. He then gathered many documents relating to the trial (some in Latin, some still in the original French) and included them in the official Latin text. Finally, he "stitched" these materials together into a single text through various means: for instance, he introduced the entire compilation with an open letter, gave headings to the documents, and provided introductions and conclusions to each day's proceedings. For further discussion of this point, see the Introduction.

I have translated the entirety of Joan's testimony, and the vast majority of the text in Cauchon's compilation. In some cases, however, I have chosen to summarize rather than translate letters and documents that deal particularly with court procedure of less immediate interest. Academic specialists will of course continue to consult the Latin original in its entirety. Readers wishing for more than the summaries can turn to the complete translation of the Latin text in W. P. Barrett, *The Trial of Jeanne d'Arc* (New York, 1932).

To clarify the components of the trial, I have supplied headings to the documents. My own summaries appear in italics after the word "Summary." Text in square brackets indicates text that I have supplied to complete the sense of the passage, or information (such as dates) that is clear from the context. The French minute does not include most of the documents found in the Latin text, or some of the interrogation. But in common passages sometimes the French minute differs from or adds to the Latin text. I have used angle brackets around passages not included in the Latin text but supplied from the French minute. When the French minute has a different reading, I have placed the French text in a note. Among the seventy articles of accusation of March 27–28, the Latin text also includes a slightly earlier Latin translation of some of Joan's responses that were placed in evidence to support these accusations. Rather than reproduce this repeated testimony, I have summarized it and noted any significant differences from the official translation. In the interrogations of Joan, the verb tenses in the Latin text shift frequently from past to present. This inconsistency reflects the circumstances of the original trial, and the fact that at the end of each day's session, the notaries (with others present) recast their notes into a text of the proceedings for that day. As a general policy, I have allowed the tenses to stand as in the original, except when doing so would confuse the meaning. The text as it stands, I hope, gives the reader a better feel for the original atmosphere of the trial.

The Trial of Joan of Arc

Introduction

The trial of Joan of Arc began on January 9, 1431, and ended with her execution on May 30. Perhaps no event of the Middle Ages created such an international sensation. "Such wonders she performed," wrote the German theologian Johannes Nider, "that not just France but every Christian kingdom stands amazed."[1] News of the trial traveled swiftly, no less than had the news of Joan's first victory at Orléans in 1429. On June 8, the ministers of the English king sent a newsletter describing the trial to all the royalty of Europe. A second letter, on June 28 to prelates and nobility in France, ordered sermons against Joan. The preaching had begun by July 4.[2] At the same time, the trial was being reported in Venice, thanks to letters sent from Bruges.[3] At least nine of the trial's judges and assessors took the news to the Council of Basel (1431–1449), which served as a network for the learned from all over Europe.[4] The outcome was probably common knowledge in Western Europe by late summer, and it immediately became a favorite topic in contemporary chronicles.

Joan had been an international celebrity for almost two years by the time the trial began. Realizing the scrutiny that such a case would attract, her judges produced the most detailed trial record of the Middle Ages. Nine years later, Joan's companion in battle Gilles de Rais was put on trial for sodomy, human sacrifice, invocation of the devil, and the murder of perhaps hundreds of children. He was then Marshal of France, the most powerful military official and one of the wealthiest men in the country, owner of many castles and keeper of a large retinue.[5] His trial is about half the length of Joan's and, like nearly all medieval trial records, survives in a single archival copy, intended only for record keeping; Joan's trial survives in dozens of manuscripts, to my knowledge the only medieval trial copied in this fashion.[6]

Much of our knowledge of Joan's life, revelations, and character depends on the text of her trial. One point therefore needs to be clear from the outset: this was not a modern trial, nor should we judge it by how closely it approximates our own legal standards. For this document to speak to us, we must enter into the spirit of the trial, its text and its procedures, and by extension into the political, cultural, and legal world of the people who produced it. I begin, then, not with the life of Joan, but with the events immediately related to her trial, its key players, and the way they produced the trial record. Next, I turn to the reliability of this text, to the legal procedures embedded there, and at last to Joan herself. The journey toward Joan through the issues surrounding the text will, I hope, be as rewarding in many ways as the study of Joan herself.

For the most part, the circumstances that led to the trial are documented in the text itself. Convinced by her voices that she was to bring about the deliverance of Orléans from an English siege, Joan persuaded a royal captain at Vaucouleurs named Robert de Baudricourt to send her to the royal court at Chinon. Once she had arrived (March 4, 1429), she provided the French king Charles VII with a sign (the subject of endless speculation among contemporaries and modern scholars), and Charles sent her to Poitiers for examination by theologians and canon lawyers. After receiving their cautious approval, he sent her to Orléans, where she arrived on April 29; in a spectacular turn of events, the French broke the siege on May 8. More than anything else she accomplished, her supporters considered this victory the great sign of Joan's authenticity.[7] A series of further victories followed, leading to the coronation of Charles VII at Reims Cathedral on July 17.

The failure to take Paris in early September marked the end of Joan's successful campaign. She was captured outside the walls of Compiègne on May 23, 1430, by a follower of Jean de Luxembourg, a French lord devoted to the duke of Burgundy and the king of England, allies at the time. Just three days later, the vice-inquisitor of France wrote to the duke of Burgundy, urging him to surrender Joan to an inquisition. A custody battle ensued, during which the University of Paris played a key role in arranging Joan's transfer from the Burgundians to the English at Rouen for trial. Although Joan was a prisoner of war, she was also accused of heresy. Pierre Cauchon, the bishop in whose diocese Joan was taken, thus had jurisdiction over the trial with the inquisitor of France, Jean Graverent, who had other commitments and appointed Jean Le Maistre in his stead.

Jean Le Maistre was a cipher whose participation was quite accidental and possibly halfhearted; Pierre Cauchon (c. 1371–1442) was master of this trial. The pattern of Cauchon's career illustrates the complete interweaving of spiritual office with temporal authority that prevailed during this period. Like many others who came of age during the civil war between Armagnacs and Burgundians (1407–1435), including most members of the University of Paris and the citizens of Paris and a good many other towns,[8] he believed that the future of France lay not with the Valois dynasty that had produced the chaotic reign of the mad king Charles VI (r. 1380–1422), but in the dukes of Burgundy who ruled one of the most powerful states of Europe and in many ways set the cultural trends for the age even more than did the Italian city-states.[9] Trained as a canon lawyer at the University of Paris, Cauchon supported John the Fearless, duke of Burgundy (r. 1404–1419) at the Council of Constance (1414–1418) in opposing the leading theologian of the age, Jean Gerson, on the issue of tyrannicide. (The duke had arranged the assassination that led to civil war in the first place.) Cauchon soon rose to become bishop of Beauvais (1420) and then Lisieux (1432). A bishop in the Middle Ages was at the nexus of spiritual *and* temporal power: on the one hand a receptacle of divine grace passed down by the apostles in direct succession, but on the other a prince of the Church endowed with wide-ranging legal and political authority and temporal possessions. The Anglo-Burgundian alliance ratified at the Treaty of Troyes in 1420 drew Cauchon into the circle of English ministers. His participation in the Great Council of Henry V of England from 1422 and of Henry VI the following year placed him among the most powerful men of his world.[10] The new French king Charles VII (r. 1422–1461) represented for Cauchon not his true sovereign but the last obstacle to a powerful, independent Burgundy allied with the king of England. From our perspective the ultimate dominance of the French king and nation might seem inevitable, merely a matter of time, and all the French who supported Burgundy might appear traitors to the fatherland. This is an illusion produced by hindsight. Cauchon was a careerist, and in this respect neither more wicked nor more virtuous than other such men.

The trial included other officials, who can be mentioned more briefly. Jean de la Fontaine, chief counsel and examiner, interrogated Joan in several sessions; according to later testimony, he drew Cauchon's anger for counseling Joan and fled Rouen. In any case, he no longer appears in the record after March 28. Another interrogator was Jean Beaupère, a respected theologian who never accepted Joan's voices, even in later years when the political winds changed. Jean d'Estivet the "promoter," or prosecutor, presented "articles of accusation" against Joan.[11] Finally, Jean Massieu served as executor of writs (sometimes called the usher in English-language scholarship), and Guillaume Colles (alias Boisguillaume) and Guillaume Manchon as notaries. In all, 131 theologians, canon lawyers, clergymen, and abbots participated, most of them as "assessors," or advisers, all but eight of them French.

The trial began with a month and a half of procedural motions and investigations. The first public session with Joan took place on February 21, followed by further sessions over the next three months. On March 27 and 28 she was asked to respond to seventy articles of accusation; these were reduced to twelve, submitted to experts for counsel, and after another round of consultation with the faculties of theology and canon law at the University of Paris, brought against Joan at last on May 23. The next day, Thursday, at the abbey cemetery of Saint-Ouen, Joan interrupted the reading of the final sentence following the public sermon and repudiated her voices and men's clothing. After signing an abjuration, she was sentenced to perpetual imprisonment. But in her cell on Friday or Saturday she resumed wearing men's clothing. The judges interrogated her in prison on Monday, when she insisted once more that her voices were authentic. On Wednesday,

May 30, Joan of Arc was condemned as a relapsed heretic and burned at the stake in the Old Market Square of Rouen.[12]

The text that gives us access to this trial is an extraordinary witness to the life of Joan, her mental outlook, the social structures of the world in which she lived, and the unfolding of her trial. But it is not a word-for-word transcript. This point bears emphasizing, given the claim in the title of an older translation that one particular manuscript offers a "verbatim report" of the trial.[13] The record of the interrogations in its original form is better described as a summary of the interrogations. Testimony given at the retrial (discussed below) provides a fairly clear picture of how the text was put together. The interrogations were conducted and recorded in French, the court's procedure in Latin. During the sessions, the notaries Manchon and Colles took notes. We should not imagine a dictation system. Often, the scribes omitted questions and collapsed an entire series of Joan's answers which then appear as streaming monologue.[14] This accounts in large part for the apparent incoherence in some of her responses. Each evening after supper, in the presence of some of the assessors, the notaries compared their notes and drafted a text of that day's proceedings. This original record is known as the French minute.

The judges in any other case would have stopped there, but nothing about Joan's case was ordinary. Soon after the end of the trial, Cauchon ordered Thomas de Courcelles, along with the notary Manchon, to gather the many documents relating to the trial, to translate the French interrogations into Latin, and to put all of this material in order as a new copy of the entire proceedings. This task involved more than just translation; it was in part a work of authorship, producing what was essentially a new text, a narrative tissue weaving together the French minute and the supporting documentation. The trial in this Latin form was intended for distribution; it has been recast in the form of an open letter, addressed "to all who will read the present letter or public instrument." The new text introduces the trial to the reader; gives headings to the many documents; provides introductions and conclusions to each day's proceedings, including the list of assessors present; omits certain consultations; summarizes various procedures and deliberations; and organizes the whole around the framework of the translated French minute. It is thus a hybrid text that has taken on what we might call both documentary and literary traits: documentary traits, in that this is still at bottom an evidentiary text, much of it a record produced as witness to an event; literary traits, in that this is also a text that consciously addresses a class of readers the producers of a "document" such as an inquisition register would never have imagined. Although medieval inquisitorial registers might be consulted and recopied for archival purposes (there are cases of accused heretics being confronted with their testimony in previous trials), they were internal documents; their publicity value or public application was "virtually non-existent outside the trial context," writes one specialist, "even when they had some circulation beyond the inquisitor's possession of them."[15] This point is crucial: the events of Joan's trial underwent a double mediation, first through the scribes at the trial, and second through the judges for distribution. The fact that the text survived is not surprising. Cauchon ordered this Latin text copied and bound into books meant to be read and preserved. We should imagine the trial record, then, as a text consciously looking for a public and attempting to justify the trial—a point I will return to later.

In persuasive intentions, it would soon have competition. The end of the trial marked the beginning of a new chapter, sketched here only in the broadest outlines. English political control soon faltered. The Anglo-Burgundian alliance ratified in 1420 collapsed in 1435 with the Treaty of Arras, which brought together Burgundy and France. Paris returned to French control the following year. Capable generals and improvements in artillery both contributed to the final outcome: Rouen fell in 1449, and by 1453, the English had been driven completely from France, with the exception of Calais.

With the English in retreat, some in the French camp saw the opportunity to revisit the condemnation of Joan. Charles VII never breathed a word about Joan of Arc after her death, except in 1450 to launch an inquest into the original trial.[16] Perhaps he had lost all faith in her after her capture, as some historians have suggested. In any case, as an order from the king, this original inquest had no authority under the canon or Church law that had passed sentence on Joan. Only seven witnesses were interviewed in Rouen—Jean Beaupère still insisted that Joan was a fraud—before the inquest was canceled for reasons unknown.[17] In 1452, the papal legate to France, Guillaume d'Estouteville, renewed the investigation into the trial, again in Rouen.[18] First twelve and then a revised twenty-seven articles were drafted as the basis for the interviews. These articles charged the original trial with harboring irregularities, such as Joan's lack of counsel, her imprisonment in a secular jail, the length of the interviews, and the falsification of the trial record. The investigation concluded with the circulation of a summary of charges, but nothing more.[19] Pope Calixtus III agreed to a formal retrial in 1455; he appointed three commissioners, all supporters of Charles VII. Moving from Paris to Rouen to Orléans, the tribunal interviewed 115 witnesses, including participants in the original trial, friends and acquaintances of Joan, bishops, members of the nobility, and others. The outcome was inevitable. On July 7, 1456, before a crowd in the archbishop's palace, a copy of the original trial was torn and burned to symbolize the official nullification of the original trial's verdict. There was no discussion whatsoever about making Joan into a saint—that was the work of the twentieth century. The king simply wanted to clear the air and put the civil war behind him. No one was punished. Documents were burned, not human beings, writes Charles VII's biographer.[20] Joan of Arc's family went away empty-handed. But in the eyes of many, she had been vindicated.

Our focus is the trial itself. The challenge posed to any close reading of the trial text will be clear from this overview. What credit do we give a text that was generated by Joan's opponents?

The Reliability of the Trial Text

At the royal inquest of 1450, the notary Guillaume Manchon stated that while taking notes during the trial, "he was sometimes pressed by the bishop of Beauvais and the judges to write according to their understanding, contrary to Joan's meaning. Sometimes when they did not like something, they said: 'Don't write that. It doesn't help the case [against her].' But in everything he wrote, [he claims] he followed only his own understanding and conscience."[21] Such accusations against Pierre Cauchon, who had died in 1442 and provided a safe target, and against the English in general were repeated many times throughout the retrial. On the strength of such testimony some scholars have expressed skepticism about the reliability of the original trial record. Yet the whole point of Manchon's testimony here is to say that he resisted the pressure of Cauchon. It is in effect a defense of the original trial record. Nor is it an isolated one. Throughout the trial, Manchon and other witnesses consistently maintained that this record—including the Latin translation by Thomas de Courcelles—was a reliable account of what had happened at the trial.[22] Some of the strongest evidence for the reliability of the text of the original trial comes from the retrial, the same procedure that condemned the judges for the original trial.

Certainly, the political nature of the original trial should put us on our guard when we are dealing with the evidence produced by its judges—and so should the political nature of the nullification trial, conducted in a highly charged atmosphere when it was in no one's interest to defend the earlier verdict, Cauchon himself, or the English. (Even Cauchon's own heirs distanced themselves, noting that they had been children at the time.)[23] The verdict was a foregone conclusion, as much as with any trial in history. Nonetheless, I believe we can approach this text with confidence in its reliability. Here is why.

We possess the original manuscripts of the Latin text. The complete Latin text was transcribed into a register that is now lost; however, five official copies were at once made of this register, three of which constitute the text of the modern Latin editions.[24] The importance of this point should not be missed. Most medieval texts survive only in later copies. Rarely, an autograph copy by a medieval author is discovered. With the Latin text of the trial, we have three copies made by the notaries themselves. These manuscripts bear every mark of authenticity: one of the notaries signed the bottom of each recto leaf, then all three copied a formal statement at the end followed by their manual sign, indicating that they had collated the text with the original register and had been present at the trial. Finally, each manuscript bore the wax seals of the two judges, Pierre Cauchon and Jean Le Maistre.[25] Manchon testified at the nullification trial that one of the copies was given to the inquisitor, a second to Henry VI, and a third to Cauchon himself.[26] A fourth was ceremonially destroyed, and the fifth copy is lost.

The Latin text was composed immediately after the trial. The dating of the Latin translation is one of the more confused issues in scholarship on the trial and has serious implications for how we approach the text. As recently as the last edition, completed in 1971, scholars agreed that the translation was not made until 1435 at the earliest. It has since been demonstrated, I think conclusively, that it was instead completed in the months immediately following the trial, by November 30, 1431, at the latest.[27] Unaware of this argument (potentially crucial but buried in an obscure journal), some scholars have continued to cite the date of 1435 as silent evidence that the translation was a kind of retrospective rewriting of the trial in later years.[28] The implication seems to be that it produced a falsified official version, perhaps in response to support for Joan and growing criticism of the trial. The earlier date of 1431 suggests rather that the Latin translation was the last stage of the trial itself, Cauchon's attempt before putting the whole matter behind him to produce a document that by dint of the bulk of its accompanying documentation, its interminable lists of learned assessors, and its obsessive concern for forms, procedures, and consultations, would make a powerful argument for the procedural correctness of the trial. Once the interrogations of Joan were translated into Latin, the text could reach a select international audience. This conscious attempt at self-justification is to my mind the most striking feature of the document as a historical and legal text.

Comparison of the Latin text with the French minute provides further evidence of the reliability of the Latin text. The original French minute has disappeared. We possess two late copies, one from the late fifteenth, the other from the early sixteenth century. The author of an earlier English translation, arguing for the superiority of the French text, claimed that in the Latin text, "Cauchon deliberately ordered Courcelles to falsify the record in order to blacken the memory of his victim."[29] Such claims have never been demonstrated, and in fact comparison of the French minute with the Latin text reveals not systematic falsification but overwhelming agreement. For the most part, the Latin text is a painfully literal word-for-word translation. Nonetheless, the two texts are not the same, and the notes to the present translation include significant differences. A general description of these differences must suffice here.

To begin with, as an official compilation, the Latin text includes much more than does the French minute: numerous letters, consultations, opinions of individual masters, and conclusions of the faculties of theology and canon law at the University of Paris, among other documents. It also includes the so-called *libellus* of the promoter Jean d'Estivet, a list of seventy charges against Joan, as well as an independent Latin translation of selected responses of Joan from the French minute. Months before Courcelles began his translation, D'Estivet had translated these responses into Latin to support the seventy articles delivered on March 27–28 against Joan; Courcelles then inserted these translated passages into the Latin text following each of the articles.[30] In other words, embedded in the Latin translation is an earlier Latin translation that provides a check on Courcelles's translation in common passages. It thus happens that much of Joan's testimony exists in two independent translations in the same text.

For its part, the French minute includes a few items omitted from the Latin text, such as the opinions of specific masters on questions of procedure, including torture. Thomas de Courcelles, the Latin translator, was one of only three who recommended in favor of torture, and some have seen this omission of his own recommendation as proof of a cover-up. This is perhaps possible, though Courcelles left out the opinions of the assessors on other matters too, a fact suggesting that the omission on torture has more to do with his style of editing the document.[31] We might assume, incorrectly, that where the two texts disagree, the French minute should be preferred. The problem with this assumption is that the text of the French minute as we have it exists in two late manuscripts, one mutilated, the other the work (according to the editor of the Latin edition) of "an editor of feeble intelligence."[32] It is also possible that the French minute contained errors from the beginning that were silently corrected in the Latin translation. Each discrepancy must therefore be evaluated on its own terms.

A few discrepancies do indicate a possible attempt by Courcelles to modify Joan's testimony. On the first day of her testimony, in a long exchange between Cauchon and Joan over the oath, Joan refused time and again to take the oath to tell the truth about what she would be asked, insisting that she would not divulge her revelations. According to the Latin text, she finally capitulated at the end and dropped her condition. This assertion directly contradicts the French text, which says that she took the oath "but refused to tell anyone about her revelations." Again on February 24 the French text (this time supported by the *libellus* d'Estivet) contradicts the Latin text by adding a qualification to her oath: "But I won't tell all I know." In the testimony concerning Franquet d'Arras, a soldier executed at Lagny near Compiègne, the Latin text directly states that Joan had him put to death, whereas the French text says only that he was executed, and this reading is supported by the *libellus* d'Estivet. One last example involves a baby at Lagny, supposedly dead, that regained consciousness through Joan's intercession. The French text first describes the boy as "the child . . . whom she visited," whereas the Latin text describes him as "the boy . . . whom she restored to life," a wording emphasizing the direct agency of Joan.

Courcelles made several blunders and omissions, the kind to be expected in any translation. So on March 12: for "she thinks that she was around thirteen when the first voice came to her" in the Latin text, the French text provides a more likely reading, "when the voice first came to her." Nonetheless, when taken as a whole, and given the vast amount of testimony translated with perfect accuracy, in my opinion this is not much on which to build a case of conspiracy. There are no devastating discoveries here. The Latin text omits very little of substance from the French minute. One exception (Article 13 on March 27) is a few lines of testimony that actually would have strengthened the case against Joan. The text that we have is reliable. Of course it is possible that testimony was omitted in the first place. But here the question moves back to the original French minute, not the Latin text, and into the realm of pure speculation.

One issue remains regarding this issue of reliability, much more difficult to resolve: the posthumous information gathered on June 7 and relating mainly to events that occurred on the morning of Joan's execution on May 30.[33] The judges claimed that in the presence of at least seven witnesses in her cell that morning, Joan, seeing she had not been rescued, admitted that her voices had failed and deceived her and agreed with the clergy that they were evil spirits. The angel that brought a crown to her king, she admitted, was she herself, who merely promised him a crowning at Reims if he put her to work. "Joan was then of sound mind," stated several witnesses.

The purpose for including this information seems clear: to show that on the morning of her execution, Joan saw that no rescue was forthcoming and, in despair, at last realized her error. Unfortunately for Cauchon, since this interview was not part of the trial, the notaries were not present. They copied the information into the record but did not sign their names: all this posthumous information appears in the manuscripts after the closing formulas, seals, and signatures. Technically, it does not belong to the official record, clearly something Cauchon understood. Perhaps because this confession was what he had wanted all along, a serious blow to Charles VII, more than anyone else, Cauchon decided to include it following the official record. Another possibility, suggested by Cauchon's biographer, is that the English heard of Joan's admission from Cauchon and, finally aware of its political usefulness, pressured him to include it in the trial record.[34] He did so on June 7. The very next day, a general letter was sent out in the name of Henry VI to "the emperor, kings, dukes, and other Christian princes," recounting Joan's history, including the confession of the morning of May 30. The close timing of the gathering of the information and this letter does not seem coincidental.

We should not overlook the strong bias of the information of May 30. Nor, I think, can we dismiss the incident as pure fabrication. We know with certainty that this account was copied by June 7, just eight days after Joan's execution. Joan was clearly under immense pressure, particularly concerning her claims that an angel had brought her king a crown in the presence of witnesses. This was all along the weakest point in her testimony and the most likely to collapse under intense scrutiny. At the nullification trial, few witnesses said anything about this last interview, including a few who had been present, and the judges seem to have ducked the issue almost entirely—puzzling behavior, given the opportunity it offered to set the record straight.

I have argued for the general reliability of the official translation, and against the notion that the text was systematically and intentionally falsified. The text is certainly not a transparent account of what happened at the trial or of what Joan believed. Beyond the problem of the notaries abridging and summarizing Joan's responses and entirely leaving out certain questions, Joan was not speaking on subjects of her own choosing, she was appearing before a hostile audience, the tone or inflection of her responses is unclear (angry? sarcastic? obliging? concessive?), it is not always possible to tell who is questioning her— and the list could go on.[35] Yet such problems of mediation and selection are hardly unique to medieval sources. Not even a photograph can be taken as an unmediated representation of reality, after all. Too radical a skepticism is ultimately incompatible with the very discipline of history. The trial text is as rich a source as any we possess for the life of a medieval woman, a source that appears strong enough to allow us to hear Joan's voice through the layers of time, custom, language, and legal tradition that separate her from us.[36]

Inquisitorial Procedure

Most discussion of the trial text has focused on its content and largely ignored questions of form and procedure.[37] The text itself seems to welcome this. The riveting exchanges between Joan and her judges seem to offer a rarity for medieval texts, a recording of voices. Joan appears confident (to some) or saucy (to others), defiant, stubborn, contemptuous, eager to turn a proverb against her accusers: "Sometimes people are hanged for telling the truth," she says, when pressed to give details about the corporeal form her voices assume. Her judges appear more elusive—cool, faceless and impersonal, emotionless, inexorable, efficient. Yet for all the inherent drama of the trial scene, this text is not as transparent as it might seem. These exchanges occurred within a very specific legal context, alien to modern sensibilities, whose terms are not apparent from the text itself. To achieve any close reading of the text, we must come to terms with this legal context, though that challenge is not always taken as seriously as it deserves. Approaching this trial requires an effort of the imagination, informed by an understanding of that legal world, but also an awareness that it is a legal world that lies more than five hundred years distant. I make no claim to offer a new interpretation of the trial in the explanation that follows, only to make the text more accessible, and specifically to provide a short introduction to its legal form and context, inquisitorial procedure in general, and a few of the problems specific to this text.

Joan's trial was an ecclesiastical procedure covered under canon law, the law governing the medieval Church (much broader than modern canon law and affecting people's lives in countless ways, from marriage to testaments to relations with Jews). Canon law is to be distinguished from civil law, the law of the state, which had been inherited from Rome through the Byzantine (or Eastern Roman) Empire and lost to the Latin-speaking West until its recovery in the eleventh century by scholars in Bologna. Unlike civil law, which had been neatly organized and codified by Justinian in the sixth century, canon law was essentially a system based on precedent, like our own common-law system. In the mid-twelfth century, a lawyer named Gratian gathered together a bewildering variety of legal canons stretching back many centuries, including sayings of the Fathers, papal pronouncements, and conciliar decrees, and organized them into a collection known as *The Concordance of Discordant Canons*, which served as the first textbook on canon law in the medieval universities. Further collections of canon law were added throughout the rest of the Middle Ages, each one followed by numerous commentaries that were not without their own legal authority. The most important of these collections was the *Liber extra* of Raymond of Peñafort (1234), commissioned by Pope Gregory IX, the closest thing to an official lawbook of the medieval Church. Still, this was seen not as a code but as a collection of individual precedents and instructions of varying authority.[38]

The trial of Joan of Arc was a heresy investigation carried out under the legal procedure known in canon law as inquisition. At its core, inquisition was a trial procedure in which the judge himself (rather than a prosecuting attorney as in the United States) brought charges against a defendant. Though grounded in Roman law, inquisition had fallen completely out of use until its gradual reintroduction in the twelfth century through a series of decretals. Pope Innocent III re-issued previous legislation and in Canon 8 of the famous Fourth Lateran Council of 1215 established inquisition as a regular procedure; by the late Middle Ages, ecclesiastical courts had adopted it for nearly all trials. Though associated today with trial for heresy, inquisition was used in the prosecution of other crimes as well, such as adultery and fornication. The procedure soon spread to the civil courts, and it gained widespread currency in France following the legal reforms of Louis IX in the thirteenth century.

The emergence of inquisitorial manuals in the period after 1230 constituted a crucial development.[39] The very existence of such manuals is evidence of the challenges that inquisitors faced in translating canon law into practical trial procedures; it was no simple task to extract and determine correct procedure from papal letters and ordinances produced over hundreds of years in a variety of contexts. Designed at first to aid inquisitors battling Cathars in southern France, the manuals clarified and simplified the procedures for trying heretics. Customarily, a good manual would include definitions of different kinds of heresy, forms for citing witnesses, for questioning, for sentencing, and for abjuring heresy (often taken from actual cases), and lists of penances to be imposed. Although the manuals had no official legal status, in practice they took on a certain authority, while distancing the inquisitor from the actual collections of canon law. Emphatically not a simple translation of canon law for practicing inquisitors, these manuals, a distinct genre, might overlook earlier legislation. In a famous series of trials in southern France between 1318 and 1325, the inquisitor Jacques Fournier relied heavily on the manual of Bernard Gui, which ignored a newly published set of decretals, the *Clementines* of 1317, that clarified rules of procedure.[40] The inquisitorial manuals often borrowed from one another. Some of Gui's most important sources were earlier manuals.[41]

The essential feature of inquisition was that the accusation against the defendant came in the form of a public outcry or general belief that the accused had committed a crime. Unlike the earlier procedure of "accusation," in which one or more persons functioned as the accuser, in an inquisition the accuser was the outcry itself. Once infamy had been established—that is, the existence of public outrage—the bishop or another ecclesiastical judge could summon the defendant and investigate the truth of the accusations. The judge was to present the defendant with a list of charges in the form of chapters or articles. The judge could then require the defendant to swear an oath to tell the truth. Especially in the fifteenth century, the judge was assisted by a "promoter" who prosecuted the case, as in the trials of Joan and of Gilles de Rais. Unlike a prosecuting attorney, the promoter was not independent of the judge but carried out one function of his office, by filling the role of accuser. The manuals encouraged the judge to ask for assistance from experts ("assessors") in law and theology, a recommendation that Pierre Cauchon took very seriously, encouraging the presence of theologians, lawyers, and other dignitaries at every opportunity, to reinforce both the authority and the legitimacy of the trial.[42] Proof of guilt could be established through the testimony of witnesses or of the accused (the primary method in Joan's case), but the ultimate proof was confession. In strictly legal terms, the long interrogation of Joan was directed toward this one end. Here a role appeared for torture, which might encourage confession. Civil courts regularly used torture, which they had recovered from Roman law. In the early fourteenth century, however, Clement V regulated its use in ecclesiastical trials after abuses occurred. Although torture seems to have been used less often in the later Middle Ages (inquisition manuals and records rarely make mention of it), it certainly did not disappear.[43] Joan of Arc herself was threatened with torture—primarily, it seems, as a strategy to encourage her confession, though three of thirteen assessors did recommend its use.

The problem for us in trying to interpret procedure in the trial of Joan of Arc is in part a matter of continuity: to what extent did the forms and procedures outlined in the manuals continue in place, and to what extent were they modified, adapted, or ignored during the later Middle Ages? As the author of the most important study on inquisitorial manuals stated, "The rights of the judge were not the same in 1230 and in 1300."[44] Although the authors of the manuals no doubt desired to adhere to the law, canon law on inquisitorial procedure never achieved the kind of static sanctity that we associate with the American Constitution or the Bill of Rights. It was sometimes quite intentionally ignored, and the procedure varied according to time and place, often influenced by local custom or reliance upon one manual or another. Older books of canon law, we know, were read alongside the new; not everyone progressed at the same rate—a feature of the medieval Church in general.[45] Some canons took on great authority, others were neglected or superseded. The reputation of the pope behind each canon mattered. A good, authoritative manual was sometimes all the inquisitor needed, and it should not really surprise us that in following the manual of Bernard Gui, Jacques Fournier, for one, ignored recent modifications to procedure in canon law. This is not to imply that his contemporaries thought procedure was unimportant: the demand for the manuals on inquisition offers an indication not only of the difficulty of the task but also of a desire to follow correct procedure. But the rules were never as clearly defined or as uniformly applied and accepted as is sometimes assumed. Procedure for inquisitions evolved over time, and to speak of the "degeneration of proper procedure" when a trial seems irregular is to assume some golden age of inquisitorial regularity that never existed.[46] Such an assumption also overlooks the office of the bishop as a source of authority in its own right, apart from canon law. Bishops saw themselves as inheritors of an authority handed down by Christ to his apostles, and although claims to papal supremacy over the course of the Middle Ages had checked episcopal power, bishops retained tremendous autonomy in ordering their dioceses and in suppressing heresy.

Some scholars have dismissed Joan's trial as a travesty of justice—in the words of a respected historian, "the best known example of a . . . court violating generally recognized inquisitorial procedures."[47] The judge, Pierre Cauchon, has been denounced as a tool of the English who was willing to sacrifice Joan to further his own career.[48] The compelling opposition—Joan the heroine, Cauchon the villain—has long since passed into literature, such as Mark Twain's *Personal Recollections of Joan of Arc*. "A brute, every detail of him," says Louis de Conte, a fictional childhood friend of Joan, speaking of Cauchon, "and when I noted that all were afraid of this man, and shrank and fidgeted in their seats when his eye smote theirs, my last poor ray of hope dissolved away and wholly disappeared."[49] Cauchon packs the jury, manufactures evidence against Joan, and at last tricks her into signing the abjuration, only to have the guards force her back into men's clothing so that he can burn her at the stake. At work here and in many popular biographies is an instinctual sympathy for Joan, a belief that any trial that could have convicted her must have been irregular. Setting aside the question of blame for Joan's death (still a major concern in scholarship on Joan of Arc), I would like in this brief interpretation to emphasize the extent to which the trial followed correct procedure. Taken as a whole, the official text is weighed down with procedural materials (hence its length); if anything, Pierre Cauchon seems to have been obsessed with correct procedure.

In this context, two general observations can be made. The first concerns the Latin text intended for distribution. The existence of a full record of the trial, unparalleled for length and detail among the inquisitorial collections of the Middle Ages, indicates that the judges took very seriously the task of recording their involvement. Beyond this, however, the fact that Cauchon ordered a translation of the trial into Latin, supplemented by numerous documents witnessing the development of the trial from beginning to end, testifies to a certain self-satisfaction on his part. This translation is powerful evidence that he believed his role in the trial would bear examination from even hostile observers. He certainly understood from the outset that this case had international significance and that the official record would have to withstand scrutiny. Cauchon embraced that opportunity, in giving the trial international reach: he ordered it translated into a language accessible not only to the French, but to English, German, and Italian readers as well. For this reason, whenever we are inclined to find fault with the procedure of the trial, it is worth remembering that it was Cauchon who felt confident enough to circulate the text throughout Europe in the first place.

The second point concerns the ultimate fate of Joan and the blame that historians have often assigned to Pierre Cauchon for her death. The desire to villainize Cauchon seems to have begun at once. The attitude was well advanced by the time of the retrial and survives today in mainstream scholarship. The most famous Joan of Arc specialist of the twentieth century, Régine Pernoud, considered Cauchon the personification of those who were out to blacken Joan's name, "the first who manipulated texts and took part in a historical lie."[50] Yet seen from another angle, this trial was Joan's only real chance at survival. The letter of Henry VI on January 3, 1431, that is included in the official trial record makes clear that the English insisted on holding Joan in their own prison throughout the proceedings, regardless of the fact that this was not a civil trial. Henry's letter states in the clearest terms that if she is not convicted, she will be returned to English custody. Judging by the time it took to surrender Joan to Cauchon, the officials of Henry VI seem to have gone along with the ecclesiastical trial only reluctantly, perhaps persuaded by the compelling argument (made by Cauchon himself?) that this was the only real way to damage the reputation of Charles VII. Had Joan been returned to the English, or had there been no trial at all, she would almost certainly have been executed. Cauchon knew this perfectly well. The text thus invites a much more nuanced reading of Cauchon than the traditional view.[51] Even granting that he may have seen this trial as a way to advance the Burgundian cause, and hence his own career, by discrediting Joan, he may well have realized that the only way for Joan to survive was through an abjuration of heresy, in which case she would necessarily have been sentenced to perpetual imprisonment. If this was his plan, he nearly succeeded, and Joan's retraction on May 28 might well have come both as a disappointment to him on Joan's behalf and as a blow to his own fortunes. Presumably, a repentant Joan of Arc wasting away in prison and admitting her errors would have represented an outcome much more damaging to Charles VII than would her execution.

Bearing this in mind, we turn now to some of the central problems in the procedure of Joan's trial. Only selected issues are considered here; others are addressed in the notes to the text.

The Legal Basis for the Trial: Establishing Notoriety

Joan of Arc was tried as a heretic not because she was a woman, although that factor played an important part, nor because she heard voices, but because she heard voices telling her to attack the English. Joan believed that God favored the French: God was on her side. This problem surfaced several times during the interrogations, most clearly on March 17 in the following exchange:

> Asked whether she knows whether Saint Catherine and Saint Margaret hate the English, she answered: "They love what God loves and hate what God hates."
> Asked whether God hates the English, she said she knows nothing about the love or hate that God has for the English, nor what he will do with their souls; but she knows for certain they will be driven from France, except those who stay and die, and that God will grant the French victory over the English.
> Asked whether God favored the English when they were prospering in France, she said she does not know whether God hated the French; but she believes he wanted them to be beaten for their sins, if they were in sin.

As long as she insisted on this point, that her voices were saints telling her to attack the English, she was doomed. Such a claim challenged the legal basis for the Anglo-Burgundian regime formed by the Treaty of Troyes in 1420 and confirmed by the coronation of Henry VI as king of England and France at Westminster in November 1429 (largely in response to Joan's early victories), and of course the position of Cauchon within that world: he was present in person at the second coronation of Henry VI at Paris in December 1431.[52] Simply executing Joan as a prisoner of war was thus insufficient. Her judges needed to show that her voices were false. The motivation for the trial was political because Joan's claims were political: if true, they would have invalidated the English claim to legitimate rule in France. Of course, exposing Joan as a fraud, or as someone deluded by evil spirits, would also have struck at the legitimacy of Charles VII, who had been crowned in a ceremony in which Joan had played a prominent role, as the trial record itself makes clear. On the other hand, the theological task of demonstrating Joan's claims to be false opened the door to all the other accusations designed to show that Joan was a heretic, such as her clothing, her fighting, and her refusal to submit to the Church. This dual nature of the trial is what makes it such a challenge to analyze. To lose sight of either the political motivation or the theological demonstration is to invite confusion and misunderstanding.

This brings us to the technical procedure in place for trying heretics. Canon law required an inquisitor to establish the bad reputation *(mala fama)* of the accused before proceeding to an inquiry into the truth. In Joan's case, no witnesses were called to establish her notoriety; it was simply asserted. According to Hostiensis (d. 1271), the most important commentator on the *Liber extra,* establishing notoriety was crucial to the integrity of an inquisition, and this instruction found its way into the manuals.[53] Nonetheless, a moment's reflection on the nature of this specific case should be enough to enable us to dismiss this concern. From the moment of her victory at Orléans, Joan had become an international celebrity. The Burgundian chronicler Enguerrand de Monstrelet claimed that the English and Burgundian soldiers were terrified of her, and at her capture "more excited than if they had captured five hundred fighting men."[54] The very first lines of the trial insist not merely that she has been accused, but that she has achieved *international* notoriety for her crimes (wearing men's clothing, since this was her most visible transgression, but also unspecified errors against the faith). Similar claims are repeated in the letter to the duke of Burgundy dated May 26, 1430, in the royal letter of surrender dated January 3, 1431, and at various points throughout the trial itself. At Joan's first appearance on February 21, Cauchon emphasized how rumor of her crimes had spread through all Christendom.[55] It seems clear, then, that Cauchon believed Joan's infamy was self-evident. Nonetheless, in building his case Cauchon did not rely exclusively on general knowledge and rumors about Joan; he ordered investigations, one of them conducted in Joan's birthplace (no easy task, given that it lay in territory controlled by Charles VII), whose results were reported to Cauchon and others on January 13; on January 23 Cauchon ordered that further information be gathered. It is likely that many of the questions at the trial, including those concerning such matters as the suit against Joan for breach of contract and her encounters with Catherine de la Rochelle, were based on information gathered during this period. The original records of these investigations were already missing by the time of the nullification trial.[56]

The Articles of Accusation

Standard procedure called for an inquisitor to charge the accused at the beginning of a trial by means of articles; the articles then formed the basis for further questioning. In Joan's case, the judges provided the articles of accusation to the defendant only after questioning her for more than a month during the "preparatory trial." We know that articles were drawn up at the beginning of the trial; they are mentioned in the session of January 23 and were read on February 19, along with testimony from witnesses. But on the first day she appeared in court, February 21, Joan was simply told to take an oath to answer the truth to questions she would be asked. While it is conceivable that the trial record never recorded the reading of articles to Joan, her response to the request to take an oath indicates that such a reading had not yet occurred: "I don't know what you wish to ask me. Perhaps you might ask me things I can't tell you." The articles were finally read to her on March 27 and 28, the second and third days of the "ordinary trial."

Part of the difficulty concerns this division of the trial into a preparatory process and an ordinary trial, not found in other, contemporary trials, though traceable to thirteenth-century commentaries.[57] Rather than launch immediately into a formal trial, Cauchon chose to begin with a long information-gathering session, ostensibly to determine whether a formal trial was justifiable, as in our grand-jury system. I suspect that this was simply one more tactic devised to elevate the trial and to place it beyond reproach. The first stage of the information-gathering ended on February 19, with the decision to summon Joan "on a matter of faith." The inquisitor was then invited to join the proceedings, and Joan was formally summoned and interrogated over the next month. The text indicates that a change in procedure occurred in the ordinary trial. It states on March 26 that the trial had thus far been a process *ex officio*.[58] In such a procedure, the judge called witnesses and examined the accused on his own initiative. From March 26 on, the trial was designated as an ordinary process, beginning the next day with the bringing of articles by the promoter, after he had taken an oath. Though appointed at the beginning of the trial, the promoter had thus far technically been unemployed. The changes in procedure at the ordinary trial, then, concerned the reading of articles to Joan and the active role of the promoter, Jean d'Estivet, in accusing her.[59]

According to testimony given by Guillaume Manchon at the inquest of 1450, sometime during Lent of 1431 the canon lawyer Jean Lohier cast doubt on the validity of the trial because, among other things, the articles had not been read to Joan.[60] One scholar has suggested that Cauchon responded to this criticism by reorganizing the trial and creating this structural division to justify the delay in reading articles.[61] If so, it is further evidence that Cauchon was trying to follow correct procedure, even if it was only to protect the trial's reputation. In any case, if Cauchon violated procedure in failing to present Joan with articles at the outset (and some scholars think he did not), he does not seem to have been aware of it. Nor do his contemporaries. This failure to provide articles attracted no criticism whatsoever at the nullification trial.

In these circumstances, the issue loses most of its historical relevance. If contemporaries did not consider it a trespass not to present the articles at the beginning of the trial, then the problem seems one of our own making.

Appeals to the Pope

During the session of March 17, Joan requested to be taken to the pope, "and then she would answer him all necessary questions," a request she repeated on May 2. Finally on May 24, the day of her first public sentencing in the cemetery of Saint-Ouen, in response to an order to submit to the Church, Joan insisted that her answers and actions be reported to the pope. She was told in reply "that this was insufficient, that it was impossible to go find the pope at such a distance.

The ordinaries were her judges, each for his diocese, and therefore she must trust to Holy Mother Church and hold to what the clerks and the other experts have said and decided about her words and deeds. And we warned her three times about this." The judges at the nullification criticized this refusal to allow Joan an appeal, stating that Joan had often asked to be sent to the pope.[62] Such appeals were legally permissible, and although they were to be made in writing, the fact that Joan made the last appeal in public in such an exceptional case as hers might have carried some weight.

From a strictly legal perspective, then, we could question the refusal to grant an appeal. Yet any interpretation of the judges' behavior must also take into account the immediate circumstances of the trial. This was not a normal ecclesiastical trial, a simple matter of determining Joan's guilt or innocence.[63] The trial occurred only thanks to a concession from the English, who stood ready to invoke the clause that returned Joan to their possession if the ecclesiastical trial did not convict her. Joan's judges were severely constrained by the circumstances.[64] The English would surely never have allowed Joan to be sent to the pope on appeal, perhaps to regain her liberty and reignite the sputtering French cause. It is also quite possible that Cauchon genuinely believed the reason he gave to Joan, that each bishop was the judge in his diocese. This was a generally held principle of great antiquity, with the corollary that appeals should be made only in exceptional cases—otherwise, the authority of the bishop would be compromised. And if we know that Joan made these appeals, it is only because Cauchon permitted them to be included in the trial record (both the French minute and the Latin text). Cauchon seems to have been quite satisfied that he had acted within the rights accruing to his office in denying Joan's appeal, and he did nothing to remove her requests from the record.

The Relapse of Joan

One of the most vexed issues surrounding the trial concerns Joan's change of clothing. Shortly after her abjuration on Thursday, May 24, probably Friday or Saturday, Joan resumed wearing men's clothes. At the nullification trial, several witnesses accused the English of foul play. They attributed the change in clothing to an attempted rape by an English lord, Joan's fear for her own modesty, and the replacement of female with male clothing by her guards at night. These claims, repeated endlessly, have taken on a life of their own in the secondary literature, sometimes at the hands of authors with little firsthand knowledge of the sources. Without denying the possibility that Joan was harassed by her guards (this seems likely), I would like to consider the explanation offered at the condemnation trial, which seems to me on the whole more satisfying. According to this text, Cauchon heard news of Joan's reversion to men's clothing and arrived with several masters at her cell on Monday, May 28. They first asked Joan why she had changed her clothing and "who had induced her to do so." She answered that she had done so of her own will, "without being forced." Since she was with men, she explained, wearing men's clothing was more fitting than wearing women's. She had done so, she added, because her judges had broken their promises to allow her to go to Mass and to release her from her chains. Cauchon had also learned that Joan was hearing voices again. Asked about this, Joan freely admitted it and said that her voices blamed her for abjuring. When she had confessed on the scaffold, she insisted, she had not intended to deny her visions, but rather had abjured out of fear. All of it was untrue. She would put back on women's clothes if they wished, but she would not deny her voices again.

According to this version of events, the change in clothing was not accidental: it reflected a personal choice and an expression of Joan's will. Further, it was the outward emblem of her restored belief in her voices. Joan's belief in her private revelations, always the fundamental problem for her inquisitors throughout the trial, emerges here as the primary cause of her relapse. By the end of the interview, the clothes have become a secondary issue; she is willing to put women's clothes back on, but she will not deny her voices.[65] Joan saw her abjuration as a personal failure, spoken in a moment of weakness, out of fear of the flames—a transgression against her voices that put her in danger of damnation. At this point in the trial, her decision was made and her judges really had no choice but to deliver her to the secular arm as a relapsed heretic. Again, it is difficult to see how this was a personal victory for Cauchon.

We have been tracing the norms of inquisitorial procedure in order to make better sense of the trial. Some studies of Joan, starting from the assumption that procedure was flawed, seem to suggest that had her judges been honest men, they could have saved Joan. That expectation implies considerable confidence in the ability of inquisitorial procedure to safeguard the rights of the accused. It also presupposes that canon law was universally accepted as the basis for determining correct procedure—to the exclusion of local custom, popular inquisitorial manuals, informal inquisitorial lore, or the right of individual bishops to pass judgments in their dioceses. The official Latin text of the trial is a monument to correct procedure; its compilers were consumed with protocol. This is exactly what makes the text, in some instances, a tedious document: Cauchon's willingness to warn Joan repeatedly of the danger she ran and to consult with everyone possible. But in the end, as even some of Cauchon's strongest critics admit, procedure was not the determining factor.[66] To dwell on apparent procedural flaws is to miss the larger issue, that Joan's claim to hear voices telling her to attack the English put her in an untenable position, given which the trial probably could not have ended otherwise.

Joan of Arc, a Fifteenth-Century Woman

I have stressed the reliability of the trial text and its legal context in part out of a belief that it is still the best source for exploring the personality and motivations of Joan of Arc. Finally we arrive at the long-awaited question: Who was Joan? What context can we find for her claims and her mission? In many ways the character of Joan of Arc still eludes historians, perhaps in part because of the many roles she is made to play: pious peasant, mystic, martyr-saint, French patriot, protofeminist, and others. Yet not all these readings find equal support in the text of her trial.

The glamour of Joan, the spectacular success and personal courage that draw us to her and make her so attractive and exciting to study, raises problems for the historian. Consider this passage about Joan by Mark Twain:

> When we reflect that her century was the brutalest, the wickedest, the rottenest in history since the darkest ages, we are lost in wonder at the miracle of such a product from such a soil. The contrast between her and her century is the contrast between day and night. She was truthful when lying was the common speech of men; she was honest when honesty was become a lost virtue; . . . she was steadfast when stability was unknown, and honorable in an age which had forgotten what honor was; . . . she was unfailingly true in an age that was false to the core; . . . she was all these things in an age when crime was the common business of lords and princes, and when the highest personages in Christendom were able to astonish even that infamous era and make it stand aghast at the spectacle of their atrocious lives black with unimaginable treacheries, butcheries, and bestialities.[67]

Twain's disdain for the Middle Ages (also apparent in *A Connecticut Yankee in King Arthur's Court*), could not, it seems, encompass Joan of Arc. She received an exemption from the sin of inhabiting the fifteenth century; she usually does.

The perceived difficulty seems to be how such an extraordinary person got trapped in such a wretched world as that of the fifteenth century. This perception of a paradox in Joan, though it is a tempting point of departure, is, I suggest, a trap. Twain's understanding of the fifteenth century as a period of decline had deep roots in European history, reaching back to Protestant critiques of the Middle Ages in general and Enlightenment hostility toward the medieval Church in particular. Twentieth-century historians made it their task to revise this account. They uncovered a renaissance of learning in the twelfth century to match that of the sixteenth, and then, working backward, a Carolingian renaissance during the eighth and ninth centuries. But only in the last generation have some historians begun to rethink the model of decline or crisis in the later Middle Ages.[68]

It thus happens that Twain's sense that Joan was a paradox or contradiction in her own world continues to resonate in modern studies of Joan of Arc. In the best-known biography of Joan, Régine Pernoud saw the battles of the Hundred Years' War as having "little in common with the chivalric warfare of the twelfth and thirteenth centuries." Joan, insists Pernoud, would have none of it: "Under the command of the Maid, even warfare had briefly changed its face back to a world of honor."[69] Joan is for others the victim of a world in decline or out of joint: growing fears about witchcraft, a university at Paris that had lost its monopoly on power and needed to reassert itself, a papacy in disarray following the Great Schism. Joan, simple, pious, passionate, true, stands as a rebuke to her world.

These are seductive oppositions in a figure who seems to defy explanation and to transcend her age. But even if a view like Twain's makes for fine rhetoric, it does not constitute good history. Clearly, Joan was exceptional; but that statement left unelaborated becomes an escape from historical analysis. Joan of Arc was not a contradiction to her world but its product, and she is comprehensible only within the terms of reference of that culture. A historical approach to Joan must come to terms not only with Joan herself—going beyond the facts of her case to broach such questions as how she regarded her mission, her king, her country, her voices, and her enemies, as well as how others saw her—but also with the norms of her society, the roles open and closed to her, the influences on her, and any precedents that might afford us a comparison. Above all, we must search within that world for points of reference.

Consider one component of Joan's legend that is central to her identity and yet extremely difficult for modern readers to approach, her claims to revelation. Joan herself said that her voices were sent directly by God; during the trial, she identified them as Saint Michael the archangel and Saints Catherine and Margaret. There is a natural tendency to mute the clarity of these voices as Joan describes them, to think of them perhaps as mere whisperings, divine suggestions, or pious inclinations, or to hide the voices and their claims to truth inside invisible brackets, to put the question out of our minds. The text of the trial scarcely allows this. The voices directed her every move. As Joan describes them, they were corporeal beings with hair, crowns, and clothing. Joan claimed that she kissed and embraced them, that they emitted a sweet scent, that they spoke French, that they were not on the side of the English, that they were in the castle during the trial, and that at Chinon, an angel brought a crown and gave it to the archbishop of Reims who gave it to the king before named witnesses (though she retracted this claim at the end, if one accepts as authentic and true the report of the meeting in her cell on May 30). Finding a way to talk about these claims is one of the greatest challenges in dealing with this text, and no interpretation that dodges the issue can be fully convincing.

Claims about special revelation through private voices, made particularly by women but by men as well, were not new. Saints Bridget of Sweden (d. 1373) and Catherine of Siena (d. 1380), both of whom called for the return of the papal court from Avignon (its residence since 1309) to Rome, are cited most often in this context. But more immediate predecessors to Joan are poorly studied and often overlooked. The Great Schism of 1378, which produced rival papacies at Avignon and Rome, seems to have provided fertile ground for revelations relating to the institutional Church, which often had a connection to politics. Around 1384 a widow named Constance of Rabastens from Albi, who claimed to have conversations with Christ, opposed the count of Armagnac for supporting the English and called on a supporter of Charles VI, Gaston Phoebus, to save France, restore full authority to the Roman pope, and lead the king on crusade. A few years later Jeanne-Marie de Maillé (d. 1414), a noble-born widow renowned for her prophecies, used her connections to members of the most powerful nobility in France—including Louis II of Anjou, who later supported Joan of Arc—to obtain secret interviews in 1395 and 1398 with Charles VI. A third mystic, the peasant woman Marie Robine (d. 1399), is somewhat better known.[70] After being healed at the tomb of Pierre de Luxembourg at Avignon, she began having visions about the Schism and the French king. "Go to the king of France," her voice told her, "and tell him to make a union in the Church through the means I have confided to him through you; and let him beware of withdrawing obedience from Benedict XIII."[71] She arrived at Paris in 1398 to see the king but, on being refused admittance, settled for an interview with Queen Isabeau; Marie died a year later.[72]

Special revelations to women on matters touching the house of France were thus by no means unprecedented. The prophetess with direct access to God was an acknowledged type in this culture, implicitly recognized in a whole literature that offered guidelines to authorities on how to distinguish authentic from inauthentic claims to revelation.[73] Joan was born into a world where, given the right combination of circumstances, female mystics could expect an audience in the highest circles. When Joan appeared at court, Charles VII had points of reference; and though Joan would turn out to be exceptional even among visionaries, she nonetheless conformed to certain patterns—perhaps not fully understood or articulated by her contemporaries, but recognizable on some level in the back of their minds. The trial of Joan itself offers evidence of competing claims among such visionaries, in this case between Joan and Catherine de la Rochelle, whose claims to special revelation from "a certain white lady" Joan completely dismissed after consulting her own saints. Even to take up arms was not unprecedented for a mystic such as Joan. The contemporary *Parisian Journal* mentions a holy woman named Pieronne of Brittany who claimed that God often appeared to her in the flesh and who apparently fought with a friend alongside supporters of Charles VII.[74] The Dominican theologian Johannes Nider even describes a holy woman from Cologne around this time who wore men's clothing and had a career as a war commander.[75]

What Joan uniquely embodied, I would submit, was the peculiar blend of the visionary and the military persona, evident in her desire to lead troops personally toward a stated goal. In her interview with Charles VII, the two elements converge; her voices provided the authority for her mission, but her leadership, she believed, was essential to its success. In this interpretation, Joan wore men's clothing because she embraced the military lifestyle. The traditional or conventional aspects of Joan's religious beliefs and piety are generally recognized: her understanding of the sacraments, her knowledge of the creed and the basic prayers, her virginity, her devotion to the saints, her conformity to parish structures (obedience to local priests, for example), her sense of liturgical time, and her awareness of holy places.[76] The trial text and testimony of contemporary witnesses reveal to how great a degree Joan appropriated traditional features of the military lifestyle, especially the clothing, arms, and horsemanship. Before she set out for Orléans, Charles VII outfitted her as a military commander, with an entire household, complete with banners, pages, heralds, and guards.[77] Joan herself stated that Charles VII gave her ten to twelve thousand gold écus to wage war, five warhorses for her own use, and seven more horses for other purposes. She took great pride in her banner and defended its prominence at the coronation at Reims. Contemporaries commented particularly on the luxury of her clothing, a point of criticism at the trial.[78] This military identity was not merely a veneer. According to various witnesses at the nullification trial, Joan was skilled in the conduct of war, at not simply directing troops, but riding a horse, wielding a lance, and even preparing gunpowder artillery.[79] The ennoblement of Joan and her family by an act of December 1429 completed her transformation from peasant girl to military leader.[80]

Of course, this military role raises other questions. Even granting that she saw herself as a war captain, why did her soldiers follow her? And when the reverses came, why did she continue to believe in her voices? The trial does not provide all the answers about Joan, but in my opinion it is the best starting point for finding the right questions to ask. The text has more to offer. I have focused on the trial as a source for understanding Joan. It is an equally rich source for exploring the attitudes of her judges. Joan's utter belief in her voices permeates her testimony; her resistance to authority is one of the reasons she is so admired today. Her confidence was crucial to her success. Yet where we might see confidence, her judges saw arrogance and pride (*superbia, fastus, arrogantia*). Besides her boasting and the nature of her claims, which made Joan into the mouthpiece of God and invalidated all human authority, the tone or manner of her responses infuriated her judges.[81] They considered more than one of her claims outlandish and strange (*insolitus*). Read as evidence of the judges' attitudes, the text suggests that they were attempting to show not merely that her claims were wrong, but that they were preposterous. Very little work has been done in this direction, though the trial lends itself to such a reading.

I have only touched on the many links between Joan of Arc and her world. To see Joan as a reflection of her times should not diminish her. She played an important role at a pivotal moment in French history. She showed extraordinary courage in a hostile setting. She transcended her world to become an "image of female heroism."[82] But to cast Joan as a paradox or contradiction is to ignore the ways in which her career reflects some of the great trends in late medieval culture: the penetration of the Church into the lives of laypeople; the problem of ecclesiastical authority and who can determine the truth of contested theological claims, particularly those made by women; the drive for participation in the life of the Church and the challenges that presented; and a growing sense of regional and national identity.[83] Joan's life and the responses she evoked in her contemporaries were forged in the great contests of her age. The study of Joan's trial, therefore, need not end with Joan herself. The trial record is an unparalleled means for taking the measure of her personality and career, but it is also a window onto the strange and brutal yet fascinating world that produced her.

1

Preparatory Trial

Joan is questioned about her voices, conduct in battle, wearing of men's clothing, and other matters. Her
judges decide to proceed to an ordinary trial.

In the name of the Lord, amen. Here begins the trial in matter of faith
against a certain late woman, Joan, commonly called the Maid.

To all who will read the present letter or public instrument, Pierre,
by divine mercy bishop of Beauvais, and Brother Jean Le Maistre, of
the Order of Friars Preachers,[1] deputy in the diocese of Rouen and especially appointed to this trial by the pious and worthy Master Jean
Graverent of the same order, distinguished professor of theology and
by apostolic authority inquisitor of the faith and of heresy for all the
kingdom of France: greeting in the Author and Finisher of our faith,[2]
our Lord Jesus Christ.

It has pleased highest Providence that a woman named Joan, commonly called the Maid, should be taken and captured by renowned
warriors within our diocese and jurisdiction. The report has now
reached many places that this woman, utterly disregarding the honor
due the female sex, throwing off the bridle of modesty, and forget-
ting all feminine decency, wore the disgraceful clothing of men, a
shocking and vile monstrosity. Her presumption reportedly grew until
she dared to perform, to speak, and to publicize many things contrary
to the catholic faith and injurious to its articles. She was said to have
committed grave transgressions both in our diocese and in many
other places in this kingdom. When these matters came to the atten-

tion of the University of Paris and Brother Martin Billorin, vice-general for the reverend inquisitor of heresy, in great urgency they at once asked the illustrious prince the duke of Burgundy, and the renowned lord Jean de Luxembourg, knight,[3] who had power and authority over this woman at the time, in the name of the vice-general mentioned above and under penalty of the law, to deliver to us, as ordinary judge, this woman so denounced and suspected of heresy.

Now, since it falls to our pastoral office, we the bishop, greatly desiring to exalt and promote the Christian faith, have determined to conduct a proper investigation into these matters so widely reported and, as law and reason dictate, to proceed with all necessary steps according with mature counsel. To this end, we have asked both the prince and Lord Jean, under penalty of the law, to surrender the woman to our spiritual jurisdiction for trial; and the most serene and Christian prince, our lord the king of France and England,[4] has asked them as well. At length, the renowned lord the duke of Burgundy and Lord Jean de Luxembourg kindly agreed to these requests, and, as good catholic Christians, desiring all that would increase the faith, they surrendered the woman to our lord the king and his agents. Then the king in his wisdom, burning with zeal for the true faith, delivered this woman to us, so that we might fully investigate her words and deeds and proceed further, according to the laws of the Church.

Having concluded these matters, we asked the excellent and renowned cathedral chapter of Rouen, which had full spiritual jurisdiction during the vacancy of the archbishop's seat, to provide us with a place here in Rouen to conduct this trial, which they graciously and generously granted. But before we continued further against this woman, we ordered a full and mature consultation of learned authorities in canon and civil law, who, by God's grace, numbered many in Rouen.[5]

Tuesday, January 9. First day of the proceedings. Tuesday, January 9, the year of our Lord 1431, according to the rite and computation of the

Church of France, the ninth indiction, the fourteenth year of Martin V, pope by divine providence, in the residence of the king's council near the castle of Rouen.[6]

We the bishop assembled here the following doctors and masters: Gilles, abbot of Holy Trinity of Fécamp, doctor of theology, and Nicolas, abbot of Jumièges, doctor of canon law; Pierre, prior of Longueville, doctor of theology, and Raoul Roussel, treasurer of Rouen Cathedral, doctor of canon and civil law; Nicolas de Venderès, archdeacon of Eu, licentiate of canon law, and Robert Le Barbier, licentiate of canon and civil law; Nicolas Couppequesne, bachelor of theology, and Nicolas Loiselleur, master of arts.[7]

When this great host of famous masters had assembled, we asked them in their wisdom to settle on a form and order of procedure and explained to them the pains that had already been taken on this score. When they fully understood the situation, they said that certain information needed to be gathered, specifically the general reports circulating about this woman's words and actions. Acknowledging this advice, we described certain information that had already been collected at our behest, and decided that more was needed— all of which would be reported to the council on a day of our choosing, that we might see more clearly what remained to do in this part of the trial. Then the lords and masters decided that dependable officers were needed who could carry out these tasks with care and diligence. Following the masters' advice, we appointed the esteemed and wise Master Jean d'Estivet, canon of the cathedral churches of Bayeux and Beauvais, as promoter or procurator general in this trial,[8] and the learned Master Jean de la Fontaine, master of arts and licentiate of canon law, as counsel, steward, and examiner. Knowledgeable and respected men were chosen as notaries and scribes: Guillaume Colles, also called Boisguillaume, and Guillaume Manchon, priest, notaries by apostolic and imperial authority, of the archbishop's court of Rouen; while the reverend Jean Massieu, priest and dean of Rouen, was named executor of our mandates and summons. All these matters are described more fully in letters drafted for the creation of these offices. We have ordered that these letters, private and public, be gathered in order and copied here, to clarify the sequence of these matters.

First, there follows the letter of the University of Paris to the duke of Burgundy.

Letter of the University of Paris to Philip, Duke of Burgundy

Summary. *Refers to a previous request to deliver Joan to the Church, to be tried for her "idolatries" and other offenses against the faith; regrets that the duke has not replied; fears that the duke's enemies are attempting to rescue Joan "by some means"; states that her escape would be an incomparable evil; pleads again for the duke to deliver Joan to the inquisitor or to the bishop of Beauvais, "in whose spiritual jurisdiction she was captured." Undated.*

Here follows a copy of the letter of the University of Paris to the noble and mighty lord Jean de Luxembourg, knight.

Letter of the University of Paris to Jean de Luxembourg

Summary. *Thanks him for capturing Joan; expresses fear about the evil that would ensue if the woman were rescued or lost; reports that their enemies are attempting to rescue her by all available means, including ransom; insists that this must not happen; because delay is "perilous," urges him to deliver Joan to the inquisitor or to the bishop of Beauvais, her judges in matters of faith. Dated July 14, 1430.*

Here follows the letter of the vice-general for the inquisitor to the lord duke of Burgundy.

Letter of the Vice-General for the Inquisitor to Philip, Duke of Burgundy

Summary. *Martin Billorin to Philip, duke of Burgundy. Notes that it is the responsibility of Christian princes to stamp out errors, and that Joan has reportedly spread many of them; urges the duke, given that Joan is in his power, to surrender her to the inquisition for trial. Dated May 26, 1430, Paris. Signed: "Lefourbeur. Hébert."[9]*

Here follows the summons made by us the bishop to the duke of Burgundy and Jean de Luxembourg.

Summons of Henry VI and Pierre Cauchon to Philip, Duke of Burgundy, and Jean de Luxembourg

This is the summons of the bishop of Beauvais to my lord the duke of Burgundy and my lord Jean de Luxembourg, and to the Bastard of Vandonne,[10] on behalf of our lord the king and of himself as bishop of Beauvais:

Let the woman commonly called Joan the Maid, prisoner, be sent to the king for handing over to the Church to stand trial, because she is suspected and accused of many crimes: sorcery, idolatry, invocation of demons, and other matters touching the faith and contrary to it. Considering these things, it seems she should not be considered a prisoner of war. Nonetheless, to reward those who captured and detained her, the king wishes to pay them generously, up to the sum of six thousand francs. For the said Bastard, who captured her, he wishes to provide a sufficient income to maintain his estate, up to two or three hundred pounds.

And since this woman was taken within his diocese and spiritual jurisdiction, the bishop asks each of the above that she be delivered to him for trial, as befits his office. He is fully ready to hear the trial with the aid of the inquisitor of the faith, if need be, doctors of theology and canon law, and other experts in judicial matters, as the case requires, so that it may be conducted in a careful, holy, and sound manner, exalting the faith and instructing those who were deceived and abused by this woman.

And finally, if some or any of the above are dissatisfied with this arrangement or refuse to obey it, since the capture of this woman is hardly equivalent to the capture of a king, prince, or other person of grand estate (whom the king could ransom if he wished for ten thousand francs, according to the right, usage, and custom of France), the bishop summons and orders these persons to hand over the said Maid, and he will offer as a security a sum of ten thousand francs in full payment. And the bishop orders that she be delivered to him as stated above, according to the law and subject to its penalties.

Report of the Delivery of the Summons

The year of the Lord 1430, July 14, the eighth indiction, the thirteenth year of the pontificate of our most holy father Pope Martin V, in the fortress of the famous prince the duke of Burgundy, his army situated before Compiègne, in the presence of the noblemen Nicolas de Mailly, bailiff of Vermandois, and Jean de Pressy, knights, and a great host of other noble witnesses.

The reverend father in Christ Pierre, by grace of God bishop and count of

Beauvais, presented to the same famous prince the duke of Burgundy a paper schedule containing word for word the five articles copied above.[11] The lord duke handed the schedule to the nobleman Nicolas Rolin, knight, his chancellor, and ordered him to give it to the mighty nobleman Lord Jean de Luxembourg, knight, the lord of Beaurevoir. So ordered, the lord chancellor did in fact hand the schedule to Lord Jean de Luxembourg when he arrived; and it appeared to me that he read the schedule.

So signed: "This was done in my presence, Triquellot, public notary by apostolic authority."

Here follows the letter of the University of Paris to us the bishop.

Letter of the University of Paris to Pierre Cauchon

To the reverend father in Christ the lord bishop and count of Beauvais.

We are amazed, reverend father, by the great delay in the case of the woman commonly called the Maid, which does great harm to the faith and ecclesiastical jurisdiction, especially since she is reportedly already in the hands of our lord the king. Christian princes have always shown favor to the interests of the Church and the true faith, such that, if some zealot opposed the dogmas of the catholic faith, they would immediately deliver him to ecclesiastical judges for correction and punishment. Perhaps had you shown keener diligence in pursuing the matter, this woman's case would already be proceeding to an ecclesiastical trial. Since you hold an illustrious bishopric in God's holy Church, you have no small concern to suppress scandals against the Christian religion, especially when they fall into your jurisdiction for judgment. Therefore, to protect the authority of the Church from the great injury of further procrastination, may it please you to strive with fatherly zeal and utmost diligence to see that this woman is quickly delivered into your power and that of the inquisitor of heresy. Should this happen, please try in due time to bring her here to Paris, where there are a great many wise and learned men, so that her case can be diligently examined and expertly judged to the edification of the Christian people and to the honor of God. May he grant you guidance in all things, reverend father, by his special care.

Written at Paris, in our general assembly solemnly celebrated on the feast of Saint Mathurin, November 21, the year of the Lord 1430. Yours, the rector and University of Paris.[12]
Signed: "Hébert."

Here follows the letter of the University of Paris to our lord the king of France and England.

Letter of the University of Paris to Henry VI

To the most excellent prince, the king of France and England, our most dread and sovereign lord and father.

We have recently heard that the woman called the Maid has been delivered into your power. We rejoice greatly in this, confident that by your good offices the woman will be brought to justice to make amends for the great evils and scandals she has notoriously brought upon this kingdom, to the great prejudice of divine honor, our holy faith, and all your good people. By virtue of our profession it is our special duty to uproot such manifest iniquities, especially when they concern our catholic faith. For this reason, we cannot ignore the long delay of justice, which must displease every good Christian, and above all your royal majesty because of the great debt you owe to God for the surpassing wealth, honors, and dignities he has granted your excellency. Now we have written you several times on this matter, and we humbly beseech you again, most dread and sovereign lord, always offering our humble and loyal service, so that we may avoid any imputation of negligence in such a propitious and urgent matter. We urgently pray you, by the honor of our Savior Jesus Christ, to order that this woman be handed over to the justice of the Church in short order—that is to the reverend father in God our honored lord the bishop and count of Beauvais, and to the inquisitor for France, who are especially concerned with her misdeeds against our faith. Then a reasonable discussion can take place about the charges against her and the appropriate remedy, to preserve the holy truth of our faith and to banish all error and all false and scandalous opinion from the souls of your good, loyal, and Christian subjects.

If it please your highness, it seems best to bring the woman to this city for a well-regarded and sure trial, for her examination would attract more attention here than in any other place because of the great number of masters, doctors, and other notables. And it would be appropriate to apply the remedy for her scandals in the place where her actions were publicized and achieved great notoriety. In so doing, your royal majesty will ensure his great loyalty to sovereign and divine majesty. May he grant your excellency continued prosperity and endless bliss.

Written at Paris, in our general assembly solemnly celebrated on the feast of Saint Mathurin, November 21, 1430. Your most humble and devoted daughter, the University of Paris.

Signed: "Hébert."

Here follows the royal letter regarding the delivery of the said woman to us, bishop of Beauvais.

Letter of Henry VI regarding the Delivery of Joan to Pierre Cauchon

Henry, by the grace of God king of France and England, to all who will see this present letter, greeting.

It is sufficiently notorious and well known how for some time past, a woman calling herself Joan the Maid abandoned women's clothes and dressed and armed herself like a man, a thing against divine law and abominable to God, and condemned and forbidden by every law. She committed cruel murders and, as reported, seduced and abused simple people by trying to convince them that she was sent by God and knew heavenly secrets, with other dangerous beliefs most scandalous and prejudicial to our holy catholic faith. While fostering these deceptions and engaging in hostilities against us and our people, she was captured fully armed before Compiègne by some of our loyal subjects, then brought to us as a prisoner. And because many have suspected and accused her of superstition, of spreading false dogmas, and of crimes of treason against divine majesty, we have been urgently entreated by the reverend father our beloved and loyal counselor the bishop of Beauvais, ecclesiastical judge and ordinary of the said Joan (since she was captured and detained within the boundaries of his diocese), and have been urged likewise by our most dearly beloved daughter the University of Paris, to surrender Joan to the reverend father for questioning and examination, so that after gathering a proper assembly, he can proceed against her according to the rules and regulations of divine and canon law.

Therefore, for the reverence and honor of God's name, and to defend and exalt his holy Church and the catholic faith, and as a true and humble son of holy Church who devoutly wishes to obey the requests of the reverend father and the exhortations of the doctors and masters of our daughter the University of Paris, we order and consent that as often as the reverend father sees fit, this Joan is to be released and delivered to him by our guards and officers, that he may interrogate and examine her, and conduct his trial according to God, reason, divine laws, and holy canons.

We therefore command our men and officers guarding Joan to release and deliver her to the reverend father, without refusal or contradiction, whenever he asks them. We further command all our men of justice, officers or subjects, both French and English, neither to hinder nor in any other way to disturb him or any others who are ordered to attend, take part in, and hear this trial; but if he should ask them, they are to give them protection, aid, defense, and comfort, under pain of severe punishment.

Nonetheless, we intend to recover the said Joan if she is not convicted or found guilty of the above crimes or any one of them, or of some other crime touching our faith.

In witness whereof we have affixed our seal to this letter, in the absence of the Great Seal.

Given at Rouen, January 3, the year of grace 1431, the ninth of our reign. Signed: "By the king in his Great Council. J. de Rinel."

Here follows the letter granting territory to us the bishop of Beauvais, from the venerable cathedral chapter of Rouen during vacancy of the archbishop's see.

Letter of the Cathedral Chapter of Rouen Granting Territory in Rouen to Pierre Cauchon

Summary. Recounts that Joan, notorious for her disgraceful behavior and errors against the faith, has been captured in the diocese of the bishop of Beauvais, but that she has now been transferred elsewhere; that the duke of Burgundy and Jean de Luxembourg have delivered Joan to Rouen and surrendered her to the bishop; that she will be tried in Rouen, and the bishop has asked for territory to accomplish this; and that the bishop is therefore granted territory in Rouen. Dated December 28, 1430. Signed: "R. Guérould."

Here follows the letter appointing the promoter.

Letter Appointing the Promoter Jean d'Estivet

Summary. In appointing Jean d'Estivet promoter, Pierre Cauchon grants him the power to present articles, questions, witnesses, letters, instruments, and all other proofs against Joan; to accuse, denounce, examine, and question her; and to perform all other functions of the office. Dated January 9, 1431, Rouen.[13] Signed: "E. de Rosières."

Here follows the letter appointing the notaries.

Letter Appointing the Notaries Guillaume Colles and Guillaume Manchon

Summary. Pierre Cauchon appoints Guillaume Colles and Guillaume Manchon notaries in the case, granting them access to Joan, to question her or hear her ques-

tioned, to receive oaths and examine witnesses, to collect the statements and confessions of Joan and the witnesses, to collect the opinions of the doctors and masters, to report them orally or in writing to the bishop, and to record everything in due form. Dated January 9, 1431, Rouen. Signed: "E. de Rosières."

Here follows the letter appointing the counselor.

Letter Appointing the Counselor Jean de la Fontaine

Summary. *Pierre Cauchon appoints Jean de la Fontaine steward and counselor-examiner of witnesses, with the power to receive, swear, examine, and absolve witnesses, record their depositions, and perform all other tasks of the office. Dated January 9, 1431, Rouen. Signed: "E. de Rosières."*

Here follows the letter appointing the executor of mandates.

Letter Appointing the Executor of Mandates Jean Massieu

Summary. *Pierre Cauchon appoints Jean Massieu executor. Dated January 9, 1431, Rouen. Signed: "E. de Rosières."*

Saturday, January 13. The following Saturday, January 13, we the bishop assembled the following doctors and masters in our residence at Rouen:[14] Gilles, abbot of Holy Trinity of Fécamp, doctor of theology; Nicolas de Venderès, licentiate of canon law; Guillaume Haiton and Nicolas Couppequesne, bachelors of theology; Jean de la Fontaine, licentiate of canon law; and Nicolas Loiselleur, canon of Rouen Cathedral.

In their presence, we explained what had been done in the previous session, and asked for their advice on subsequent procedure. We further ordered the reading of evidence collected about this woman in her birthplace and in many other places, as well as specific notes on this evidence and on other things that were commonly reported. The masters then decided that articles should be drafted in due form, that we might arrive at a clearer understanding of the case so ordered, and that we might be more certain whether the evidence was sufficient to summon anyone in a trial of faith. On the advice of the masters, we therefore decided to proceed with the composition of these articles, and we entrusted the task to worthy and learned experts in canon and civil law, along with the notaries. And they diligently complied with our decision and undertook the composition of articles on the days following—Sunday, Monday, and Tuesday.

Tuesday, January 23. On Tuesday, January 23, there appeared in our residence at Rouen the reverend masters Gilles, abbot of Fécamp, Nicolas de Venderès, Guillaume Haiton, Nicolas Couppequesne, Jean de la Fontaine, and Nicolas Loiselleur.

In their presence, we ordered the reading of articles drafted at our command, and asked for their wise counsel on the articles and on subsequent procedure. They replied that the articles had been gathered and drafted in good and proper form, that a formal set of questions corresponding to the articles should be drawn up, and that we the bishop should proceed to gather information about the words and actions of the prisoner. Agreeing, we ordered this preparatory information to be gathered, but because we were otherwise engaged, we appointed the esteemed and wise Master Jean de la Fontaine, licentiate in canon law, to carry out this task.

Tuesday, February 13. On Tuesday morning, February 13, there appeared in our residence the reverend masters Gilles, abbot of Fécamp, Jean Beaupère, Jacques de Touraine, Nicolas Midi, Pierre Maurice, and Gérard Feuillet, doctors of theology; Nicolas de Venderès and Jean de la Fontaine, licentiates of canon law; Guillaume Haiton, Nicolas Couppequesne, and Thomas de Courcelles, bachelors of theology; and Nicolas Loiselleur, canon of Rouen Cathedral.

We summoned the officials already named and appointed in this case: the reverend Jean d'Estivet, promoter; Master Jean de la Fontaine, steward; Guillaume Boisguillaume and Guillaume Manchon, notaries; and the reverend Jean Massieu, executor of our mandates and summons. And we asked them all to take an oath to perform their offices faithfully; complying with our request, they swore between our hands to do so.[15]

[February 14–17.] Preparatory information gathered: Wednesday, Thursday, Friday, and Saturday. The following Wednesday, Thursday, Friday, and

Saturday, Jean de la Fontaine, steward, assisted by the two notaries, gathered the preparatory information as ordered.

Monday, February 19. On Monday, February 19, the year of our Lord 1431, about eight o'clock in the morning, there appeared at our residence <in the house of Master Jean Rubé, canon of Rouen,> the reverend masters Gilles, abbot of Fécamp, Jean Beaupère, Jacques de Touraine, Nicolas Midi, Pierre Maurice, and Gérard Feuillet, doctors of theology; Nicolas de Venderès and Jean de la Fontaine, licentiates of canon law; Guillaume Haiton, Nicolas Couppequesne, and Thomas de Courcelles, bachelors of theology; and Nicolas Loiselleur, canon of Rouen Cathedral.

We the bishop explained that after drafting articles based on reports about the words and actions of the woman whom our king had entrusted to us, as stated above, we had established a preliminary inquiry to determine whether there was sufficient cause to summon this woman in a trial of faith. Then we ordered the reading of these articles and the witnesses' depositions included in this information. After hearing and fully considering these matters, the reverend masters held long and mature consultation. Finally, on their advice, we decided that we had sufficient evidence to justify summoning this woman, and we ordered her called and summoned on a matter of faith to answer certain questions. Furthermore, to conduct the trial with all due dignity and profit, and out of respect for the Holy Apostolic See, which has appointed inquisitors of heresy especially to correct errors against the true faith, we have decided, on the advice of our experts, that the reverend inquisitor of heresy for the kingdom of France should be invited to join us in this trial of faith, according to his pleasure and interest. But since he was absent from Rouen, we ordered that his deputy at Rouen should be called and summoned.

The same day in the afternoon. The same Monday, about four in the afternoon, at our request there appeared in our residence the esteemed and wise Brother Jean Le Maistre of the Order of Preachers, deputy of the reverend inquisitor for the kingdom of France and appointed by him for the city and diocese of Rouen. Now, we had summoned the vicar, and we asked him to join and proceed with us in this matter, offering to take counsel with him about everything we had done or would do in the future. Le Maistre answered that he was prepared to show us his commission or letters of appointment that the reverend inquisitor had given him, and that he would gladly perform what the matter required for the office of holy inquisition, according to the commission. But since he was appointed specifically to the diocese and city of Rouen and since, although we had been granted territory in this city, we had received the authority to proceed in the matter by reason of our jurisdiction over Beauvais, he doubted that his commission extended to this trial. We told him to return to us tomorrow, and we would meanwhile take counsel on the issue.

Tuesday, February 20. The following Tuesday, February 20, there appeared before us in our residence Brother Jean Le Maistre, deputy of the reverend inquisitor, and Masters Jean Beaupère, Jacques de Touraine, Nicolas Midi, Nicolas de Venderès, Pierre Maurice, Gérard Feuillet, Thomas de Courcelles, Nicolas Loiselleur, and Brother Martin Lavenu of the Order of Friars Preachers.

We reported that we had seen the commission of the reverend inquisitor to Brother Jean Le Maistre and that, according to the experts to whom we showed it, since it covered the city and the entire diocese, he could join us and take part in the proceedings here in Rouen. Nonetheless, to ensure complete regularity in the proceedings, we decided to summon the inquisitor in letters patent, asking him either to come to Rouen himself to conduct the trial or to appoint a deputy with clearer and more specific authority, as appears more fully in the letters included below.

Brother Jean Le Maistre replied that for peace of conscience and for the smoother conduct of the trial, he would not participate in the proceedings until he had received authority to do so, and then only to the extent permitted him. Yet to the extent permissible, he was happy for us to continue the proceedings until he had complete instructions about whether his commission allowed him to officiate. Then once again we offered to inform him of all past and future proceedings. Next, on the counsel's advice, we ordered the woman to be summoned before us by letters of citation, transcribed below, on the following Wednesday, February 21.

First follows the letter appointing Brother Jean Le Maistre as vice-inquisitor.

Letter Appointing Jean Le Maistre as Vice-Inquisitor

Summary. *Jean Graverent appoints Jean Le Maistre vice-inquisitor. Dated August 21, 1424, Rouen.*

Here follows the letter that we the bishop sent to the reverend inquisitor of heresy.

Letter of Pierre Cauchon to Jean Graverent, Inquisitor of France

Summary. *Pierre Cauchon to Jean Graverent. Recounts that Joan has been taken and delivered to the bishop for trial, and that the bishop has been granted territory in Rouen to conduct the trial. With theologians, canon lawyers, and other experts assembled, the trial has begun. But as a matter of heresy, this trial particularly concerns the inquisitor, and therefore the bishop entreats the inquisitor to come to Rouen so that the trial may proceed. If the inquisitor is occupied, he may appoint his vice-inquisitor, Jean Le Maistre, or some other deputy, in order to avoid the charge of delaying the trial. Dated February 22, 1431, Rouen. Signed: "G. Boisguillaume, G. Manchon."*

Wednesday, February 21. First public session. On Wednesday, February 21, about eight in the morning, we the bishop arrived at the royal chapel of the castle of Rouen, where we had ordered Joan to appear at that day and hour. And we were seated in judgment, assisted by reverend fathers, lords, and masters: Gilles, abbot of Holy Trinity of Fécamp, Pierre, prior of Longueville-Giffard, Jean de Châtillon, Jean Beaupère, Jacques de Touraine, Nicolas Midi, Jean de Nibat, Jacques Guesdon, Jean le Fèvre, Maurice du Quesnay, Guillaume le Boucher, Pierre Houdenc, Pierre Maurice, Richard Praty, and Gérard Feuillet, doctors of theology; Abbots Nicolas de Jumièges, Guillaume de Sainte-Catherine, and Guillaume de Cormeilles, as well as Jean Guérin, doctors of canon law; Raoul Roussel, doctor of canon and civil law;

Guillaume Haiton, Nicolas Couppequesne, Jean Le Maistre, Richard de Grouchet, Pierre Minier, Jean Pigache, and Raoul le Sauvage, bachelors of theology; Robert Le Barbier, Denis Gastinel, Jean le Doux, Nicolas de Venderès, Jean Basset, Jean de la Fontaine, Jean Bruillot, Aubert Morel, Jean Colombel, Laurent du Busc, and Raoul Anguy, licentiates of canon law; and André Marguerie, Jean Alespée, Geoffroi du Crotay, and Gilles Deschamps, licentiates of civil law.

In their presence the letter from the king, detailing the woman's surrender and her delivery to us, was read, then the letter from the chapter of Rouen granting us territory; these letters are given above. Then the reverend Jean d'Estivet, our promoter for this trial, reported that the woman named Joan had been summoned by our official executor to appear on this day and hour to answer questions according to the law, as shown by the executor's report attached to our summons.

Here follow the summons and report.

Summons from Pierre Cauchon, Ordering Joan to Appear

Pierre, by divine mercy bishop of Beauvais, holding territory in the city and diocese of Rouen from the cathedral chapter during the vacancy of the archbishop's seat, in order to conduct and conclude the matter described below, to the rural dean of Rouen and to all priests of this city and diocese who read this letter, whether charged with care of souls or not: greeting in the Author and Finisher of our faith, our Lord Jesus Christ.

A certain woman commonly called Joan the Maid was caught and taken in our diocese of Beauvais, and our most serene and Christian prince the king of France and England delivered and released her entirely to us, under grave suspicion of heresy, that we might initiate proceedings against her in matters of faith. And since reports of her damaging words and acts had spread not only throughout France but even to all Christian lands, we gathered evidence and sought learned counsel, wishing to proceed in this matter with mature reflection; and we have ordered that this Joan be summoned, cited, and heard upon the articles and formal questions prepared against her, and upon matters of faith. We charge each one of you, if summoned, not to wait for someone else, nor to excuse himself. Therefore, peremptorily summon the said Joan, so gravely suspect of heresy, to appear before us in the royal chapel of the castle of Rouen at eight o'clock in the morning of Wednesday, February 21, to answer the truth to the articles and questions and to other accusations, and to be dealt with according to law and reason; and intimate that we shall excommunicate her if she does not appear on that day. You who execute the summons, send us a faithful report.

Given at Rouen under our seal, the year of the Lord 1431, Tuesday, February 20. Signed: "G. Boisguillaume, G. Manchon"

Report of the Executor Jean Massieu That the Summons Was Carried Out

Summary. Jean Massieu, executor, reports to Pierre Cauchon that Joan has been cited to appear at eight o'clock in the morning on Wednesday, February 21, in the royal chapel of Rouen. She has replied that she will willingly appear and answer the truth to the questions asked her. She has also requested "that you would assemble as many clergy from France as from England" and further asked to hear Mass tomorrow before her appearance, and that the bishop be informed of these requests. Dated February 20, 1431. Signed: "Jean."

The Promoter's Petition

Then, after the reading of these letters, the promoter urgently requested that the woman be ordered to appear before us in judgment, according to her summons, to be examined on specific articles of faith; and we granted this request. In the meantime, since the woman had asked to hear Mass first, we explained to the assembly that we had consulted with worthy lords and masters, and that, given the crimes of which she was accused and the shameful attire she insisted on wearing, they had decided we should postpone permission for her to hear Mass or attend divine office.

Joan Is Led to the Audience

As we spoke, the executor led in the woman. Now that she had appeared at court, we explained that this Joan had been taken and captured recently within our diocese of Beauvais, that reports in nearly every Christian land told of her many actions harming the true faith, committed not just in our diocese but in many other places, and that a short time ago, the most serene and Christian prince, our lord the king, had brought and delivered her to us, that a procedure might be brought against her in matters of faith, in accordance with law and reason. So after considering the common report and public rumors, as well as the reliable information mentioned above, and after mature counsel with experts in canon and civil law, we ordered that this Joan be summoned in writing to answer truthfully the questions put to her in matters of faith, and that she act according to law and reason, as set forth in letters shown by the promoter.

The First Exhortation Made to Joan

Desiring then to fulfill our duty in this trial to protect and exalt the catholic faith, and with the kind aid of Jesus Christ, whom this trial concerns, we kindly advised and requested Joan, seated before us, to answer the full truth to questions in matters of faith, both to expedite the trial and to unburden her own conscience; and to avoid subterfuge or stratagems that would prevent honest replies.

Request to Take an Oath

What is more, by virtue of our office we judicially requested Joan to take an oath in due form, touching Holy Gospels, to tell the truth concerning the things she would be questioned about, as mentioned earlier.[16]

Joan answered: "I don't know what you wish to ask me. Perhaps you might ask me things I can't tell you."

But when we said to her: "You will swear to tell the truth about the things we ask you that concern the faith, and <all the other things> that you know," she answered in reply that she would gladly swear concerning her father and mother and the things she had done after her journey had taken her to France, but that she had never told or revealed to anyone the revelations to her from God, except to Charles alone, whom she calls her king, nor would she reveal them, even were it necessary to cut off her head; that she believed her visions or her secret counsel forbade her to reveal them to anyone and that within eight days she would know very well whether she should reveal them.

And once again and then several more times, we the bishop advised and requested Joan please to take an oath to tell the truth in things touching our faith. Then kneeling and placing both hands on a book, a missal, Joan swore to tell the truth about the things to be asked her that she knew concerning the faith, but she said nothing about the condition mentioned previously, namely that she would neither tell nor reveal to anyone the revelations made to her.[17]

First Interrogation after the Oath

After she took the oath in this way, we questioned Joan about her given name and surname. She answered that she was called Jeannette in her region, and Joan [Jeanne] after she came to France. But of her surname she said she knew nothing.

Asked her birthplace, she replied that she was born in the village of Domrémy, which is adjacent to the village of Greux, and the principal church is in Greux.[18]

Asked the names of her father and mother, she replied that her father was called Jacques d'Arc, her mother Isabelle.[19]

Asked where she was baptized, she replied, in the church of Domrémy.

Asked who her godfathers and godmothers were, she said that one of her godmothers was named Agnes, another Joan, another Sibylle; and one of her godfathers was named Jean Lingué, and another Jean Barrey. She heard from her mother that she had many other godmothers.

Asked what priest had baptized her, she replied that she thought it was the reverend Jean Minet.

Asked whether he was alive, she said yes, to the best of her belief.

Asked how old she was, she replied, around nineteen years, so it seems. She said further that she had learned the Our Father, the Hail Mary, and the creed from her mother, and that she had learned her beliefs only from her mother.

Asked by us to say the Our Father, she said that if we would hear her confession, she would gladly say it to us. And after we asked her many times to say it, she replied that she would not say the Our Father unless we heard her confession. Then we said we would gladly provide her with one or two notable men of the French tongue[20] to hear her say the Our Father. But Joan replied that she would say it to them only in confession.

Then we the bishop forbade Joan to return from her prison cells in the castle of Rouen without our leave, under pain of conviction of the crime of heresy. But she said she did not accept this prohibition and stated further that if she escaped, no one could accuse her of breaking or violating her oath, since she had never given an oath to anyone. Finally, she complained of being bound in iron chains and fetters. We told her that in other places she had often tried to escape from prison, and for this reason, to guard her more safely and securely, an order had been given to shackle her with iron chains. She replied: "It's true that I wanted to escape from other prisons and that I still do, as is allowable for any captive or prisoner."

Then we committed Joan to the safekeeping of the nobleman John Grey, squire of the body of our lord king, and of John Berwoit and William Talbot with him, charging them to guard Joan well and faithfully, and to let no one talk with her without our leave. With their hands on Holy Gospels, they solemnly swore to do so.

At last, we scheduled Joan to appear the next day, Thursday, at eight o'clock in the morning, in the robing chamber at the end of the great hall of the castle of Rouen.

Thursday, February 22. Second session. The Thursday immediately following, February 22, we the bishop went to the robing chamber at the end of the great hall of the castle of Rouen, where reverend fathers, lords, and masters were assembled together with us: Gilles, abbot of Holy Trinity of Fécamp, Pierre, prior of Longueville-Giffard, Jean de Châtillon, Jean Beaupère, Jacques de Touraine, Nicolas Midi, Jean de Nibat, Jacques Guesdon, Jean le Fèvre, Maurice du Quesnay, Guillaume le Boucher, Pierre Houdenc, Pierre Maurice, Richard Praty, and Gérard Feuillet, doctors of theology; Abbots Nicolas de Jumièges, Guillaume de Sainte-Catherine, Guillaume de Cormeilles, along with Jean Guérin, doctors of canon law; Raoul Roussel, doctor of canon and civil law; Guillaume Haiton, Nicolas Couppequesne, Jean Le Maistre, Richard de Grouchet, Pierre Minier, Jean Pigache, Raoul le

Sauvage, bachelors of theology; Robert Le Barbier, Denis Gastinel, Jean le Doux, licentiates of canon and civil law; Jean Basset, Jean de la Fontaine, Jean Bruillot, Aubert Morel, Nicolas de Venderès, Jean Pinchon, Jean Colombel, Laurent du Busc, Raoul Anguy, licentiates of canon law; André Marguerie, Jean Alespée, Geoffroi du Crotay, and Gilles Deschamps, licentiates of civil law; the abbot of Préaux and Brother Guillaume Lermite; Guillaume Desjardins, doctor of medicine; Robert Morellet and Jean le Roy, canons of Rouen Cathedral.

In their presence we explained that we had summoned and requested Brother Jean Le Maistre, vice-inquisitor, then present, to take part in the present trial, and that we had offered to communicate to him all that had happened so far and that would happen; and that the vicar had answered that the reverend inquisitor had enlisted and deputed him only for the city and diocese of Rouen but that now we had moved the trial into borrowed territory, by reason of our jurisdiction of Beauvais. Therefore, so as not to invalidate the trial, and for peace of conscience, he had put off taking part until he should receive fuller counsel from the reverend inquisitor, as well as fuller authority or a commission; yet as far as he was concerned, the vicar was content for us to proceed in the matter without interruption.

On hearing our account, the vicar answered: "What you say is true. As far as I am concerned, you may proceed."

Then, with Joan before us, we requested and advised her under penalty of the law to take the oath she had made the day before and to swear simply and completely to answer the truth to questions on the matter for which she was accused and denounced. She answered that she had taken an oath yesterday, and that ought to be sufficient.

Again we advised her to swear, for no one who is questioned in a matter of faith, not even a prince, can refuse to take an oath. She answered again: "I took an oath for you yesterday; that should be quite enough for you. You overburden me." Finally, she took an oath to tell the truth on matters touching the faith.

After this, the distinguished professor of sacred theology Master Jean Beaupère, by our order and command, questioned Joan on the following subjects.

He first urged her to answer the questions truthfully, as she had sworn. She answered: "You may well ask me some things that I will answer truthfully, and others that I will not." And she added: "If you were well informed about me, you would wish me out of your hands. I have done nothing but through revelation."

Asked next how old she was when she left her father's house, she said she did not know for certain.

Asked whether she had learned any skill in her youth, she said yes, to sew linen and to spin; and she feared no woman in Rouen for sewing and spinning. Further, she admitted that for fear of the Burgundians, she left her father's house and went to the village of Neufchâteau in Lorraine, to the home of a certain woman named La Rousse, where she stayed around fifteen days.[21] She added that while she was at her father's house, she attended to household chores and did not go to the fields with the sheep and other animals.[22]

Asked whether she confessed her sins each year, she answered, yes, to her own parish priest; and when her parish priest could not, she confessed to another priest, by leave of the parish priest. Several times—two or three times, she thought—she had also confessed to mendicants; and this was at the town of Neufchâteau. And she received the sacrament of Eucharist at Easter.

Asked whether she received the sacrament of Eucharist on feasts other than Easter, she told the interrogator to go on to the next question. She declared further that when she was thirteen, she heard a voice from God helping her to behave. And at first she feared greatly. And the voice came around noon in the summer, in her father's garden; and Joan had not fasted the previous day.[23] She heard a voice on her right, toward the church, and she seldom hears it without light. This light comes from the same side where she hears the voice, but all around in that place there is a great light. When she came to France, she often heard the voice.

Asked how she saw the light she spoke of, since the light was at her side, she did not answer, but passed on to other subjects. She said that if she was in a wood, she would clearly hear the voices coming to her. It seemed a worthy voice, and she believed that the voice was sent by

God; after she heard the voice three times, she knew it was the voice of an angel. She said that the voice always protected her well and she understood the voice well.

Asked what instruction the voice gave her for her soul's salvation, she said that it taught her to behave herself and go to church, and said to her, Joan, that she must come to France. And Joan told the interrogator that he would not learn from her at this time what the voice looked like when it appeared to her. She declared that the voice told her two or three times a week that she must leave and come to France, and that her father knew nothing of her departure.[24] She also said that the voice told her to come to France and not to stay where she was any longer. The voice told her that she must raise the siege of the city of Orléans. She said next that the voice told her that she, Joan, must go to Vaucouleurs to find Robert de Baudricourt, the captain there, and he would supply her with men;[25] she answered that she was a poor girl who knew nothing of riding or waging war. She went to her uncle,[26] and he told her that he wanted her to stay with him for a little while, and she stayed for about eight days; then she told her uncle that she had to go to Vaucouleurs, and he took her there.

Then she said that when she reached Vaucouleurs, she recognized Robert de Baudricourt, even though she had never seen him before; and she knew Robert through her voice, for the voice told her it was he; and she, Joan, told Robert she must come to France. But Robert twice turned her away and rebuffed her, but the third time heeded her and gave her men; and it was just as the voice had told her it would happen.

Then she declared that the duke of Lorraine had sent for her.[27] She went and told him she wanted to go to France. The duke questioned her about the recovery of his health, but she said she knew nothing about it. She told him very little about her journey. Yet she told him to give her his son and men to escort her to France and she would pray to God for his health. Joan went to the duke under safe conduct and returned to Vaucouleurs.

Then she said that upon her departure from Vaucouleurs, she wore men's clothing and carried a sword that Robert de Baudricourt had given her, with no other weapons. Accompanied by a knight, a squire, and four servants, she reached the village of Saint-Urbain and spent the night there in the abbey.

She said that on that voyage she passed through the village of Auxerre, and heard Mass there in the great church.[28] She often heard her voices then, with the one mentioned above.[29]

Asked to tell on whose advice she began wearing men's clothing, she refused many times to reply. Finally she said she blamed no one for this; and she changed her answer often.

She said that Robert de Baudricourt made the men of her escort swear to guide her well and securely. And Robert told Joan when she left him: "Go, and let come what may."

Joan also said she knows very well that God loves the duke of Orléans,[30] and that she even had more revelations about him than about any other living person, except for the one she calls her king. She said, besides, that she had to exchange her clothes for men's. She believes her counsel spoke well.

She said she sent a letter to the English at Orléans telling them to depart, as recorded in a copy of the letter that was read to her in this town of Rouen[31]—except that there are two or three wrong words in this copy. So this copy says, "Deliver to the maiden," when it should read, "Deliver to the king"; and the words "body for body" and "war chief" were not in the original letter.[32]

Joan added that she went to the one she calls her king, with no hindrance. And when she reached Sainte-Catherine de Fierbois, first she sent to the one she calls her king; then she went to the village of Château-Chinon, where the one she calls her king was staying.[33] She arrived there around noon and lodged at a certain inn. After lunch, she went to the one she calls her king, who was in the castle. She says that when she entered her king's chamber, she recognized him among the others by the counsel of her voice, which revealed him to her. And she told her king that she wanted to make war on the English.

Asked whether on this occasion, when the voice revealed her king to her, there was any light in that place, she answered: "Go on to the next question."

Asked whether she saw an angel over her king, she answered: "Spare me, go to the next question." Yet she said that before her king put her to the task, he had many apparitions and beautiful revelations.

Asked what kind of revelations and apparitions her king had, she answered: "I will not tell you this. It is not yet time. But send to the king, and he will tell you."

She said her voice promised her that soon after she had gone to her king, he would meet her. She said that those on her side knew very well that the voice was sent to Joan by God, and they saw and knew the voice—Joan claimed she knew this very well. She also said that her king and many others heard and saw voices coming to her; Charles of Bourbon and two or three others were there.[34]

Joan said that not a day passes when she does not hear the voice, and she needs to very much. She never asked the voice for any last reward but the salvation of her soul. Joan stated further that the voice told her to stay at Saint-Denis in France;[35] and she wanted to, but the lords took her away against her will. Had she not been injured, she would not have left; she was injured in the trenches at Paris after arriving there from Saint-Denis.[36] But she was healed in five days. She declared that she brought about an attack—*escarmouche* in French—before Paris.

Asked whether that was on a feast day, she said she well believes it was.

Asked whether this was the right thing to do, she answered: "Go to the next question."

When these matters were concluded, since it seemed enough for one day, we the bishop scheduled the next session for the very next Saturday at eight o'clock in the morning.

Saturday, February 24. Third session. The following Saturday, February 24, we the bishop arrived at the castle of Rouen, the same chamber, where Joan appeared before us in judgment in the presence of many reverend fathers, doctors, and masters: Gilles, abbot of Holy Trinity of Fécamp, Pierre, prior of Longueville-Giffard, Jean de Châtillon, Erard Emengart, Jean Beaupère, Jacques de Touraine, Nicolas Midi,

Jean de Nibat, Jacques Guesdon, Maurice du Quesnay, Jean le Fèvre, Guillaume le Boucher, Pierre Houdenc, Pierre Maurice, Richard Praty, Jean Charpentier, Gerard Feuillet, and Denis de Sabrevois, doctors of theology; Abbots Nicolas de Jumièges, Guillaume de Sainte-Catherine, Guillaume de Cormeilles, along with Jean Guérin, doctors of canon law, and Raoul Roussel, doctor of canon and civil law; Nicolas Couppequesne, Guillaume Haiton, Thomas de Courcelles, Jean Le Maistre, Nicolas Loiselleur, Raoul le Sauvage, Guillaume de Baudribosc, Nicolas le Mire, Richard le Gagneux, Jean Duval, Guillaume Le Maistre, and Guillaume Lermite, bachelors of theology; the abbot of Saint-Ouen, the abbot of Saint-Georges, the abbot of Préaux, the prior of Saint-Lô, and the prior of Sigy, along with Robert Le Barbier, Denis Gastinel, and Jean le Doux, licentiates of canon and civil law; Nicolas de Venderès, Jean Pinchon, Jean de la Fontaine, Aubert Morel, Jean Duchemin, Jean Colombel, Laurent du Busc, Raoul Anguy, Richard des Saulx, licentiates of canon law; André Marguerie, Jean Alespée, Geoffroi du Crotay, Gilles Deschamps, Nicolas Maulin, Pierre Carrel, Bureau de Cormeilles, licentiates of civil law; Robert Morellet and Jean le Roy, canons of Rouen Cathedral; and Nicolas de Foville.

In their presence we first requested Joan to swear simply and completely to tell the truth about what she would be asked, with no condition to the oath; and we advised her three times about this. Joan answered: "Allow me to speak." Then she said: "By my faith, you could ask me things I would not tell you." She said again: "Perhaps, among the many things you may ask me, I will not answer the truth to the questions about revelations. For you might drive me to say something that I've sworn not to say, and so I would commit perjury— something you should not wish." She added: "I tell you, mind well what you say, that you are my judge, because you are taking on a heavy burden, and you overburden me." She also said that swearing the oath twice seemed plenty.

Asked again to swear, simply and absolutely, she answered: "You can leave the matter. I've sworn twice; that's plenty," adding that all the clergy of Rouen or Paris would not know how to condemn her, except through law.[37] She said she would gladly tell the truth about her arrival, but not about everything, and that eight days would not be enough to tell all.

But we the bishop told her to take the advice of the assessors whether or not to swear. She answered again that she would gladly tell the truth about her arrival, but nothing else, and that there was no need to speak further to her about it.

Then we told her that she would open herself to suspicion if she would not swear to tell the truth. She answered as before.

Again we requested her to swear briefly and absolutely. She answered that she would gladly tell what she knows, but not all. She said further that she came from God and that she has no business here; and she asked to be sent back to God from whom she came.

Asked and advised again to swear, under penalty of being convicted of what was imputed to her, she answered: "Continue to the next question."

Finally, we asked her again to swear, and we advised her at length to tell the truth in what concerns the trial, telling her she was exposing herself to great danger by refusing. She answered: "I'm ready to swear to tell the truth about what I know that concerns the trial. <But I won't tell all I know.>"[38] And she swore to this.

Then by our order Joan was questioned by the distinguished doctor Master Jean Beaupère, mentioned above. He first asked her when she had last eaten or drunk. She answered that she had not eaten or drunk since yesterday afternoon.

Asked when she last heard the voice come to her, she answered: "I heard it yesterday and today."

Asked what time yesterday she heard the voice, she said she heard it three times that day, once in the morning, once at vespers, and a third time when the bell rang for the Hail Mary at night; and she hears it many more times than she says.

Asked what she did yesterday morning when the voice came to her, she answered that she was sleeping, and the voice woke her.

Asked whether the voice woke her by touching her arms, she said it woke her without touching her.

Asked whether the voice was in her room, she said she thinks not, but it was in the castle.

Asked whether she thanked the voice and genuflected, she said she thanked it, seated on her bed, and clasped her hands. This was after she had asked for help. Moreover, the voice told her, Joan, to answer boldly.

Asked what the voice told her when she was awake, she said she asked the voice to counsel her how to answer and told the voice to seek counsel from the Lord; and the voice told her to answer boldly and God would help her.

Asked whether the voice said anything to her before she asked it, she said the voice told her things, but she did not understand them all. Nonetheless, after she was awake, the voice told her to answer boldly.

She told us the bishop: "You say that you are my judge. Take care what you do, for in truth I am sent from God, and you put yourself in great peril"—*en grant dangier* in French.

Asked whether the voice did not sometimes change its advice, she said she never knew it to contradict itself. She also said she heard it that night telling her to answer boldly.

Asked whether the voice forbade her to answer all that she was asked, she answered: "I won't answer you that. I have revelations touching the king that I won't tell you."

Asked whether the voice forbade her to tell her revelations, she answered: "I haven't been advised about this. Give me fifteen days and I'll answer you." And when she asked again for time to respond, she added: "What would you say if the voice has forbidden me?"

Asked again whether this was forbidden her, she answered: "Believe me, it wasn't men who forbade me." She said she would not respond that day, and she does not know whether to reply until it is revealed to her.[39] She said she firmly believes—as firmly as she believes in the Christian faith and believes that God redeemed us from the pains of hell—that the voice comes from God and by his command.

Asked whether the voice that she said appears to her is an angel or comes directly from God or is the voice of a saint, she answered: "The voice comes from God; and I believe I'm not telling you all I know. I fear to fail by saying something that may displease the voices more than I fear answering you. As for this question, I request a delay."

Asked whether she believes that telling the truth displeases God, she answered: "The voices told me to say certain things to the king and not to you." She said that <the voice> told her many things that night for the good of her king, things she wished the king to know even then, and that she would not drink wine until Easter. For then, she said, he would dine more happily.

Asked whether it might be possible to make the voice wish to obey her and to bear her king a message, she said she did not know if the voice would obey her, unless it was God's will and God allowed it. And if it pleases God, she said, he could very well send the revelations to her king. "And I would be perfectly happy with this."

Asked why the voice no longer speaks to her king as it did when Joan was in his presence, she said she did not know whether it was God's will. And she added that if not for the grace of God, she could do nothing.

Asked whether her counsel revealed to her that she would escape from prison, she answered: "Do I have to tell you?"

Asked whether that night the voice counseled and advised her what to answer, she said that if the voice revealed anything to her, she did not understand it.

Asked whether any light appeared on the last two days she heard voices, she said that the light comes in the name of the voice.[40]

Asked whether she sees anything else with the voices, she answered: "I may not tell you all; I don't have leave, and my oath does not cover this. The voice is good and worthy, and I'm not bound to answer." She then asked that the points that she was not answering be given to her in writing.

Then she was asked whether the voice from which she asked counsel had vision and eyes. She answered: "You won't learn that yet." She said little children have a saying: Sometimes people are hanged for telling the truth.

Asked whether she knows she is in the grace of God, she answered: "If I'm not, may God put me there; and if I am, may God keep me in it.[41] I would be the most miserable person in the world if I knew I was not in the grace of God." She said further that if she were in a state of sin, she believes the voice would not come to her; she wishes that everyone could understand it as well as she can. She thinks she was around thirteen when the first voice came to her.[42]

Asked whether she used to play in the fields with other children when she was young, she said sometimes she certainly did, but she does not know at what age.

Asked whether the villagers of Domrémy took the side of the Burgundians or the other side, she said she knew only one Burgundian there, and she would gladly have seen his head cut off, so long as it pleased God.

Asked whether there were Burgundians or enemies of the Burgundians at the village of Maxey, she said Burgundians.

Asked whether, when she was young, the voice told her to hate Burgundians, she said that after she understood that the voices were for the king of France, she did not love the Burgundians. She said the Burgundians will have war unless they do what they ought; she knows this from the voice.

Asked whether, when she was young, she had a revelation from the voice that the English should come to France, she said the English were already in France when the voices started coming to her.

Asked whether she was ever with little children who fought for the side she supports, she said no, not that she remembers; but she certainly did see some children from Domrémy who fought against others from Maxey, sometimes returning home quite wounded and bleeding.

Asked whether, when she was young, she fully intended to pursue the Burgundians, she said she had a great will or desire that her king should have his kingdom.

Asked whether she had wanted to be a man when she was supposed to come to France, she said she had answered that already.[43]

Asked whether she took animals to the fields, she said she had already answered that. After she had grown up and had more judgment, in general she did not look after the animals, but, fearing the soldiers, she did help lead them to the meadows and to a castle called the Island. But she does not recall whether she looked after them when she was younger.

Asked about a certain tree near her village, she said that close by the village of Domrémy is a tree called the ladies' tree, and others call it the tree of the fairies, *fées* in French, which is near a spring. She heard that those sick with the fever drink from the spring,[44] and they go in search of its water for healing. She saw this herself, but she does not know whether they are cured. She said she heard that when they can lift themselves up, the sick go to the tree to walk about there. It is a large beech tree, from which they get the May, in French *le beau mai*.[45] And it belonged by custom to Lord Pierre de Bourlémont, knight. She said that sometimes she went for a walk with the other girls and made wreaths near the tree for the image of Blessed Mary of Domrémy. And many times she heard the old folk (not those of her family) say that the fairies gathered there. And she heard from a woman named Joan, the wife of Mayor Aubery of that town and her own godmother, that she had seen the fairies there; but Joan did not know whether or not this was true. She said she never saw fairies near the tree, as far as she knew. She saw young girls put wreaths in the branches, and sometimes she did so with other girls; sometimes they took them away, sometimes they left them. After she knew she was supposed to come to France, she spent little time in games or strolls, as little as possible. And she does not know whether she danced near the tree after she reached the age of discretion; but sometimes she may well have danced there with the children, but she sang more than danced. She says there is a wood called the Oak Wood, *le Bois chesnu* in French, visible from her father's door, less than half a league away. She does not know, nor has she ever heard, that the fairies gathered there; but she heard from her brother that it was reported in the countryside that she, Joan, received her message at the fairies' tree. But she says she did not, and she contradicted him. She says further that when she came to her king, some of them asked her whether there was a wood in her area called *le Bois chesnu* in French, because there were prophecies saying that a maiden who would perform wonders was supposed to come from that wood. But Joan said that she put no faith in this.

Asked whether she wanted a woman's dress, she answered: "Please give me one garment; I'll take it and go. Otherwise, I won't take it, and I'm content with this, since it pleases God that I wear it."

After these matters were brought to a close, we ended the interrogation for that day and scheduled the Tuesday following to continue the interrogation with all present, at the same hour and at the same place.

Tuesday, February 27. Fourth session. Tuesday, February 27, we the bishop arrived as on previous days at the chamber of the castle of Rouen, where we had sat in judgment. There also appeared reverend fathers, lords, and masters: Gilles, abbot of Holy Trinity of Fécamp, Pierre, prior of Longueville-Giffard, Jean Beaupère, Jacques de Touraine, Nicolas Midi, Pierre Maurice, Gérard Feuillet, Jean de Nibat, Jacques Guesdon, Maurice du Quesnay, Jean le Fèvre, Guillaume le Boucher, Pierre Houdenc, Jean de Châtillon, Erard Emengart, Jean de Fano, Denis de Sabrevois, Nicolas le Mire, and Jean Charpentier, doctors of theology; Abbots Nicolas de Jumièges, Guillaume de Sainte-Catherine, Guillaume de Cormeilles, along with Jean Guérin, doctors of canon law; Raoul Roussel, doctor of canon and civil law; Guillaume Haiton, Nicolas Couppequesne, Guillaume de Baudribosc, Richard de Grouchet, Pierre Minier, Thomas de Courcelles, Jean Le Maistre, and Jean le Vautier, bachelors of theology; the abbot of Préaux; Guillaume Desjardins, doctor of medicine; Robert Le Barbier, Denis Gastinel, Jean le Doux, Nicolas de Venderès, Jean Pinchon, Jean Basset, Aubert Morel, Jean Duchemin, Jean de la Fontaine, Jean Colombel, Jean Bruillot, Raoul Anguy, licentiates of canon law; Jean Alespée, Geoffroi du Crotay, Gilles Deschamps, Nicholas Caval, Pierre Carrel, Nicolas Maulin, licentiates of civil law; and Nicolas Loiseleur and Robert Morellet, canons of Rouen Cathedral.

In their presence we first requested Joan to take an oath to tell the truth on matters touching the trial. She said she would gladly swear to tell the truth about matters touching the trial, but not everything she knows.

Again we asked her to tell the truth about everything that she would be asked. She answered as before: "You should be content, I have sworn enough."

Then by our order, Jean Beaupère began to question her. First he asked her how she had been doing since the previous Saturday. She answered: "You see very well how I've been doing. As best I can."

Asked whether she would fast during Lent, she answered by asking: "What does this have to do with your trial?"

And when she was told that this concerned the trial, she answered: "Yes, truly, I've been fasting throughout Lent."

Asked whether, since Saturday, she had heard the voice that comes to her, she answered: "Yes, truly, I've heard it many times."

Asked whether she heard it on Saturday in the hall where she was interrogated, she answered: "This doesn't concern your trial." And later she said that she had heard it there.

Asked what the voice told her on Saturday, she answered: "I didn't understand the voice very well; I understood nothing I could repeat to you, until I returned to my room."

Asked what the voice told her in her room when she returned, she answered: "It told me to answer you boldly." She said she sought counsel from the voice about what was asked of her. She also said that she will gladly speak about what the Lord allows her to reveal; but without leave from her voice, she will say nothing about her revelations concerning the king of France.

Asked whether the voice forbade her to tell all, she said she had not fully understood.

Asked what the voice last told her, she said that she had sought counsel about things she had been asked.

Asked whether the voice gave her counsel on certain points, she said she received counsel on certain points; and they might ask her questions that she will not answer without leave. If she were to answer without leave, she might not have the authorization—*garant* in French—of the voices. But when the Lord gives her leave, she will not fear to speak, for she will certainly have authorization.

Asked whether the voice that spoke to her was an angel's voice or a saint's or direct from God, she said it was the voice of Saint Catherine and Saint Margaret.[46] And their forms are crowned with beautiful crowns, in rich and precious fashion. "And I have leave from the Lord about this," she says. "If you doubt this, send to Poitiers where I was interrogated on another occasion."[47]

Asked how she knows there are two saints, how she clearly knows one from the other, she said she knows very well who they are and clearly knows one from the other.

Asked how she knows one from the other, she answered that she knows them by their greeting to her. She also said that a good seven years have passed since they undertook to guide her. She knows the saints because they tell her their names.

Asked whether the saints are dressed in the same cloth, she answered: "I will tell you nothing else; I don't have permission to reveal it. If you don't believe me, go to Poitiers." She said there are some revelations that concern the king of France, not those who interrogate her.

Asked whether the saints are the same age, she answered that she had no leave to say.

Asked whether the saints speak together, or one after the other, she answered: "I don't have permission to say; but I always receive counsel from them both."[48]

Asked which one first appeared to her, she answered: "I didn't know them immediately; I knew this at one time, but now I've forgotten. If I have leave, I'll gladly tell; it's recorded in the register at Poitiers." She added that she had received comfort from Saint Michael.[49]

Asked which of these apparitions came to her first, she said Saint Michael.

Asked whether much time had passed since she first heard the voice of Saint Michael, she answered: "I do not name the voice of Saint Michael to you, I speak rather of great comfort."

Asked which voice first came to her, when she was thirteen or thereabouts, she said she saw Saint Michael before her eyes; and he was not alone, but was well attended by angels from heaven. She said she came to France only by God's command.

Asked whether she saw Saint Michael and the angels bodily and really, she answered: "I saw them with my bodily eyes, just as well as I see you; and when they left me, I wept and truly wished they had taken me with them."

Asked what shape Saint Michael took, she answered: "I haven't yet answered you this and still have no leave to speak of it."

Asked what Saint Michael said to her that first occasion, she answered: "You'll get no further answer today." She said that the voices told her to answer boldly. On one occasion she certainly did tell her king all that had been revealed to her, because it concerned him. Nonetheless, she says she does not yet have leave to reveal what Saint Michael told her. She sorely wishes her interrogator had a copy of the book at Poitiers, provided that it pleased God.

Asked whether the voices told her not to speak of her revelations without their permission: "I'll answer you no further about that. I'll gladly answer where I have leave to speak. But if the voices have forbidden it, I haven't understood."

Asked what sign she gives to show that the revelation comes from God, and that she is speaking with Saint Catherine and Saint Margaret, she answered: "I've told you often enough that they are Saint Catherine and Saint Margaret; believe me if you wish."

Asked whether she was forbidden to say this, she answered: "I haven't clearly understood whether or not this is forbidden."

Asked how she knows the difference, to answer some things and not others, she said she sought permission for some points, and for some she received it. She says further that she would rather be torn asunder by horses than have come to France without God's permission.

Asked whether she had been commanded to wear men's clothing, she said that the clothing is a small matter, one of the least. She put on men's clothing not by counsel of a man of this world; she has not taken clothing, nor has she done anything else, but by command of God and the angels.

Asked whether it seemed to her that this command to take on men's attire was lawful, she answered: "All that I have done is by the Lord's command. If he commanded me to put on something else, I would do it, since this would be by God's command."

Asked whether she did so at the order of Robert de Baudricourt, she answered no.

Asked whether she thinks she has done well to take men's attire, she said that all she has done by the Lord's command, she believes she has done well, and she trusts for good sanction and aid from it.

Asked whether she thinks she has done well in this particular case, in taking men's attire, she said she did nothing in the world but by God's command.

Asked whether, when she saw the voice come to her, there was light with it, she said there was much light all around, and this seemed fitting. She further told the interrogator that all the light did not reach her.[50]

Asked whether there was an angel over her king's head when she first saw him, she answered: "By Blessed Mary! If so, I don't know and I didn't see it."

Asked whether there was a light there, she answered: "There were more than three hundred knights and fifty torches there, not counting the spiritual light. I seldom have revelations without light."

Asked why her king put faith in her words, she said he had good signs—and through the clergy.

Asked what kind of revelations her king had, she answered: "You will not learn them from me this year." She said she was questioned by clergy for three weeks at Chinon and Poitiers. Her king had a sign about her mission before he would believe her. And the clerks of her side held the opinion that, as it seemed to them, there was only good in her mission.

Asked whether she was ever at Sainte-Catherine de Fierbois, she said yes, she heard three masses there on the same day and then went to Chinon. She says she sent her king a letter asking to enter the town where her king was, saying she had made good progress over 150 leagues to reach him for his aid, and that she knew many things to his benefit. She thought the letter said that she would know her king from all the others quite clearly. She says she had a sword that she took at Vaucouleurs. When she was at Tours or at Chinon, she added, she sent to find a sword in the church of Sainte-Catherine de Fierbois, behind the altar; and it was immediately found, completely rusted.

Asked how she knew the sword was there, she said the sword was in the ground, rusted, bearing five crosses; she knew from the voices that it was there, and she never saw the person who went in search of the sword. She wrote to the clergy of the place asking them to please let her have the sword, which they sent her. It was buried not very deep, behind the altar, she thought. She does not rightly know whether it was in front of or behind the altar, but she thinks that at the time she wrote to say it was behind the altar. She says as soon as the sword was found, the clergy there rubbed it and at once the rust fell off effortlessly. An armorer of Tours went looking for it, and the clergy and the citizens of Tours together gave Joan a scabbard, and they ordered two scabbards: one of red velvet, *velours vermeil* in French, and another of cloth of gold. She herself had another made of stiff leather. She says she did not have the sword with her when she was captured. She carried the sword continuously from the time she received it until she left Saint-Denis, after the assault on Paris.

Asked what blessing she pronounced or directed to be pronounced upon the sword, she said she never blessed it there or had it blessed, nor would she know how to do so. She treasured the sword because it had been found in the church of Saint Catherine, whom she loved very much.

Asked whether she was ever at the town of Coulange-la-Vineuse, she said she did not know.[51]

Asked whether she sometimes placed her sword upon the altar, she said no, as far as she knows, at least not so that it should have better fortune.

Asked whether she ever prayed that her sword would have better fortune, she answered: "It's good to know that I would have wished my armor"—*mon harnois* in French—"to have good fortune."

Asked whether she had her sword when she was captured, she said no, but she had a sword that was taken from a Burgundian.

Asked where the sword was and in what town, she said she offered a sword and arms in the abbey of Saint-Denis, but not that sword. She had it at Lagny, and took it from there to Compiègne, since it was a good battle sword, good for giving hard strokes and blows, in French *de bonnes buffes et de bons torchons*. But she says that to tell where she left it does not concern the trial, and she will not answer this for now. Her brothers have her possessions, horses, and sword, she thinks, and other things more than 12,000 écus in value.[52]

Asked whether, when she went to Orléans, she had a banner—*estandart* or *banière* in French—and what color it was, she said she had a banner with a field sown with fleurs-de-lis; it pictured the world with two angels on either side; it was white, made of white linen or fine buckram. The names Jesus, Mary were written there, she thought; and it was fringed with silk.[53]

Asked whether the names Jesus, Mary were written above, below, or to the side, she said on the side, it seemed to her.

Asked which she preferred, her banner or sword, she said she was much fonder, indeed forty times fonder, of the banner than of the sword.

Asked who persuaded her to make the picture on the banner, she answered: "I have told you often enough that I have done nothing but by God's command." She carried the banner when she attacked the enemies, to avoid killing anyone; she says she never did kill anyone.

Asked what forces her king gave her when he set her to the task, she said ten or twelve thousand men, and at Orléans she went first to the fortress of Saint-Loup, and then to the fortress at the bridge.[54]

Asked to which fort she ordered her men to retreat, she said she does not remember. She says she was quite certain from her revelation that she would lift the siege of Orléans; she told her king so before going there.

Asked whether, at the moment of attack, she did not tell her troops that she would receive all arrows, bolts, and rocks from the catapults and cannons, she said no; on the contrary, a hundred or more men were wounded. But she did indeed tell her men to have no fear, they would raise the siege. She says that during the attack on the fort at the bridge, she was wounded in the neck by an arrow or bolt; but she had great comfort from Saint Catherine and was healed within fifteen days. But she did not give up riding and working because of the wound.

Asked whether she knew well in advance that she would be wounded, she said she knew very well and told her king, but nonetheless she would not abandon her responsibilities. The voices of two saints revealed it to her, Blessed Catherine and Blessed Margaret. She was the first to put the ladder against the fort at the bridge; she was wounded in the neck by the bolt while raising the ladder.

Asked why she did not conclude a treaty with the captain of Jargeau,[55] she said the lords of her party told the English that they would not get the delay of fifteen days they had requested, but that they should take their horses and leave within the hour. For her part, she says she told the people from Jargeau that if they wished, they could leave in their doublets and tunics and escape with their lives; otherwise they would be taken by storm.

Asked whether she had any conversation with her counsel—that is to say, her voices—about whether or not to grant the delay, she said she does not remember.

With these matters concluded, further interrogation was postponed, and we scheduled the following Thursday for further inquiry and interrogation.

March 1. Fifth session. Thursday, March 1, we the bishop arrived at the accustomed chamber of the castle of Rouen; and Joan appeared before us in judgment, in the presence of reverend fathers, lords, and masters: Gilles, abbot of Holy Trinity of Fécamp, Pierre, prior of Longueville-Giffard, Jean de Châtillon, Erard Emengart, Jean Beaupère, Jacques de Touraine, Nicolas Midi, Denis de Sabrevois, Pierre Maurice, Gérard Feuillet, Maurice du Quesnay, Guillaume le Boucher, Pierre Houdenc, Jean de Nibat, Jean le Fèvre, Jacques Guesdon, doctors of theology; Abbots Nicolas de Jumièges, Guillaume de Sainte-Catherine, Guillaume de Cormeilles, as well as Jean Guérin, doctors of canon law; Raoul Roussel, doctor of canon and civil law; the abbots of Saint-Ouen and Préaux, the prior of Saint-Lô, Guillaume Haiton, Nicolas Couppequesne, Thomas de Courcelles, Guillaume de Baudribosc, Jean Pigache, Pierre Minier, Richard de Grouchet, Jean Le Maistre, and Jean le Vautier, bachelors of theology; Nicolas de Venderès, Jean Bruillot, Jean Pinchon, Jean Basset, Jean de la Fontaine, Raoul Anguy, Jean Colombel, Richard des Saulx, Aubert Morel, Jean Duchemin, Laurent du Busc, Philippe le Maréchal, licentiates of canon law; Denis Gastinel, Jean le Doux, Robert Le Barbier, licentiates of canon and civil law; André Marguerie, Jean Alespée, Gilles Deschamps, Nicholas Caval, Geoffroi du Crotay, Pierre Cave, Nicolas Maulin, licentiates of civil law; Robert Morellet and Nicolas Loiselleur, canons of Rouen Cathedral.

In their presence we summoned and requested Joan to swear to tell the truth, simply and absolutely, about the things she was to be asked.

She said that she was ready to swear to tell the truth about all she knew that concerned the trial, as she had already said. She said she knows much that does not concern the trial, and she need not speak of those things. She said once again: "Everything I know that truly concerns the trial I will gladly tell."

Again summoned and requested to take the oath, she answered: "What I know to answer truly, I'll gladly tell, as far as what touches the trial." So she swore, touching Holy Gospels. Then she said: "I'll gladly tell the truth about what I know that touches the trial; and I'll tell you just what I would tell if I were before the pope in Rome."

Asked what she says about our lord the pope, and who she believes is the true pope, she answered by asking if there were two.

Asked whether she had received a letter from the count of Armagnac asking which of the three popes he should obey, she said the count had written her a letter about this and she had responded by saying, among other things, that she would give him an answer when she was at Paris, or when she had time elsewhere.[56] She was about to mount her horse when she answered him.

Then we ordered to be read in court a copy of the letters from the count and from Joan, and Joan was asked whether this was her response in the copy. She answered that she supposed that she had made this reply in part, but not all of it.

Asked whether she had claimed to know, by the counsel of the King of kings, what the count should think on this matter, she said she knew nothing about it.

Asked whether she had any doubt about whom the count should obey, she said she did not know what to tell him about whom to obey, because the count wanted to know whom God would have him obey. But as for her, Joan, she holds and believes that we should obey our lord the pope in Rome. She added that she told the count's messenger more than is in this copy of the letter; had not the messenger left at once, he would have been hurled into the water, but not by her. She said that in regard to his question about whom God wished him to obey, she replied that she did not know; but she gave him many instructions not put in writing. As for her, she believes in the pope at Rome.

Asked why she wrote that she would reply some other time, since she believed in the pope at Rome, she answered that she had said this about another matter, not the three popes.

Asked whether she had said that she would receive counsel on the matter of the three popes, she said she had never written or caused to be written anything on the matter of the three popes. She swore this by her oath: never had she written or ordered to be written anything at all.

Asked whether she customarily put in her letters the names Jesus, Mary with a cross, she said that in some she did, in some she did not. Sometimes she placed a cross as a signal to someone of her party not to do what her letter said.

The content of the letters that the counts and Joan wrote to one another is included below among the articles of the promoter.[57]

Then she was read the letters she had sent to the lord our king, to the duke of Bedford, and to others; the content of these letters is also included below among the articles of the promoter.[58]

Next she was asked whether she recognized the letters. She said yes, except for three phrases: where it says "give to the Maiden" it should say "give to the king"; where it says "war captain"; and a third passage that says "body for body." These words were not in the letter she sent. No lord ever dictated these letters, she says, but she dictated them before sending them, though certainly she showed them to some of her party.

She says that before seven years have passed, the English will lose a greater stake than they did at Orléans, and all they have in France. Further, the English will suffer a greater loss than they ever had in France, through a great victory that God will give the French.

Asked how she knows this, she answered: "I know quite well by a revelation made to me, and that it will happen within seven years; and I might well be angry that it should be delayed so long." She added that she knows this by revelation, just as plainly as she knows we are there before her.

Asked when this will happen, she said she does not know the day or the hour.

Asked what year it will happen, she answered: "You will not yet learn that; but truly I wish it were before the feast of Saint John."[59]

Asked whether she said it would happen before Martinmas, she answered that she had said that many things would come to pass before Martinmas; and possibly the English would be overthrown.[60]

Asked what she said to John Grey, her jailer, about Martinmas, she answered: "I've told you that."

Asked through whom she knew this would happen, she said she knew this by Saint Catherine and Saint Margaret.

Asked whether Saint Gabriel was with Saint Michael when he came to her, she said she did not remember.

Asked whether she had spoken with Saint Catherine and Saint Margaret since last Tuesday, she said yes, but she did not know at what hour.

Asked on what day, she answered, yesterday and today; not a day passes but she hears them.

Asked whether she always sees them in the same clothing, she said she always sees them in the same shape; their figures are richly crowned. She does not speak of the rest of their appearance. She knows nothing of their robes.

Asked how she knows whether the apparition is a man or woman, she said she knows very well and recognizes them by their voices, and they revealed themselves to her; she knows nothing but by revelation and command of God.

Asked what shape she sees there, she said she sees a face.

Asked whether the saints that appear to her have hair, she answered: "It's a good thing to know, yes."

Asked whether there was anything between their crowns and their hair, she said no.

Asked whether their hair was long and flowing, she answered: "I know nothing about it." She added that she does not know whether they have something in the way of arms or other members. They spoke exceedingly well and beautifully, and she understood them perfectly.

Asked how they spoke, if they have no other body parts, she answered: "I leave that to God." She says further that the voice is lovely, pleasant, and low, and speaks in French.

Asked whether Saint Margaret does not speak English, she answered: "Why would she speak English, when she is not on the English side?"

Asked whether the heads with crowns wore rings in the ears or somewhere else, she answered: "I know nothing about this."

Asked whether she, Joan herself, has any rings, she directed her answer to us the bishop:[61] "You have one of mine, give it back to me." She said that the Burgundians have another ring, and asked us, if we have the ring, to show it to her.

Asked who gave her the ring that the Burgundians have, she said her father or mother; and she seems to recall the names Jesus, Mary written on it. She does not know who caused it to be written, nor, she thinks, does it have a stone; she was given the ring at Domrémy. She says her brother gave her the other ring that we have; she charged us to give it to the church. She says she never healed anyone with her rings.

Asked whether Saint Catherine and Saint Margaret spoke to her beneath the tree mentioned earlier, she answered: "I know nothing about that."

Asked whether they spoke to her at the spring near the tree, she said yes, she heard them there. But she does not know what they said to her.

Asked what the saints promised her, there or elsewhere, she said they promised her nothing except by God's leave.

Asked what promises they made her, she answered: "This has nothing at all to do with your trial." Among other things, they told her that her king would be restored to his kingdom, whether his enemies wanted it or not. Further, she said they promised to bring her, Joan, to paradise, and she asked them to do so.

Asked whether she had any other promises, she said there is another one, but she will not tell it, and it has nothing to do with the trial. She says she will reveal another promise within three months.

Asked whether the voices told her that she would be freed from prison in three months, she answered: "This has nothing to do with your trial; nonetheless, I don't know when I will be freed." She said that those who want to remove her from this world might well depart first.

Asked whether her counsel did not tell her that she will be set free from prison, she answered: "Talk to me in three months, and I'll answer you." She added: "Ask the assessors on their oath whether this concerns the trial."

After this, the assessors took counsel, and they all agreed that it did. Then Joan said: "I have always told you quite clearly that you don't know everything, and at some point there will come a time when I must be freed. I wish for permission if I am to tell you; so I ask for a delay."

Asked whether the voices forbade her to tell the truth, she answered: "Do you want me to tell you what is intended for the king of France? Many things do not concern the trial." She said she knows very well that her king will regain the kingdom of France, just as clearly as she knows we are seated before her in judgment. She would have died but for the revelation that comforts her each day.

Asked what she had done with her mandrake, she said that she does not nor ever did have a mandrake.[62] She heard that there is one near her village, but she has never seen it. She heard that it is a dangerous and wicked thing to keep. She does not know its proper use.

Asked where this mandrake is that she has heard of, she said she had heard it is near the tree she mentioned earlier, but she does not know the location. She has heard that a hazel grows on top of the mandrake.

Asked what she has heard the mandrake is good for, she said she had heard that it attracts money, but she does not believe it. Her voices never told her anything about this.

Asked what shape Saint Michael took when he appeared to her, she said she did not see his crown and knew nothing of his garments.

Asked whether he was naked, she answered: "Do you think God can't find him clothes?"

Asked whether he had hair, she answered: "Why would it be cut off?" She added that she had not seen Saint Michael since she left the castle of Crotoy,[63] nor does she see him often. She said at last that she does not know whether he has hair.

Asked whether he was holding a scale,[64] she answered: "I know nothing about that." She added that she feels great joy when she sees him; and it seems to her that she is not in mortal sin when she sees him. Saint Catherine and Saint Margaret gladly have her confess from time to time, each in turn. She says that if she is in mortal sin, she is not aware of it.

Asked whether, when she confesses, she believes she is in mortal sin, she said she does not know whether she has been in mortal sin, and she does not believe she has done anything to warrant it. "Please God," she said, "I never have been, and may it please him I never will do such things as might burden my soul."

Asked what sign she gave her king that she was from God, she answered: "I have always told you that you will not drag that out of me. Go ask him."

Asked whether she swore not to reveal what would be asked concerning the trial, she answered: "I have already said that I won't speak to you about matters meant for our king. I won't talk about what concerns him directly."

Asked whether she does not know the sign she gave her king, she answered: "You won't learn this from me." Then, when she was told that this concerns the trial, she answered: "I won't tell you what I've promised to keep secret." And she added: "I promised and can't tell you without perjury."

Asked to whom she made this promise, she said Saint Catherine and Saint Margaret, and it [the sign] was shown to the king. She promised these two saints of her own free will. She herself, Joan, made this request, for too many people would have questioned her had she not made the promise to the saints.

Asked whether there was anyone else in the king's company when she showed him the sign, she said she thought not, although plenty of people were nearby.

Asked whether she saw a crown on the king's head when she showed him the sign, she answered: "I can't answer that without perjury."

Asked whether her king had a crown when he was at Reims, she said she thought her king took the crown that he found at Reims with great pleasure. But a really rich one was brought later. He did this to hasten his deed [that is, his coronation], at the request of the people of Reims, to avoid the burden of armed men. Had he waited, he would have had a crown a thousand times richer.

Asked whether she had seen this richer crown, she answered: "I can't tell you without risking perjury. If I haven't seen it, I have heard that it is so rich and splendid."

With these matters concluded, we ended for that day and scheduled Saturday at the hour of eight in the morning for the continuance. And we requested those present to gather in the same place at that day and hour.

Saturday, March 3. Sixth session. On Saturday, March 3 immediately following, at the place designated above, Joan appeared before us, in the presence of reverend fathers, lords, and masters: Gilles, abbot of Holy Trinity of Fécamp, Pierre, prior of Longueville, Jean de Châtillon, Erard Emengart, Jean Beaupère, Jacques de Touraine, Nicolas Midi, Denis de Sabrevois, Nicolas Lami, Guillaume Erard, Pierre Maurice, Gérard Feuillet, Maurice du Quesnay, Pierre Houdenc, Jean de Nibat, doctors of theology; Guillaume, abbot of Notre-Dame de Cormeilles, doctor of canon law; Guillaume Desjardins, Gilles Quenivet, Roland l'Ecrivain, and Guillaume de la Chambre, doctors of medicine; the abbot of Saint-Georges de Préaux, the prior of Saint-Lô, along with Nicolas Couppequesne, Thomas de Courcelles, Guillaume Le Maistre, Guillaume de Baudribosc, Jean Pigache, Raoul le Sauvage, Richard de Grouchet, Pierre Minier, bachelors of theology; Jean le Doux, doctor of canon and civil law; Jean Duchemin, Jean Colombel, Raoul Anguy, Aubert Morel, licentiates of canon law; Geoffroi du Crotay, Bureau de Cormeilles, Nicolas Maulin, licentiates of civil law; and Nicolas Loiselleur, canon of Rouen Cathedral.

In their presence we requested Joan to swear to tell the truth, simply and absolutely, about the things she was to be asked. She answered: "I'm ready to swear as I've done formerly." And so she swore, touching Holy Gospels.[65]

Then, because she had stated that Saint Michael had wings,[66] and yet she had said nothing about the bodies and members of Saint Catherine and Saint Margaret, she was asked what she wished to say about them. She answered: "I have told you what I know, and I have nothing else to tell you." She added that she had seen Saint Michael and the other saints so clearly that she knew they were saints of paradise.

Asked whether she saw anything besides their faces, she answered: "I've told you all I know about this; and while telling all I know, I'd rather you had cut my throat." She said she will gladly tell all she knows that concerns the trial.

Asked whether she believes that Saint Michael and Saint Gabriel have natural heads,[67] she answered: "I saw them with my own eyes, and I believe they were there as surely as I believe there is a God."

Asked whether she believes that God made them in the same manner and shape[68] in which she sees them, she said yes.

Asked whether she believes that God created them from the beginning in that manner and shape, she answered: "You will get nothing more for now than what I've already answered."

Asked whether she knew by revelation that she would escape, she answered: "This doesn't concern your trial. Do you want me to speak against myself?"

Asked whether her voices told her anything about it, she answered: "This doesn't concern your trial; I trust to God. If everything concerned you, I would tell you all." She added that, upon her oath, she does not know the day or the hour when she will escape.

Asked whether the voices spoke to her about this in general, she answered: "Yes, in truth. They told me I would be freed, but I don't know the day or the hour; and I should boldly put on a cheerful countenance."

Asked whether, when she first approached her king, he asked her whether her revelation ordered her to change her attire, she answered: "I've answered you this; I don't remember if that was asked of me. It's written down at Poitiers."

Asked whether she remembered whether the masters who examined her in the other obedience, some for a month, others for three weeks, questioned her about her change of attire, she answered: "I don't remember. They asked me where I took up men's clothing, and I told them Vaucouleurs."

Asked whether these masters asked her whether she had taken men's clothing at the command of her voices, she answered: "I don't remember."

Asked whether, on her first visit, her queen[69] had asked her about her change of attire, she answered: "I don't remember."

Asked whether her king, queen, and others of her party did not sometimes ask her to set aside her men's garments, she answered: "This does not concern your trial."

Asked whether she had not been asked to do so at the castle of Beaurevoir,[70] she answered: "Yes indeed, and I said I would not set them aside without God's leave." <She said that the demoiselle of Luxembourg requested the lord of Luxembourg that Joan not be surrendered to the English.>[71] She said that the demoiselle of Luxembourg and the lady of Beaurevoir offered her women's clothing, or cloth to make some, and they asked her to put it on. She said she did not have God's permission, that it was not yet time.

Asked whether Lord Jean de Pressy and others at Arras offered her women's clothing, she said that he and many others often entreated her to wear it.[72]

Asked whether she believes that she would have committed a fault or sinned mortally in taking women's dress, she said that it is better to obey and serve her supreme lord, that is, God. She said if she had been obliged to wear women's dress, she would have done so at the request of those two ladies more readily than of any others in France, save her queen.

Asked whether, when God revealed to her that she should change her clothing to men's clothing, this was by the voice of Saint Michael or by the voice of Saint Catherine or Margaret, she answered: "You will get nothing more out of me now."

Asked whether, when her king set her to work and she had her banner made, other soldiers had not had pennons made in the style of hers, she answered: "It's good to know that the lords take care of their arms." She said that some of her companions-at-arms had pennons made, others did not.

Asked what material they used, linen or wool, she said white satin, with lilies on some. Joan herself had only two or three lances in her company; but her companions-at-arms sometimes had pennons like hers made, but only to distinguish themselves from others.

Asked whether the pennons were often restored, she answered: "I don't know. When the lances were broken, new pennons were made."

Asked whether she sometimes said that pennons made like hers were lucky, she said she did indeed sometimes say to those of her party: "Go boldly among the English," and she did the same thing herself.

Asked whether she told them to bear the pennons boldly and they would have good luck, she said she did in fact tell them what had happened and what would happen again.

Asked whether she sprinkled the pennons with holy water or had others do so when they were first carried, she answered: "I know nothing of that. If this was done, it was not by my command."

Asked whether she saw them sprinkled with holy water, she answered: "This doesn't concern your trial. If I saw it done, I am not advised to answer you now."

Asked whether her comrades-at-arms had the names Jesus, Mary put on her pennons, she answered: "By my faith, I do not know."

Asked whether she had carried, or had others carry, cloth for the pennons around an altar or church, in the manner of a procession, she said no, nor did she see it happen.

Asked what she was wearing at the back of her helmet when she was before the town of Jargeau, and whether it was something round, she answered: "By my faith, there was nothing there."

Asked whether she ever knew Brother Richard, she answered: "I never saw him until I came before Troyes."[73]

Asked what sort of greeting this Brother Richard made her, she said that the inhabitants of Troyes, she thinks, sent him to her, saying that they doubted that Joan was coming on behalf of God; and when the friar approached her, he made the sign of the cross and sprinkled holy water. And she told him: "Approach boldly—I won't fly away."

Asked whether she had seen or had had made any images or paintings of herself, after her likeness, she said she saw a painting at Arras[74] in the hands of a Scotsman; it showed her fully armed, presenting letters to her king, with her knee bent. She said she never saw or had made any other image or painting of herself.

Asked whether, in her host's house at Orléans, there was a painting showing three women, with the inscription "Justice, Peace, Union," she said she knew nothing about that.[75]

Asked whether she knew that members of her party had ordered that a service, Mass, and prayers be performed in her honor, she said she knew nothing of this; if they have had any service performed, she did not order it. But if they have prayed for her, she thinks they did nothing wrong.[76]

Asked whether the members of her party firmly believe that she has been sent by God, she answered: "I don't know whether they believe, and I leave it to their judgment; but if they don't believe, I have still been sent by God."

Asked whether she thinks they believed well, in believing that she has been sent by God, she answered: "If they believe I am sent by God, they are not deceived."

Asked whether she knew the thoughts of the members of her party, when they kissed her feet, hands, and clothing, she said that many gladly saw her and that they kissed her hands as little as she could manage. The poor gladly came to her, for she brought them no displeasure, but rather helped them to bear [their misfortune].[77]

Asked what honor the citizens of Troyes paid her upon her entrance into the town, she said they paid no honor. She added that, as she remembers, Brother Richard entered Troyes with her and her party; but she does not recall whether he saw her enter.[78]

Asked whether Brother Richard preached a sermon when she arrived, she said she did not stay there long;[79] as for a sermon, she knows nothing of it.

Asked whether she spent many days at Reims, she said she believes that she and her party were there five or six days.[80]

Asked whether she acted as godmother to a child there, she said she did so for one at Troyes; but she does not remember doing so at Reims or at Château-Thierry. She did so for two children at Saint-Denis in France. She gladly named the boys Charles, in honor of her king, and the girls Joan; sometimes she named them as the mothers wished.

Asked whether the women of the town did not touch their rings to the ring that Joan wore on her finger, she answered: "Many women touched my hand and rings, but I don't know with what thought or intention."

Asked what members of her party caught butterflies using her standard before Château-Thierry,[81] she said her party had never done that—the other side had invented it.

Asked what she did at Reims with the gloves her king was wearing when he was consecrated, she said that a gift of gloves was to be given to the knights and nobles; one person there had lost his gloves, but she did not say she would find them.[82] She said her standard was in the church at Reims; as she remembers, it was quite near the altar where her king was consecrated, and she supported it there for a short while. She does not know whether Brother Richard held it.

Asked whether, when she went through the country, she often received the sacraments of Eucharist and penance when she was in good towns, she said yes, occasionally.

Asked whether she took the sacraments in men's attire, she said yes; but she does not remember taking them in arms.

Asked why she took the hackney—*haquenée* in French—of the bishop of Senlis, she said that that palfrey was purchased for two hundred saluts.[83] She does not know whether or not he received the sum, but there was an arrangement, or he was paid. She wrote again to the bishop to say that he could take back his hackney if he wanted to, that she did not want it—it was worthless for carrying a load.

Asked how old the boy was whom she restored to life at Lagny,[84] she said he was three days old. He was placed before the image of Blessed Mary in Lagny, and Joan was informed that the girls of the town were there at the image, and that she might wish to go and pray to God and the Blessed Virgin to give life to the infant. Then she went with the other girls and prayed, when at last life appeared in the boy, who yawned three times and then was baptized. And immediately he died and was buried in consecrated ground. It was said that the boy had shown no signs of life for three days, and he was as black as her cloak. But when he yawned, his color began to return. Joan was with the girls, praying on her knees before Our Lady.

Asked whether it was reported in that town that she had caused the resurrection,[85] and that it happened because of her prayer, she said she did not ask about this.

Asked whether she had known or seen Catherine de la Rochelle, she said yes, at Jargeau and Montfaucon, in the duchy of Berry.[86]

Asked whether this Catherine had shown her a certain lady clothed in white, who she said sometimes appears to her, she said no.

Asked what Catherine had said to her, she said that Catherine told her that a certain white lady came to her, dressed in cloth of gold, and told her to go through the good towns with heralds and trumpets the king would give her, to proclaim that anyone having gold, silver, or hidden treasure should bring it forward at once; and that she would know those who had anything hidden and did not bring it forth, and would be able to find it quite easily. And thus would she pay Joan's men-at-arms. At this, Joan told Catherine to go back to her husband and do her housework—*son mesnage* in French—and take care of her children. To know for certain about the claim of this Catherine, Joan spoke to Saint Catherine and Saint Margaret, who told her that it was all folly and there was nothing to it. She wrote to her king telling him what to do about it;[87] and when she met him, she told him that it was folly and that there was nothing whatsoever to the claim of this Catherine. Yet Brother Richard wanted Catherine to be put to work, so Brother Richard and Catherine were unhappy with Joan.

Asked whether she had spoken to Catherine about going to La Charité-sur-Loire, she said that Catherine had not advised her to go, and that it was too cold; she told Joan she would not go. Joan told Catherine, who wanted to go to the duke of Burgundy to make peace, that she believed that peace would be found only at the point of a lance. She said she asked Catherine whether the white lady who appeared to her came every night; in order to see her [the white lady], she said, she wanted to sleep in the same bed with her. And Joan lay down and watched until midnight, and saw nothing; then she slept. When morning came, she asked Catherine whether the white lady had come to her. She said yes, while Joan was sleeping, but she could not wake her. Then Joan asked her whether the lady would come the following night, and Catherine said yes. So Joan slept that day, to stay awake the entire next night. And that night she went to bed with Catherine, and watched all night. But she saw nothing, though she often asked Catherine whether the lady would come or not, and Catherine replied: "Yes, any minute."

Then Joan, asked what she had done in the trenches at La Charité, said that she ordered an assault there, but that she did not sprinkle holy water, or order any to be sprinkled.

Asked why she did not enter La Charité, when she had been so commanded by God, she answered: "Who told you I was commanded so by God?"

Asked whether she had had counsel from her voice, she said that she had wished to come to France, but the men-at-arms told her that it would be better to go first to La Charité.[88]

Asked whether she had been long in the tower of Beaurevoir, she said she spent four months or so there and that when she learned that the English were coming to seize her, she was furious. Yet the voices often forbade her to leap from the tower. At last, fearing the English, she leaped and commended herself to God and Blessed Mary, and was wounded. After she had leaped, the voice of Saint Catherine told her to be of good cheer, and that the people of Compiègne would lend her aid. She said further that she always prayed to her counsel for the people of Compiègne.

Asked what she said after she leaped, she answered that some people had said she was dead. And as soon as the Burgundians saw that she was alive, they told her that she had leaped.

Asked whether, at that point, she said that she would rather die than fall into the hands of the English, she said she had stated that she would rather deliver her soul to God than fall into the hands of the English.

Asked whether she was angry then and blasphemed the name of

God, she said she never cursed the saints and had never had the habit of swearing.

Asked about Soissons and the captain who had surrendered the town, whether she had denied God when she said that if she had gotten hold of the captain, she would have ordered him to be drawn and quartered, she said she had never denied the saints, and those who said or reported that she did had misunderstood.[89]

With these matters concluded, Joan was led back to her prison cell. Then we the bishop stated that in continuing the trial without interruption, we would call certain doctors and experts in canon and civil law, who would gather from the things that Joan had confessed whatever should be gathered from her responses, which had been put into writing. And after these had been examined and gathered, if there remained certain statements of Joan that called for further questioning, she would be interrogated by individuals of our choosing, without troubling the entire body of assessors. And everything would be put into writing, so that the doctors and lawyers might, whenever fitting, deliberate and give their opinions and offer counsel. And we told them that they might study and privately consider the case and what they had heard at the trial, and conclude what should be done, in their opinion, and report back to us or our deputies; or they might keep to themselves, in order to deliver their opinions at a suitable time and place after more thoughtful and careful deliberation. We forbade, moreover, each and every assessor to leave Rouen without our permission before the close of the trial.

Sunday, March 4. End of the public sessions for this first time. Sunday, March 4, immediately following, and the very next Monday, Tuesday, Wednesday, Thursday, and Friday.

We the bishop, with many solemn doctors, masters, and experts in divine and canon law assembled at our house in Rouen, ordered all Joan's confessions at trial and her responses to be gathered up and an extract to be made of those answers which were insufficient and seemed to call for further questioning. After these were gathered and carefully extracted, upon the advice and deliberation of these experts we decided to proceed to further interrogation of the said Joan. And since by reason of our many obligations we could not always attend the interrogations, we assigned the esteemed and wise man Jean de la Fontaine, master of arts and licentiate of canon law, to interrogate Joan judicially in our place; and we entrusted him with this task on Friday, March 9, in the presence of doctors and masters Jean Beaupère, Jacques de Touraine, Nicolas Midi, Pierre Maurice, Thomas de Courcelles, Nicolas Loiseleur, and Guillaume Manchon.

Saturday, March 10. First session in prison. On Saturday, March 10, immediately following, we the bishop arrived at a room in the castle of Rouen that was assigned to Joan as a prison cell. There, assisted by Master Jean de la Fontaine, our appointed representative, with esteemed doctors and masters of theology Nicolas Midi and Gérard Feuillet and with witnesses present—Jean Secard, lawyer, and the reverend Jean Massieu, priest—we requested Joan to make and to take an oath to tell the truth about what she would be asked.

She answered: "I promise you to tell the truth about what concerns your trial. The more you force me to swear, the longer I'll take to tell you."

Then Joan was questioned by Master Jean de la Fontaine, whom we had particularly chosen and designated for this task. And he asked her, upon the oath she had taken, where she had come from the last time she went to Compiègne. She said she had come from Crépy-en-Valois.[90]

Asked whether she passed many days in Compiègne before she left or made a "sally," she said she had come at a secret hour in the morning and entered the town without her enemies' knowledge, she thought. The evening of the same day, she made a sally—*saillie* in French—when she was captured.[91]

Asked whether the bells were rung when she attacked, she said that if so, it was not by her command or with her knowledge, nor did she give any thought to this; she does not even remember saying they were rung.

Asked whether she ordered the sally at the command of her voice, she said that Easter week last, while in the trenches of Melun, her voices—that is Saint Catherine and Saint Margaret—told her she would be taken before the feast of Saint John, that it must be so, that she should not be overwhelmed, but should take it in good part and God would help her.[92]

Asked whether since Melun her voices had told her that she would be captured, she said yes, quite often, nearly every day. She asked of her voices that when she should be taken, she might die at once, without the long distress of imprisonment. And the voices told her to take it all in good part, that it must be so; but they did not tell her the hour. Had she known the hour, she would not have gone. She often asked her voices the hour of her capture, but they would not tell her.

Asked whether she would have gone if her voices had ordered her to attack from Compiègne, and had signified that she would be taken captive, she answered that had she known the hour of her capture, she would not have gone willingly; nonetheless, she would have obeyed the command of the voices, whatever should happen to her.

Asked whether, when she made the sally from Compiègne, she had it from her voice or revelation that she should go and make the sally, she said that on that day she did not know she would be captured, nor had she any command to go forth; but she had always been told that she must be taken prisoner.

Asked whether she crossed the bridge of Compiègne when she made the sally, she said that she crossed the bridge and the boulevard, and went with a company from her party against the people of my lord Jean de Luxembourg. Twice she drove them back to the camp or lodging of the Burgundians, reaching halfway the third time. Then the English who were there cut Joan and her company off from the road. And while Joan was retreating, she was captured in the fields on the side nearest Picardy, near the boulevard. Between the place where she was captured and Compiègne there was nothing but the river and the boulevard with a trench.[93]

Asked whether the world and two angels, etc., were painted on the banner she was carrying, she said yes, she never had but one.

Asked what this meant, to paint God holding the world, and two angels, she said that Saint Catherine and Saint Margaret told her to take the banner and bear it boldly, and to have the King of Heaven painted there. She told her king this, most unwillingly. She knows nothing more about its meaning.

Asked whether she had a shield and arms, she said she never did, but her king gave arms to her brothers, a shield of azure bearing two golden lilies with a sword between.[94] And in this town [of Rouen], she described these arms to a painter who had asked her what arms she bore. She said her king gave them to her brothers <for their pleasure>, without her asking and without revelation.

Asked whether she had a horse when she was captured, whether a charger or a hackney, she said she was riding a horse, a demi-charger—*ung demi coursier* in French.

Asked who gave it to her, she said that her king or his people gave it to her out of the king's treasury. She had five chargers out of her king's treasury not counting the hacks, which numbered more than seven.

Asked whether she ever had other riches from her king besides the horses, she said she asked nothing from her king but good arms, good horses, and money to pay the people of her household.

Asked whether she had a treasury, she said she had ten or twelve thousand écus, but it was not much for carrying on a war, rather it was too little. Her brothers have it, she thinks. What she has, she says, is her king's own money.

Asked what sign she gave her king when she came to him,[95] she said one that is fair, honorable, most trustworthy and good, the richest in the world.

Asked why she has no desire to tell or reveal the sign, as she wished to see the sign of Catherine de la Rochelle, she said that she would not have asked to know the sign of Catherine if it had been shown to important churchmen as much as Joan's sign had been—to archbishops and bishops, such as the archbishop of Reims and others whose names she does not know, as well as Charles of Bourbon, my lord of Trémoille, the duke of Alençon, and many other knights who saw and heard the sign as clearly as Joan sees people talking to her and standing before her today.[96] And yet she already knew from Saint Catherine and Saint Margaret that the claim of Catherine de la Rochelle was utter nonsense.

Asked whether the sign still exists, she said that it is a good thing to know; it will endure a thousand years and beyond. She says the sign is in her king's treasury.

Asked whether it is gold, silver, a precious stone, or a crown, she answered: "I won't tell you anything else. No one could describe a thing as precious as this sign. All the same, the sign you need is that God will deliver me from your hands, and it is the most certain one he could send you." She says that when she was to leave to go see her king, her voices told her: "Go boldly! When you stand before the king, he will have a good sign to receive and believe in you."

Asked what reverence she made the sign when it came to her king, and whether it came from God, she said she thanked God for delivering her from the hostility of clerks in her own party who opposed her; she genuflected many times. She says that an angel of God and no other gave her king a sign, and she gave thanks to God for it many times. The clerks stopped opposing her when they received the sign.

Asked whether the churchmen of her party had seen the sign, she said that when her king and those with him saw the sign and the very angel who gave it, she asked her king whether he was satisfied, and he said yes. Then she left and went to a chapel close by. And after she left, she heard that more than three hundred people saw the sign. She added that for love of her, and so that people might stop questioning her, God wanted to allow those members of her party who did in fact see the sign to witness it.

Asked whether she and her king paid reverence to the angel when he brought the sign, she said she did, and she knelt and bared her head.

Monday, March 12. Second session. The following Monday, March 12, there appeared in our dwelling at Rouen the religious and wise man Brother Jean Le Maistre, of the Order of Friars Preachers, vice-inquisitor of heresy in the kingdom of France, in the presence of esteemed and wise men: the reverend masters Thomas Fiefvet and Pasquier de Vaux, doctors of canon law; Nicolas de Hubent, apostolic secretary; and Brother Ysambard de la Pierre, of the Order of Friars Preachers.

We the bishop explained to the vice-inquisitor that at the beginning of the trial that we had begun in a matter of faith against a certain woman Joan, commonly called the Maid, we had summoned him and asked him to participate, and we offered to share with him the acts, documents, and everything else pertaining to the matter and trial. But the vice-inquisitor then raised a difficulty concerning his participation in the trial, because he had been appointed only for the city and diocese of Rouen; now the trial had fallen to us by virtue of our jurisdiction of Beauvais, in borrowed territory. Therefore, to settle the matter more surely, and taking all precautions, we had decided to write to the reverend inquisitor and ask him to come to Rouen or to appoint a vicar especially for this case, with complete authority to conduct and conclude the trial on his behalf, as reported in greater detail above. After the reverend inquisitor had received our letter, he kindly consented to our request, for the honor and exaltation of the true faith, and especially appointed and delegated Brother Jean Le Maistre to conduct and conclude this case, by his letters patent secured and authenticated by his seal, whose contents follow below. We therefore summoned and requested Brother Jean Le Maistre to join himself to this trial, according to his commission. He replied that he would gladly see the commission addressed to him, the trial record signed by the notaries, and other documents that we would share with him. After he had seen and examined them, he would reply and do his duty on behalf of holy inquisition. And we told him that he had already been present for much of the trial and had heard many of Joan's responses; and we were satisfied and would gladly share with him the trial record and all that had been done in the matter, for his study and examination.

Here follows the letter of commission sent by the reverend inquisitor, mentioned above.

Letter of Jean Graverent Appointing Jean Le Maistre Vice-Inquisitor for the Trial

Summary. *Jean Graverent to Jean Le Maistre. Since Graverent is prevented from coming himself, he appoints Le Maistre vice-inquisitor for the trial. Dated March 4, 1431, Coutances. Signed: "C. Ogier."*

The same Monday. The same Monday in the morning, we the bishop entered the room assigned to Joan as her prison in the castle of Rouen, where esteemed and wise men gathered with us: the reverend masters Jean de la Fontaine, our chosen representative; Nicolas Midi and Gérard Feuillet, doctors of theology; witnesses Thomas Fiefvet and Pasquier de Vaux, doctors of canon law; and Nicolas Hubent, apostolic secretary.

In their presence, we asked Joan to swear to tell the truth about the things she was to be asked. She replied that she would gladly tell the truth "about what touches your trial," as she had said on other occasions. And so she swore.

Then, by our order, she was first asked by Master Jean de la Fontaine whether the angel who had brought her king a sign, as mentioned above, had not spoken. She said yes, and he told the king to put Joan to work, and the country would straightaway be relieved.

Asked whether the angel that brought the sign to her king was the same that had first appeared to her <or if it were another>, she said he is always one and the same, and he never fails her.

Asked whether the angel did not in fact fail her with respect to her good luck when she was captured, she said that since it pleased God, it was better for her to be captured.

Asked whether the angel had not failed her in the blessings of grace, she answered: "How could he fail me when he comforts me each day?" She understands, as she says, that this comfort comes from Saint Catherine and Saint Margaret.

Asked whether she calls out to Saint Catherine and Saint Margaret, or whether they come without being summoned, she said they often come without being summoned. On other occasions, if they did not come, she would at once ask God to send them.

Asked whether sometimes the saints did not come when she summoned them, she said that never did she have need of them and not have them.

Asked whether Saint Denis ever appeared to her, she said no, as far as she knows.

Asked whether she spoke to God when she promised him to keep her virginity, she said that it ought to be enough to make this promise to those sent from God, namely Saint Catherine and Saint Margaret.

Asked what persuaded her to summon a man from Toul in an action for marriage,[97] she answered: "I didn't have him summoned; he had me summoned. I swore there before the judge to tell the truth," and finally she said that she had made him no promise. She says further that the first time she heard her voice, she took a vow to keep her virginity, so long as it pleased God; she was around thirteen years old. She says her voices assured her of winning her case in Toul.

Asked whether she ever spoke to her priest or to any other clergyman about the visions she says she has, she said no, only to Robert de Baudricourt and to her king. She says further that her voices did not compel her to keep this secret; but she dreaded to reveal them for fear of the Burgundians, that they would hinder her journey. She especially feared her father, that he would keep her from making her journey.

Asked whether she believes she did well in leaving without her father and mother's permission, since she should honor her father and mother,[98] she said that she obeyed her father and mother very well in all other matters, except for that journey; later, she wrote to them about this, and they forgave her.

Asked whether she thought she was sinning when she left her father and mother, she said that since God had commanded her, it had to be done. She says further that since God commanded her, had she one hundred fathers and mothers, and were she the king's daughter, still she would have left.

Questioned whether she had asked her voices if she should tell her father and mother of her leaving,[99] she said that with regard to her father and mother, the voices would have been well pleased that she should tell them, were it not for the trouble they would have caused had she done so. For herself, she would not have told them for anything. She says the voices let her decide whether to tell her father and mother of this or to remain silent.

Asked whether she made reverence to Saint Michael and the angels when she saw them, she said yes, and she kissed the ground they passed over after they left.

Asked whether the angels stayed long with her, she said they often come unseen among Christians. She often sees them among Christians.

Asked whether she had received letters from Saint Michael or from her voices, she answered: "I do not have leave to speak to you of this. Within eight days I will gladly tell you what I know."

Asked whether her voices had ever called her daughter of God, daughter of the Church, daughter great-hearted, she said that before the lifting of the siege of Orléans and every day since, when they spoke to her they frequently called her Joan the Maid, daughter of God.

Asked why, though she calls herself daughter of God, she does not willingly say the Our Father, she said she would gladly say it. Formerly, when she refused, she did so intending that we the bishop should hear her in confession.

The same Monday afternoon. The same Monday in the afternoon, there appeared in Joan's prison reverend masters: Jean de la Fontaine, our chosen representative; Nicolas Midi and Gérard Feuillet, doctors of theology; Thomas Fiefvet and Pasquier de Vaux, doctors of canon law; and Nicolas Hubent, apostolic secretary.

Joan was interrogated by the said La Fontaine by our command, first concerning the dreams her father reportedly had about her before she left his house. She replied that when she was still in her father and mother's house, her mother often told her that her father spoke of having dreamed that Joan, his daughter, would leave with men-at-arms. From that time, her father and mother took great care to guard her, and kept her in great subjection. She obeyed them in all matters, except for the trial at Toul in the cause of marriage. She says she heard her mother say that her father told her brothers: "Truly, if I believed what I fear for my daughter would happen, I should wish you to drown her; and if you would not, I would drown her myself." Her mother and father nearly lost their senses when she left for Vaucouleurs.

Asked whether these thoughts or dreams came to her father after she had had her visions, she said yes, more than two years after she had first heard the voices.

Asked whether it was at the request of Robert de Baudricourt or at her own prompting that she took men's clothes, she said it was of her own will, and not at the request of any living person.

Asked whether the voice instructed her to take men's garb, she answered: "Everything good that I have done has been at the instruction of my voices. As for my clothing, I will answer at another time; I have not been advised at present, but will answer this tomorrow."

Asked whether she did not think she was doing wrong in taking men's garb, she said no. Even now, if she were still with her own people and dressed in men's clothing, it seems to her that it would be for the great good of France to do as she did before her capture.

Asked how she would have freed the duke of Orléans, she said she would have taken enough English prisoners to ransom him. And had she not taken enough on this side [of the sea], she would have crossed the sea, to rescue him from England by force.

Asked whether Saint Catherine and Saint Margaret had told her absolutely and unconditionally that she would take enough prisoners to ransom the duke of Orléans in England, or that she would cross the sea at another time to rescue him, she said yes, and she had told her king this, and that he would let her deal with the English lords who were prisoners. Given three years without obstacles, she would have freed the duke. This was a task of less than three years and more than one; but she does not remember [exactly how long].

Asked what the sign was that she gave her king, she said she would take counsel with Saint Catherine about this.

Tuesday, March 13. On Tuesday, March 13, immediately following, we the bishop arrived at the prison. And there, at the same hour, appeared the esteemed and wise man Brother Jean Le Maistre, accompanied by esteemed and wise men, the reverend masters Jean de la Fontaine, Nicolas Midi, and Gérard Feuillet; and as witnesses Nicolas de Hubent and Ysambard de la Pierre, of the Order of Friars Preachers.

Brother Jean Le Maistre, having now seen the letter addressed to him by the reverend inquisitor with the other documents for consideration, joined with us in the trial, ready to proceed to a decision in the case, according to law and reason. We kindly explained this to Joan herself, urging and advising her for her soul's salvation to tell the truth in the trial about all things she would be asked. Then the vice-inquisitor, wishing to proceed further in the case, appointed the reverend Jean d'Estivet, canon of the churches of Bayeux and Beauvais, as promoter of the holy inquisition; the nobleman John Grey, squire of the body of our lord the king, and Jean Berwoit as jailers; and the reverend Jean Massieu, priest, as executor of citations and summons. We the bishop appointed and ordained all of these to their offices, as related more fully in the bishop's letters above and in the vice-inquisitor's letters below, confirmed by our seals. All of these officers took an oath to the vice-inquisitor to exercise their offices faithfully.

Here follows the letter of appointment of the promoter by the vice-inquisitor.

Letter of Jean Le Maistre Appointing Jean d'Estivet Promoter for the Inquisition

Summary. Jean Le Maistre appoints Jean d'Estivet as promoter on behalf of the inquisition. Dated March 13, 1431, Rouen. Signed "Boisguillaume, Manchon."

Here follows the letter whereby the vice-inquisitor appointed the reverend Jean Massieu priest, executor of summons and citations in this trial.

Letter of Jean Le Maistre Appointing Jean Massieu Executor for the Inquisition

Summary. Jean Le Maistre appoints Jean Massieu executor. Dated March 13, 1431, Rouen. Signed: "Boisguillaume, Manchon."

When this was concluded, we the bishop and Brother Jean Le Maistre, vice-inquisitor, proceeded to examine Joan as above.

First, at our command, Joan was asked what the sign was that she gave her king. She answered: "Do you want me to perjure myself?"

Asked <by my lord the vice-inquisitor> whether she had sworn and promised Saint Catherine not to speak of that sign, she answered: "I have sworn and promised not to speak of the sign of my own accord, since people troubled me so much to speak of it." And then she promised to speak no further of this to anyone. She says the sign was that an angel, in bringing her king a crown, assured him that he would have the kingdom of France whole and entire with the help of God and the labors of Joan herself. He should put Joan to work, that is give her men-at-arms, or he would not so soon be crowned and consecrated.

Asked whether she had spoken with Saint Catherine since yesterday, she said she had heard her since then; and still she told her many times to answer the judges boldly about what they would ask her touching her trial.

Asked how the angel bore the crown mentioned earlier, and whether he placed it on the head of her king, she said that the crown was given to an archbishop, namely the archbishop of Reims, she thinks, in her king's presence. And the archbishop took it and gave it to her king; and Joan herself was there. The crown was put into her king's treasury.

Asked where the crown was brought, she said to her king's chamber in the castle of Chinon.

Asked on what day and at what hour, she said she knows nothing of the day; as for the hour, it was late, but otherwise she does not remember. It was in April or March, she thinks. And she said: "From next April or the present month of March, it is two years ago, and it was after Easter."[100]

Asked whether, on the day she saw the sign, her king also saw it, she said yes, and her king himself received it.

Asked what the crown was made of, she said it is good to know that it was made of pure gold. The crown was so rich or splendid that she knew not how to count or fathom its richness. And the crown signified that her king would hold the kingdom of France.

Asked whether it had precious stones, she answered: "I've told you what I know of this."

Asked whether she held or kissed the crown, she said no.

Asked whether the angel that brought the crown came from on high or from the earth, <she answered: "He came from on high." And she understood that he came by the commandment of our Lord, and entered the room by the door. Asked whether the angel came from the earth and entered the room by the door,>[101] she said that when the angel came before her king, he bowed before him, bending down and pronouncing the words about the sign that Joan mentioned above. And with that, the angel recalled to the king the sweet patience he had shown through the great trials that had afflicted him. From the door, the angel walked upon the ground and came toward her king.

Asked how far it was from the door to her king, she said she believes the length of a lance; the angel went out as he had come in. When the angel came, she accompanied him by the stairs to her king's chamber. The angel entered first, then Joan; and Joan said to her king: "Sire, here is your sign; take it."

Asked where the angel appeared to Joan, she answered: "I was almost always praying that God would send the king's sign, and I was in my lodging in the house of a good woman near the town of Chinon when the angel came; afterward, he and I went to the king together. This angel was well attended by other angels, which no one saw." She said further that were it not for love of her and to remove her from the trouble caused by her opponents, she truly believes, the angel would not have made himself visible to many who saw him.

Asked whether all who were there with her king saw the angel, she said she believes the archbishop of Reims and the lords d'Alençon, de la Trémoille, and Charles of Bourbon saw him. As for the crown, many clergymen and others saw it who did not see the angel.

Asked about the appearance and size of the angel, she said she has no leave to speak of this and would answer tomorrow.

Asked whether all the angels who attended the angel had the same appearance, she said that some were very like each other, and others not, in the way that she saw them; some had wings and some were crowned <and others not>.[102] In that company were Saint Catherine and Saint Margaret, together with the angel and other angels, who filed right into her king's chamber.

Asked how the angel left her, she said he left her in a certain small chapel. She was very angry at his departure; she cried and would gladly have gone with him—that is, her soul would have gone.

Asked whether she remained joyful <or frightened and in great fear>[103] after the angel's departure, she said he did not leave her in fear or trembling, but she was angry at his leaving.

Asked whether it was for any merit of Joan herself that God sent her his angel, she said that the angel came for a great purpose, in the hope that her king would believe the sign and people would cease opposing Joan, and to help the good people of Orléans, as well as for the merits of her king and the good duke of Orléans.

Asked why this happened to her instead of someone else, she said that it pleased God to do this through a simple maid, to drive back the king's enemies.

Asked whether she had been told whence the angel had taken the crown, she said that it was brought by God, and that no goldsmith in the world could have made one so rich and fair. But as to the question whence the angel took the crown, Joan trusts to God and knows nothing more about it.

Asked whether the crown had a pleasing scent, and whether it shone, she said she does not remember and will seek counsel. But then she said it had a pleasing scent, and will have as long as it is well kept, as is seemly. It was in the shape of a crown.

Asked whether the angel had written her letters, she said no.

Asked what sign her king had and those with him and she herself, to persuade them that an angel brought the crown, she said her king believed it by the guidance or teaching of the clergy present, and by the sign of the crown.

Asked how the clergymen knew it was an angel, she said they knew it from their learning, and because they were clerks.

Asked about a priest with a concubine and about a lost cup that she was said to have revealed, she said she knows nothing of all these matters, nor has she ever heard of them before.[104]

Asked whether, when she went to Paris, she did so on account of the revelation of her voices, she said no, she went at the request of nobles who wanted to undertake an assault, *une escarmouche* in French, or an assault-at-arms. She fully intended to go farther and to cross the trenches of Paris.

Asked whether she had a revelation about going to the town of La Charité, she said no, she went at the request of men-at-arms, as she replied before.

Asked whether she had a revelation about going to Pont-l'Evêque,[105] she said no, after she had a revelation at the trenches of Melun that she would be captured, she turned over most of the conduct of war to the captains; yet she did not tell them of her revelation, that she would be captured.

Asked whether it was right to attack Paris on the Nativity of Blessed Mary,[106] a feast day, she said that it is good to keep the feasts of Blessed Mary; it seems good to her in her conscience to keep the feasts of Blessed Mary from beginning to end.

Asked whether she had not said before Paris: "Surrender this town to Jesus!"[107] she said no, she had said: "Surrender it to the king of France."

Wednesday, March 14. The following Wednesday, March 14, we, Brother Jean Le Maistre, vicar of the lord inquisitor, trusting to the diligence and integrity of that esteemed and wise man the reverend Nicolas Taquel, priest of the diocese of Rouen sworn in as imperial notary public and notary at the archiepiscopal court of Rouen, and having full trust in the Lord, have retained, chosen, and named the said Nicolas notary and secretary for this trial, as shown more fully in our letters patent transcribed below, sealed with our seal and bearing the manual signs of the notaries public. And the next day, in Joan's prison where we had appeared, the reverend Nicolas took an oath before us to faithfully exercise his office as we had requested him, in the presence of Masters Jean de la Fontaine, Nicolas Midi, Gérard Feuillet, Guillaume Manchon, and many others.

Here follows the letter retaining the notary.

Letter of Jean Le Maistre Appointing Nicolas Taquel
Notary for the Inquisition

Summary. Jean Le Maistre appoints Nicolas Taquel notary. Dated March 14, 1431, Rouen. Signed: "Boisguillaume, G. Manchon."

The same day. Master Jean de la Fontaine, deputy appointed by us the bishop, and we, Brother Jean Le Maistre, presiding in Joan's prison in the castle of Rouen. Joan was examined before esteemed and wise men, the reverend masters Nicolas Midi and Gérard Feuillet, doctors of theology, along with Nicolas de Hubent, apostolic secretary, and Brother Ysambard de la Pierre, witnesses.

First she was asked why she leaped from the tower of Beaurevoir.

She replied that she had heard it said that everyone in Compiègne above the age of seven was to be put to fire and sword, and she would rather die than live after such a destruction of good people. This was one reason she leaped. The other was that she knew she had been sold to the English, and she would rather have died than fall into the hands of her enemies the English.

Asked whether she leaped by the counsel of her voices, she said that Saint Catherine told her almost every day not to jump and God would help her and the people of Compiègne. And Joan told Saint Catherine that since God was to help the people of Compiègne, she wished to be there. Then Saint Catherine told her: "You must bear this gladly; you will not be freed until you have seen the king of the English." And Joan answered: "Truly, I don't want to see him; I'd rather die than fall into English hands."

Asked whether she had told Saint Catherine and Saint Margaret such words as these: "Will God let the good people of Compiègne die so horribly?" she replied that she had not said "so horribly," but had spoken to them thus: "How can God let these good people of Compiègne die who have been and are so loyal to their lord?"

She said that following her leap from the tower, she had no desire to eat for two or three days, and she was so injured from the fall that she could not eat or drink. Yet she was comforted by Saint Catherine, who told her to confess and ask forgiveness from God for leaping, and without fail the people of Compiègne would receive help before the winter feast of Saint Martin. Then she began to get better and to eat and was soon healthy.

Asked whether, when she leaped, she believed she was killing herself, she said no, in leaping she commended herself to God. She believed by this leap that she would escape being handed over to the English.

Asked whether, when her speech returned, she denied God and his saints, as it states in the evidence, she said she has no memory of ever denying or cursing God and the saints, then or any other time. <She does not admit this; she does not remember what she said or did.>

Asked whether she wished to refer to the evidence, she answered: "I trust to God and no other, and to good confession."

Asked whether her voices ask her for a delay before answering, she said that sometimes Saint Catherine answers,[108] and sometimes Joan fails to understand her because of the noise in the prison and the uproar from her guards. And when she makes a request to Saint Catherine, then Saint Catherine and Saint Margaret make the request to God, and then they give Joan the answer, according to God's command.

Asked whether, when the saints come, a light comes with them, and whether she saw the light when she heard the voice in the castle, not knowing whether it was in her room, she said that not a day goes by when they do not come to the castle, nor do they come without light. As to the time in question, she does not remember whether she saw the light, or whether she saw Saint Catherine. She says she asked for three things from her voices: one was her deliverance; another was that God would help the French and protect the towns subject to them; the third was her soul's salvation. She asks that if she is taken to Paris, she may have a copy of her questions and answers, so that she may give them to people at Paris and say: "Look how I was interrogated at Rouen, and my answers"; and that she may not be troubled again with so many questions.

And since she said that we the bishop were putting ourselves in grave danger—*en grant dangier* in French—for putting her on trial, she was asked what this meant, what was the peril or danger into which we were placing ourselves, we and the others. She answered that she had told us the bishop: "You say you're my judge; I don't know whether you are, but take good care not to judge me wrongfully, for you would put yourself in grave danger. I'm warning you so that if God punishes you, I'll have done my duty in telling you."

Asked what the peril or danger is, she said that Saint Catherine told her she would have help;[109] she does not know whether this means she will be freed from prison, or whether while she is on trial, some disturbance will happen to free her; she supposes it will be one or the other. For the most part the voices have told her that she will be freed by a great victory. Later, the voices say to her: "Take it all in good part; have no thought for your martyrdom; at the last, you will come to the kingdom of heaven." The voices told her this simply and clearly, without faltering. She says "martyrdom" because of the pain and trials she suffers in prison. She does not know if she will suffer greater pain, but leaves this to God.

Asked whether, since her voices told her that in the end she will come to heaven, she believes herself assured of salvation and that she will not be damned in hell, she said she firmly believes what the voices have told her—namely, that she will be saved—as firmly as if she were already there.

Asked whether, after this revelation, she believes she cannot commit a mortal sin, she answered: "I know nothing about it, but commit myself entirely to God."

And when it was told her that this answer had great consequence, she said that she too reckons it a great treasure.[110]

The same Wednesday afternoon. The same Wednesday afternoon, there appeared in the same place esteemed and wise men, reverend masters: Jean de la Fontaine, appointed by us the bishop, and by us, Jean Le Maistre, vice-inquisitor; assisting with us Nicolas Midi and Gérard Feuillet, doctors of theology; and Brother Ysambard de la Pierre and Jean Manchon, witnesses.

Joan spoke first concerning the article on the certainty of her salvation, on which she was questioned this morning: that she meant by this, provided she keeps the oath and promise she made to God to keep her virginity in both body and soul.

Asked whether she need confess, since she has a revelation from her voices that she will be saved, she said she does not know that she has sinned mortally, but if she is in mortal sin, she thinks that Saint Catherine and Saint Margaret would abandon her at once. And in answer to the question, she believes that one cannot cleanse one's conscience too much.

Asked whether she has denied or cursed God since arriving in this prison, she said no, and sometimes when she says in French: "God willing," or "Saint John," or "Our Lady," those who have reported her words have misunderstood them.

Asked whether it is a mortal sin to take someone for ransom and to put him to death as a prisoner, she said she did not do this.

And since Franquet d'Arras was mentioned, whom she had put to death at Lagny,[111] she said that she consented to his death if he deserved it, for he confessed that he was a murderer, a thief, and a traitor. She said his trial lasted two weeks, and he was judged by the bailiff of Senlis and the magistrates of Lagny. She said she asked to exchange this Franquet for a man from Paris, the owner of the tavern called At the Bear.[112] And when she heard he was dead, and when the bailiff told her that she would be doing a great injury to justice by freeing this Franquet, she told the bailiff: "Since the man I want is dead, deal with this one as justice requires."

Asked whether she gave money or had money given to the one who captured this Franquet, she said she is not the mintmaster or treasurer of France, to hand out money.

And after reminding her that she had attacked Paris on a feast day, that she had taken the lord bishop of Senlis's horse, that she had flung herself from the tower of Beaurevoir, that she is wearing men's clothes, and that she agreed to the death of Franquet d'Arras, they asked her whether she believes she has committed a mortal sin. She said to the first, the attack on Paris, that she does not believe she is in mortal sin; and if she is, it is for God to know it, and the priest in confession.

Second, regarding the horse, she said she firmly believes that she did not sin against God in this, for the horse was valued at two hundred gold saluts, for which the bishop had received an allotment. But the horse was sent back to Lord La Trémoille to return to the bishop of Senlis; the horse was useless to her for riding. And she was not the one who took it from the bishop. She did not want it, she added, because she had heard that the bishop was angry that his horse had been taken; besides, the horse was useless to men-at-arms. In conclusion, Joan does not know whether the bishop was paid the allotment, nor whether he has gotten back his horse, but she thinks not.

Third, regarding the leap from the tower of Beaurevoir, she answered: "I did it not out of despair, but in the hope of saving my body and to help the many good people in need. After leaping, I took confession and asked the Lord for forgiveness," and she received forgiveness from the Lord. She believes it was not good, but wrong, to do so. She knows she was forgiven after she took confession, by revelation from Saint Catherine; it was by the advice of Saint Catherine that she confessed.

Asked whether she had to do heavy penance for this, she said she bore a large part of the penance in the injury she sustained in falling.

Asked whether she believes that the wrong she did in leaping was a mortal sin, she said she knows nothing about it, and commits herself to God.

Fourth, regarding the men's clothing, she answered: "Since I do this by God's command and in his service, I don't think I'm doing evil. And the minute it pleases God to command it, I'll remove these clothes."

Thursday, March 15. The Thursday morning immediately following, March 15, at Joan's prison. There presiding, Master Jean de la Fontaine, appointed by us the bishop, and by us, Brother Jean Le Maistre, vice-inquisitor; assisted by esteemed men, the reverend masters Nicolas Midi and Gérard Feuillet, doctors of theology; and Nicolas de Hubent, apostolic secretary, and Brother Ysambard de la Pierre, witnesses.

With kind entreaties, Joan was warned and requested to yield to the decision of Holy Mother Church, to whom she should yield if she has done anything against the faith. But she replied that her answers may be seen and examined by clerks, and then let her be told if they include anything against the faith. She will be able to tell what it is quite well, and then she will tell what she has learned from her counsel. But should there be anything against the Christian faith that God has commanded, she would not wish to uphold it, and she would be quite vexed to find herself in opposition.

The difference between the Church triumphant and the Church militant was explained to her, what each one was. And she was advised henceforth to submit herself to the decision of the Church about what she has said and done, whether good or evil. She answered: "I won't reply further at present."

Then Joan was advised, under her oath, to tell how she tried to escape from the castle at Beaulieu between two planks of wood.[113] She said that she had never been a prisoner anywhere but she would gladly have escaped. When she was in that castle, she would have locked her guards in the tower had it not been for the porter, who saw and prevented her. She said regarding this incident that it seemed to her that it was not God's will for her to escape, and that she must see the king of the English as her voices told her, as recorded above.

Asked whether she has leave from God or her voices to leave prison whenever she wants, she answered: "I've asked for it many times, but so far I don't have permission."

Asked whether she would leave right now if she saw the chance, she said that if she saw the door open she would go; this would be God's permission. And she firmly believes that if she saw the door open and her guards and the other Englishmen unable to oppose her, she would take this as her permission, that God would send her help. But she would not go without leave, unless she undertook an attack—*une entreprise* in French—to see whether God was pleased. She quoted the French proverb "God helps those who help themselves."[114] And she says this so that if she escapes, no one can say she went without leave.

She was asked, since she had requested to hear Mass, whether she does not think it would be more decent to put on women's clothing. And she was asked which she would prefer: to wear women's clothing and hear Mass, or stay in men's clothing and not hear Mass. She answered: "Promise me that I'll get to hear Mass if I wear women's clothes, and I'll answer you."

Then the interrogator told her: "I promise that you will hear Mass if you wear women's clothing."

She answered: "And what do you say if I've promised our king and sworn not to remove these clothes? Nonetheless, I say, make me a long robe that touches the ground, with no train, and give it to me for Mass. Then when I come back I'll put back on these clothes I'm wearing."

Asked again whether she would wear women's clothing to go hear

Mass,[115] she answered: "I'll take counsel on this and answer you later." She further asked that for the honor of God and Blessed Mary she might hear Mass in this good town.

And the questioner told her to put on women's clothing once and for all. But she answered: "Give me a garment befitting a citizen's daughter—that is, a long greatcoat—and I'll wear it <and a woman's hood> to go hear Mass." She asked further, with greatest urgency, that she be allowed to hear Mass in the clothes she was wearing, without changing.

Asked whether she would submit and refer all she has said and done to the decision of the Church, she answered: "All my words and deeds are in God's hands, and I wait on him in these things. I assure you, I would not do or say anything against the Christian faith. If I had said or done anything, or if there were anything on my body that clerks could say was against the Christian faith the Lord established, I would not uphold it but would reject it."

Asked whether she would submit on this point to the decree of the Church, she answered: "I won't answer anything further now. But send the clerk to me on Saturday, if you don't want to come yourself, and with God's help I'll answer him, and it will be put into writing."

Asked whether, when her voices come, she does them absolute reverence, as to a saint, she said yes; if sometimes she did not, she asked their pardon afterward. She does not know how to pay them the great reverence that befits them, for she firmly believes they are Saint Catherine and Saint Margaret. And she said the same for Saint Michael.

Asked whether, since candles are commonly offered to saints in heaven, she has never offered burning candles or other things to the saints who visit her, in church or elsewhere, or whether she has never had masses said, she said no, except in offering [a candle] into the priest's hand at Mass, in honor of Saint Catherine. She believes she is one of those who appear to her. She has not lit as many candles as she gladly would for Saint Catherine and Saint Margaret in paradise, who she believes steadfastly are the ones who come to her.

Asked whether, when she puts candles before the image of Saint Catherine, she does so in honor of the one that appears to her, she answered: "I do it in honor of God, Blessed Mary, and Saint Catherine in heaven, and she who reveals herself to me."

Asked whether she places these candles in honor of the Saint Catherine who reveals herself or appears to her, she said yes, and she sees no difference between the one who appears to her and the one who is in heaven.

Asked whether she always does and carries out what her voices command her, she said that with all her might she has fulfilled the command of God revealed to her by her voices, what she can understand of it. The voices instruct her to do nothing without God's blessing.

Asked whether she has done anything in battle without counsel from her voices, she answered: "You have my answer to this. Read your book very carefully and you'll find it." Still, she said that at the request of the men-at-arms, she had staged an armed attack on Paris, and on La Charité at the request of her king. This was neither for nor against the command of her voices.

Asked whether she had ever done anything against the will and command of the voices, she said she did her best at whatever she could do and knew how to do. As for the leap from the tower of Beaurevoir, which she made against their command, she could not help herself. When the voices saw her need, that she could not help it, they saved her life and kept her from killing herself. No matter what she has done, the voices have always helped her in her great enterprises; and this is a sign they are good spirits.

Asked whether she has any other sign that the voices are good spirits, she said that Saint Michael assured her of it before the voices came.

Asked how she knew it was Saint Michael, she said by his speech and by the angelic language; and she firmly believes they were angels.

Asked how she knew they were angels,[116] she said she believed it almost right away, and desired to believe it. She said that when Saint Michael came, he told her that Saint Catherine and Saint Margaret would visit her and that she should follow their counsel; they were appointed to lead her and advise her in the tasks ahead, and she should believe what they told her, for this was by God's command.

Asked how, if the devil took the shape or appearance of a good angel, she would know it was a good or an evil angel, she said she would know very well if it was Saint Michael or a counterfeit in his likeness. The first time, she had grave doubts that it was Saint Michael, and she was very frightened. She saw him many times before she knew it was Saint Michael.

Asked how she knew that it was Saint Michael then, rather than the first time he appeared to her, she said that the first time, she was just a young girl, and frightened. After that, Saint Michael taught her and showed her so much that she firmly believed it was he.

Asked what doctrine he taught her, she said that above all he told her to be a good child and God would help her. And among other things, he told her she should go help the king of France. The greater part of what the angel taught her is in this book;[117] and the angel recounted to her the distress of the kingdom of France.

Asked the height and bearing of the angel, she said she would answer this on Saturday, along with the other answers she has to give, if it pleases God.

Asked whether she does not believe it is a great sin to displease Saint Catherine and Saint Margaret who visit her, and to act against their commands, she said yes, but amends can be made.[118] She displeased them most by her leap at Beaurevoir, so she sought their forgiveness for this and for her other offenses against them.

Asked whether Saint Catherine and Saint Margaret would take bodily vengeance for that offense, she said she does not know and has not asked them.

Asked whether, since she said on another occasion that one is sometimes hanged for telling the truth, she knows some crime or offense for which she could or should die if she confessed it, she said no.

Saturday, March 17. Saturday, March 17 immediately following, presiding in Joan's prison, Master Jean de la Fontaine, appointed by us the bishop, and by us, Jean Le Maistre, vice-inquisitor, was assisted by esteemed and wise men, the reverend masters named above, Nicolas Midi and Gérard Feuillet, doctors of theology; and Ysambard de la Pierre and Jean Massieu, present. The said Joan was asked to take an oath, and she did.

Asked the form and shape, appearance and dress in which Saint Michael came to her, she said he took the shape of a most righteous man; she will say nothing more about his clothing and other matters. As for the angels, she saw them with her own eyes, and nothing more will be said about them. She says she believes the words and deeds of Saint Michael who appeared to her, just as surely as she believes that our Lord Jesus Christ suffered and died for us. What leads her to believe is the good counsel, comfort, and teaching he gave Joan.

Asked whether she will submit all her deeds to the judgment of Holy Mother Church, for better or worse, she said that as for the Church, she loves it and would support it with all her might for our Christian faith; she is not the one who should be kept from going to church or hearing Mass. As for her good works and her mission, she must trust to the King of Heaven who sent her to Charles, son of Charles, king of France, who was king of France.[119] "And you'll see," she said, "that soon enough the French will win a great enterprise that God will send them, and the whole kingdom of France will shake," *branlera* in French. She is saying this so that when it happens, people will remember that she said it.

Asked to specify when, she answered: "In this I wait upon the Lord."

Asked whether she would submit her deeds and words to the decision of the Church, she answered: "I submit to God, who sent me, to Blessed Mary, and to all the saints of heaven. It seems to me that God and the Church are one and the same, and there should be no difficulty. Why do you make this a difficulty?"

Then she was told that there is the Church triumphant, where dwell God, the saints, the angels, and those souls already saved; there is also the Church militant, in which are the pope, God's vicar on earth, the cardinals, the prelates of the Church, the clergy and all good catholic Christians. When assembled, this Church cannot err and is governed by the Holy Ghost. Therefore she was asked whether she would submit to the Church militant, that which is on earth, as it had now been explained. She replied that she came to the king of France from God, the Blessed Virgin Mary, and all the saints of heaven and the Church victorious above, and at their command; and she submits all her good deeds and all that she has done and will do to that Church. And as to whether she will submit to the Church militant, she says she will not answer at this time.

Asked what she has to say about the women's clothes they offered her so that she could go hear Mass, she said that as to the women's clothes, she would not take them until it pleased God. And if she must be brought to judgment <and stripped>,[120] she asks the lords of the Church to grant her the grace of a woman's gown and a hood for her head. She would rather die than deny what God gave her to do. She firmly believes that God will not let her be brought so low but he will help her by a miracle.

Asked why, since she says she wears her clothing by God's command, she asks for a woman's gown in her final hour, she answered: "It only needs to be long."

Asked whether her godmother who saw the fairies, *les fées* in French, is considered a wise woman, she said that she is considered an upright woman, not a fortune-teller or sorceress.

Asked whether it was pleasing to God, her saying that she would take women's clothing if they let her go, she said that if they let her go in women's clothing, she would immediately put men's clothes back on and do what the Lord had commanded her. She said this at another time; and not for anything would she take an oath not to arm herself or wear men's clothing to do the Lord's command.

Asked about the age and garments of Saint Catherine and Saint Margaret, she answered: "You've already heard the answer you'll hear from me, and you won't hear another. I've answered you as best I can."

Asked whether she believed before today that fairies were evil spirits, she said she knows nothing about it.

Asked whether she knows whether Saint Catherine and Saint Margaret hate the English, she answered: "They love what God loves and hate what God hates."

Asked whether God hates the English, she said she knows nothing about the love or hate that God has for the English, nor what he will do with their souls; but she knows for certain they will be driven from France, except those who stay and die, and that God will grant the French victory over the English.

Asked whether God favored the English when they were prospering in France, she said she does not know whether God hated the French; but she believes he wanted them to be beaten for their sins, if they were in sin.

Asked what promise and help she expected to receive from the Lord for wearing men's clothes, she said that for her clothing and her other deeds, she expected nothing but the salvation of her soul.

Asked what arms she offered in the church of Saint-Denis in France, she said she offered a complete suit of white armor, *un blanc harnois* in French, suitable for a man-at-arms, with a sword she won at Paris.

Asked why she offered those arms, she said out of devotion, according to the custom of soldiers when they are wounded. Since she was wounded at Paris, she offered them to Saint Denis, because that is the battle cry of France.

Asked whether she did it so that her arms might be worshipped, she said no.

Asked the purpose of the five crosses that were on the sword she found at Sainte-Catherine de Fierbois, she said she knows nothing about it.

Asked what moved her to have angels painted on her banner, complete with arms, feet, legs, and garments, she answered: "You already have my answer to this."

Asked whether she had had the angels that visit her painted, she said she had them painted the way they are painted in churches.

Asked whether she has ever seen them the way they were painted, she answered: "I will tell you nothing else."

Asked why she did not have the light painted that comes to her with the angel or voices, she said that this was not commanded.

The afternoon of the same day. The same Saturday in the afternoon, we the bishop and vice-inquisitor, presiding, were assisted by esteemed and wise men: the reverend masters Jean Beaupère, Jacques de Touraine, Nicolas Midi, Pierre Maurice, and Gérard Feuillet, doctors, and Thomas de Courcelles, bachelor of theology; Jean de la Fontaine, licentiate of canon law appointed by us the bishop—in the presence of Brother Ysambard de la Pierre and of John Grey.

Joan was asked whether the two angels painted on her banner represented Saint Michael and Saint Gabriel. She answered that they were only there to glorify God, who was painted on the banner. She had the two angels represented only to glorify God, who was shown holding the world.

Asked whether the two angels pictured on her banner were the two angels who guard the world, and why there were not more, seeing that God had commanded her to take the banner, she said that the whole banner was commanded by God through the voices of Saint Catherine and Saint Margaret, who told her: "Receive this banner in the name of the King of Heaven." And because they told her: "Take this banner in the name of the King of Heaven," she had God and the angels pictured and colored there. She did everything by God's command.

Questioned as to whether she had then asked the two saints whether, by the power of that banner, she would win all battles she fought and be victorious, she said they told her to take it boldly and God would aid her.

Asked whether she helped the banner more than the banner helped her, she said that whether the victory was hers or her banner's, it was all for the Lord.

Asked whether the hope of victory was founded on the banner or on Joan herself, she said that it was founded on the Lord and no other.

Asked, if someone else had carried the banner, whether he would have had as good luck as Joan, she answered: "I know nothing about it; I wait upon God."

Asked, if a man of her party or especially her king had given her his banner, whether she would have carried it, and whether she would have put as much faith in it as in her own banner, which was commanded for her by God, she answered: "I carried more gladly what was ordained for me by God. Still, I trust myself entirely to God."

Asked the purpose of the sign she put in her letters, and the names Jesus, Mary, she said that the clerks who wrote her letters put them there; some of them told her that it was proper to write the two names Jesus, Mary.

Asked whether it had not been revealed to her that if she lost her virginity, she would lose her good fortune and her voices would no longer come to her, she said it had not been revealed to her.

Asked whether she thinks the voices would come to her if she were married, she answered: "I don't know. I trust myself to God."

Asked whether she judges and firmly believes that her king did right when he murdered <or ordered the murder of> the lord duke of Burgundy,[121] she said that this brought great harm to the kingdom of France; but whatever had happened between those two princes, God had sent her to help the king of France.

Asked, since she told us the bishop that she would answer us and our representatives as she would our holy father the pope and yet she chooses not to answer many questions, whether she would not answer the pope more fully than she answers us, she said that she has answered everything as truly as she can; and if something came to mind that she has omitted, she would gladly tell it.

<Asked the age, size, and clothing of the angel who brought the sign to her king.>[122]

Asked whether she does not think that she would have to tell the truth to our father the pope, vicar of God, about everything she would be asked touching the faith and the state of her conscience, more fully than she answers us, she said that she wants to be taken to our father the pope, and then she will answer him all necessary questions.

Asked about the material of one of her rings on which the words "Jesus, Mary" are written, she said she does not know for sure. If it is gold, it is not pure gold. She does not know whether it was gold or brass. She thinks it had three crosses, and no other sign that she knew of, except the names Jesus, Mary.

Asked why she looked fondly at the ring when she went into battle, she said it was out of pleasure, and in honor of her father and mother. While she was wearing the ring on her hand and finger, she touched Saint Catherine who appeared to her.

Asked what part of Saint Catherine she touched, she answered: "You will get no other answer."

Asked whether she had ever kissed or embraced Saint Catherine and Saint Margaret, she said she embraced them both.

Asked whether they had a pleasant fragrance, she said it is a good thing to know, they had a pleasant fragrance.

Asked whether she felt warmth or anything else when she embraced them, she said one could not embrace them without feeling and touching them.

Asked what part she embraced, the upper or lower, she said it is more proper to embrace them below than above.

Asked whether she had not given them garlands or chaplets, she said that in their honor she often placed garlands before images or likenesses of them in churches. She does not recall giving any to those who appear to her.

Asked whether, when she hung these garlands on the tree mentioned earlier, she did so to honor those who appear to her, she said no.

Asked whether she made reverence to the saints by kneeling and bowing when they came to her, she said yes, as much as she could she showed them reverence, for she knows full well that they are in the kingdom of heaven.

Asked whether she knows anything of those who consort with fairies, she said she never did such a thing, nor does she know anything about it; but she did hear rumors of them, and that they went on Thursdays. But she does not believe in it and thinks it is just sorcery.

Asked whether someone caused her banner to wave above her king's head when he was crowned at Reims, she said no, not that she knows.

Asked why her banner was carried in the church at Reims at the coronation before the banners of other captains,[123] she said that her banner had been through perils; it made good sense that it should have the honor.

Passion Sunday, March 18. On Passion Sunday, March 18, we the bishop and Brother Jean Le Maistre, vice-inquisitor, presiding in the bishop's residence at Rouen, assisted by reverend fathers, lords, and masters: Gilles, abbot of Fécamp, Pierre, prior of Longueville, Jean Beaupère, Jacque de Touraine, Nicolas Midi, Pierre Maurice, and Gérard Feuillet, doctors of theology; Raoul Roussel, doctor of canon and civil law;

Nicolas de Venderès and Jean de la Fontaine, licentiates of canon law; and Nicolas Couppequesne and Thomas de Courcelles, bachelors of theology.

We the bishop recalled how Joan had been examined for many days and that many of her confessions and answers had been put in writing, and we asked the assessors to advise us how to proceed. Next, we ordered the reading of many assertions that some of the masters had extracted from Joan's testimony at our command, to let them consider the case more clearly and deliberate with greater certainty about what to do next.

The masters then took solemn and mature counsel. And after hearing each of their opinions, we decided that each one should inspect and diligently study authoritative books for the opinions of the doctors on these kinds of assertions, to reassemble on Thursday to offer advice. Meanwhile, we directed that articles be drafted for presentation to us, the judges, for use against Joan at trial.

Thursday, March 22. The following Thursday, March 22, in the bishop's residence at Rouen, esteemed and reverend masters appeared before us the bishop and Brother Jean Le Maistre, vice-inquisitor: Jean de Châtillon, Erard Emengart, Guillaume le Boucher, Pierre, prior of Longueville, Jean Beaupère, Jacques de Touraine, Nicolas Midi, Maurice du Quesnay, Pierre Houdenc, Jean de Nibat, Jean le Fèvre, Pierre Maurice, Jacques Guesdon, and Gérard Feuillet, doctors of theology; Raoul Roussel, treasurer of Rouen Cathedral, doctor of canon and civil law; Nicolas de Venderès, archdeacon of Eu in Rouen Cathedral, and Jean de la Fontaine, licentiates of canon law; Guillaume Haiton, Nicolas Couppequesne, and Thomas de Courcelles, bachelors of theology; Nicolas Loiselleur, canon of Rouen Cathedral, and Brother Ysambard de la Pierre, of the Order of Friars Preachers.

Many of the doctors and masters presented, with great display of learning, extracts and comments that they had gathered on the case. After carefully considering each of their opinions and holding long conference with them, we concluded and ordered that the extracts from the register of Joan's confessions should be reduced to a smaller number of articles in the form of statements and propositions. These articles should then be given to all the masters to make it easier for them to give their opinions. As for the rest—that is, whether Joan should be examined any further—we should proceed so that with God's help, the trial is conducted to the praise of God and the exaltation of his faith, and so that these proceedings will be blameless.

Saturday, March 24. The following Saturday, March 24, in Joan's prison, Master Jean de la Fontaine presiding, appointed by us the bishop and by us, Brother Jean Le Maistre, vice-inquisitor; assisted by esteemed and reverend masters: Jean Beaupère, Nicolas Midi, Pierre Maurice, and Gérard Feuillet, doctors of theology; Thomas de Courcelles, bachelor of theology; and Master Enguerrand de Champrond, official of Coutances.

The register containing the questions to Joan and her answers was read to her in French by the notary Guillaume Manchon. But before the reading had begun, the promoter offered to prove that the contents of the register, both questions and answers, had been uttered and made as stated, in case Joan denied any of her answers written there. Then Joan took an oath to add nothing to her answers unless it was true.

During the reading, she said her surname was d'Arc or Rommée, and that in her region, girls took their mother's surname. She then asked that the questions and answers be read in order; unless she contradicted them, she considered them to be true and confessed.

She added these words to the article about taking women's clothes: "Give me a woman's robe to go to my mother's house, and I'll take it." This was so she could escape from prison, and when she was outside, she would take counsel about what to do next.

Finally, after the reading of the register, Joan acknowledged that she readily believed that she had said what had been written in the register and read to her. She did not contradict anything else from its contents.

Palm Sunday, March 25. The following day, the morning of Palm Sunday, March 25, at Joan's prison in the castle of Rouen, we the bishop spoke to Joan in the presence of Masters Jean Beaupère, Nicolas Midi, Pierre Maurice, doctors of theology; and Thomas de Courcelles, bachelor of theology. We told her that often and especially yesterday she had asked to be allowed to hear Mass on Palm Sunday because of the solemnity of the days and the season.[124] We therefore asked her whether, if we let her do so, she would abandon her men's clothes and take women's, such as she used to wear in her region and as the women there normally wear.

Joan replied by asking to hear Mass in her men's clothes and to take the Eucharist at Easter. We told her to answer the question whether, if we let her do so, she would set aside men's clothes. But she said that she had not been advised on this, nor could she wear women's garments.

We asked her whether she wanted to take counsel with her saints about wearing women's clothes. She said that dressed as she was, she might be allowed to hear Mass, and she supremely desired it. But she could not change her garb; the decision was not hers.

Then the masters urged her, for such a good thing as this and for the devotion she seems to have, to take clothing appropriate to her sex. Joan answered again that this was out of her power; if it were up to her, she would do it right away.

Then she was told to speak with her voices to learn whether she could assume women's clothing to take the sacrament at Easter. Joan answered that, as far as in her lay, she would not receive the sacrament by changing into women's clothes. She asked to be allowed to hear Mass in men's clothes, saying that these clothes did not burden her soul and that wearing them was not against the Church.

The reverend Jean d'Estivet asked for an official record of this entire session, in the presence of Masters Adam Milet, royal secretary, William Brolbster, and Pierre Orient, of the dioceses of Rouen, London, and Châlons.

2

Ordinary Trial

Joan is formally accused of heresy but refuses to submit to the Church. Upon sentencing, she recants and receives a sentence of perpetual imprisonment.

Monday, March 26. Here begins the ordinary trial following the trial conducted *ex officio.*[1]

On the Monday, March 26, after Palm Sunday, at our residence at Rouen, there appeared before us the bishop and Brother Jean Le Maistre, vice-inquisitor, esteemed lords and masters: Jean de Châtillon, Jean Beaupère, Jacques de Touraine, Nicolas Midi, Pierre Maurice, Gérard Feuillet, doctors of theology; Raoul Roussel, treasurer of Rouen Cathedral, doctor of canon and civil law; André Marguerie, archdeacon of Petit-Caux, licentiate of laws; Nicolas de Venderès, archdeacon of Eu, and Jean de la Fontaine, licentiates of canon law; Thomas de Courcelles, bachelor of theology; and Nicolas Loiselleur, canon of Rouen Cathedral. In their presence we ordered the reading of certain articles that the promoter was to bring against Joan.

Then it was decided that in addition to the preparatory trial conducted by virtue of our office, we the bishop and the vice-inquisitor had decided and concluded that an ordinary trial must and would proceed against Joan; that these articles were well considered and that Joan would be questioned and heard on them; that the articles would be brought on behalf of the promoter by a worthy lawyer or by himself; and that if Joan refused to answer them after she had been canonically warned, they could be taken as confessed. And after many other matters, we concluded that the next day the promoter would deliver the articles and Joan would be questioned and heard on them.

Tuesday, March 27. The Tuesday, March 27, after Palm Sunday in the chamber near the great hall at the castle of Rouen.

We the bishop and Brother Jean Le Maistre, vice-inquisitor, presiding, assisted by reverend fathers, lords, and masters: Gilles, abbot of Fécamp, Pierre, prior of Longueville, Jean Beaupère, Jacques de Touraine, Nicolas Midi, Pierre Maurice, Gérard Feuillet, Erard Emengart, Guillaume le Boucher, Maurice du Quesnay, Jean de Nibat, Jean le Fèvre, Jacques Guesdon, Jean de Châtillon, doctors of theology; Raoul Roussel, doctor of canon and civil law; Jean Guérin, doctor of canon law; Robert Le Barbier, Denis Gastinel, Jean le Doux, licentiates of canon and civil law; Nicolas de Venderès, Jean Pinchon, Jean Basset, Jean de la Fontaine, Jean Colombel, Aubert Morel, Jean Duchemin, licentiates of canon law; André Marguerie, archdeacon of Petit-Caux, Jean Alespée, Nicolas Caval, Geoffroi du Crotay, licentiates of civil law; Guillaume Desjardins and Jean Tiphaine, doctors of medicine; Guillaume Haiton, bachelor of theology; Guillaume de la Chambre, licentiate of medicine; Brother Jean Duval, Brother Ysambard de la Pierre of the Order of Friars Preachers, William Brolbster and John Hampton, priests.

Jean d'Estivet, canon of the churches of Bayeux and Beauvais, our appointed promoter in this trial, appeared judicially before us; and in the presence of Joan, who was led before us, brought a petition in French, whose tenor, translated literally into Latin, is as follows:

My lords, reverend father in Christ, and you, vicar, especially appointed by the reverend inquisitor, who is established and chosen for all the kingdom of France, to oppose those wandering from the Catholic faith: I, your appointed and ordained promoter in this trial, according to true information and examinations made by you and on your behalf, do state, affirm, and declare that Joan here present has been brought to answer what I shall choose to ask, state, and declare against her touching the faith. And I undertake to examine [her] if need be, by affirmations and to the ends and conclusions set forth more fully in the register before you, the judges in this trial; I present and deliver against Joan the facts, laws, and reasons declared in the articles written and specified in this register. And I beseech and request you to make Joan swear and declare that she will answer the articles, each one individually, as she believes or does not believe. And if she refuses to swear, if she is reluctant or delays overmuch after you have instructed and summoned her to do this, may she be deemed at fault and contumacious in her presence; and as her obstinacy requires, may she be declared excommunicated for manifest offenses. Then, let a definite and brief term be assigned for her responses to the articles, through an announcement to her that if she does not answer them, or certain of them, by the appointed day, you will consider the articles to which she has not responded as confessed, even as law, practice, use, and common observance wish and require.

After the petition, the promoter presented the written accusation against Joan in the form of demonstrated articles transcribed below.[2] Then we the judges asked the assessors for advice on the next course of action. After the petition of the promoter had been seen and the opinions of each heard, we concluded that the articles furnished by the promoter should be read and explained to Joan in French, and that Joan should answer what she knows to each article; and if she asked for a delay to answer certain ones, a sufficient delay should be granted her.

<To begin, Master Nicolas de Venderès said, to the first point, that she should be made to take the oath. To the second, the promoter is also right to require it, and she should be found contumacious if she refuses to swear. To the third, he thinks she should be excommunicated. And if she receives a sentence of excommunication, they should proceed against her according to law. Likewise, if she refuses, she should receive a sentence of excommunication.

Master Jean Pinchon said the articles should be read to her first, before deliberation.

Master Jean Basset said the articles should be read before the sentence of excommunication.

Master Jean Guérin said the articles should be read.

Master Jean de la Fontaine agreed with Nicolas de Venderès.

Master Geoffroi du Crotay said he thought she should be given a triple delay, at least, before she is excommunicated, and that she should be found convicted if she refuses to swear, especially since in civil law three delays are granted for swearing *de calumnia.*[3]

Master Jean le Doux agreed.

Master Gilles Deschamps said the articles should be read and a day appointed for her to come and answer, after she has considered the matter.

Master Robert Le Barbier agreed.

The reverend abbot of Fécamp said he thought she should be required to swear to tell the truth in all things touching the trial. And if she has not considered the matter, she should have a suitable delay. A day should also be set for her to appear, after she has had time for consideration.

Master Jean de Châtillon said she should be required to tell the truth, especially where it concerns her conduct.

Master Erard Emengart agreed with the reverend Fécamp.

Master Guillaume le Boucher agreed with him.

The reverend prior of Longueville said that on articles that she does not know how to answer, she should not be compelled to answer by saying she believes or does not believe.

Master Jean Beaupère said that in those articles where she is certain and which concern her conduct, she should be required to tell the truth. But on those which she does not know how to answer truthfully or which would imply a legal assertion, she should be granted a delay if she asks for one.

Master Jacques de Touraine agreed.

Master Nicolas Midi also agreed, adding that he yields to the lawyers as to whether she ought now to be made to swear unconditionally.

Master Maurice du Quesnay agreed with the reverend Fécamp.

Master Jean de Nibat said that as to the articles, he yields to the lawyers, and as to the oath, she ought to swear to tell the truth about those matters touching the trial and the faith; and if in other matters she raises any difficulty about answering truthfully, and asks for a delay, one should be granted her.

Master Jean le Fèvre yields to the lawyers.

Master Pierre Maurice said she should answer what she knows.

Master Gérard said she should be required to reply under oath.

Master Jacques Guesdon agreed.

Master Thomas de Courcelles said she should be required to answer; the articles should be read to her, and she should answer during the reading. As to a delay, she should be given one if she asks for it.

Master André Marguerie was of the opinion that she should swear to everything touching the trial. A delay should be granted for doubtful points.

Master Denis Gastinel said she should take the oath, and the promoter is right to ask for one. As to how to proceed if she refuses to swear, he wishes to consult several books.[4]

Master Aubert Morel and Master Jean Duchemin said she should be required to swear.>

Then the promoter took before us the oath *de calumnia* and swore <namely, that he declares that the accusations included in the register or in the articles and in this procedure against Joan proceed not from partiality, malice, fear, or hatred, but from zeal for the faith>. Next, we told Joan that all present were learned churchmen, knowledgeable in canon and civil law, who wished and strove to proceed with her in all piety and meekness, as they had always intended, seeking not revenge or corporal punishment, but her instruction and return to the path of truth and salvation. And since she was not sufficiently learned and instructed in letters and such difficult matters to serve as her own counsel about what to say or do, we therefore suggested that she choose one or more of the assessors present; or, if she knew not how to choose, we could appoint some of them to counsel her about what to do or reply, it being understood that she would have to speak truthfully for herself about her conduct; and we requested that Joan take an oath to tell the truth about her conduct.

Joan answered: "First, I thank you and the entire assembly for advising me on my own welfare and on our faith. I thank you also for the counsel you offer. But I don't intend to depart from the counsel of God. As for the oath you wish me to take, I'm ready to tell the truth about everything that touches your trial." And so she swore, touching Holy Gospels.

Then, at our command, the articles produced by the promoter were read, and the contents of the articles or the register were explained to Joan in French, both Tuesday and the following Wednesday.[5]

Wednesday, March 28. On Wednesday, there were present reverend fathers, lords, and masters: Gilles, abbot of Fécamp, Pierre, prior of Longueville, Jean Beaupère, Jacques de Touraine, Erard Emengart, Maurice du Quesnay, Nicolas Midi, Pierre Maurice, Guillaume le Boucher, Jean de Nibat, Jean le Fèvre, Jean de Châtillon, Jacques Guesdon, and Gérard Feuillet, doctors of Holy Writ; Raoul Roussel, doctor of canon and civil law; Robert Le Barbier, licentiate of canon law; Guillaume Haiton, Nicolas Couppequesne, bachelors of theology; Jean Guèrin, Denis Gastinel, Jean le Doux, licentiates of canon and civil law; Jean Pinchon, Jean Basset, Jean de la Fontaine, Jean Colombel, Jean Duchemin, licentiates of canon law; André Marguerie, archdeacon of Petit-Caux, Jean Alespée, Nicolas Caval, Geoffroi du Crotay, licentiates of civil law; Guillaume Desjardins, Jean Tiphaine, doctors of medicine; Guillaume de la Chambre, licentiate of medicine; William Brolbster and John of Hampton, priests.

Here follow word for word the contents of the articles of the *libellus* and of the answers given by Joan, together with the answers she gave elsewhere, to which she refers.[6]

The *Libellus* d'Estivet

[Tuesday, March 27.] I come before you, competent judges in this affair—reverend father and lord in Christ Lord Pierre, by divine mercy bishop of Beauvais, ordinary judge possessing territory in the city and diocese of Rouen; and religious Master Jean Le Maistre, of the Order of Friars Preachers, bachelor of theology, vicar in this city and diocese, and in this trial especially appointed by Master Jean Graverent, distinguished doctor of theology of the same order, inquisitor of heresy for the kingdom of France appointed by the Apostolic See—I come before you for this reason: a certain woman named Joan, called *la Pucelle* in the vernacular, was recently found, captured, and detained within your territory and diocese of Beauvais, reverend father. She was surrendered, handed over, delivered, and restored to you, as

her ecclesiastical and ordinary judge, by our most Christian lord the king of France and England, as your subject, under your jurisdiction and subject to your correction. She was greatly suspect, slandered, and grievously and notoriously denounced by upright and eminent persons for the things that follow. Let her be pronounced and declared, O judges, a sorceress, diviner, false prophetess, conjurer of evil spirits, superstitious, entangled in and practicing the magic arts, evil-thinking in the catholic faith, schismatic, doubting and misled in the article "One holy Church," etc.,[7] and other articles of the faith, sacrilegious, idolatrous, apostate from the faith, evil-speaking and maleficent, blaspheming God and his saints, scandalous, seditious, a disturber of peace and an obstacle to it, inciting wars, cruelly thirsting for human blood and encouraging its shedding, wholly forsaking the decency and reserve of her sex, utterly without modesty and shamelessly having taken the disgraceful clothing and state of armed men; for these and for other reasons an abomination to God and man, a transgressor of divine and natural laws and ecclesiastical discipline, seductress of princes and peoples; permitting and allowing herself to be worshipped and adored in injury and contempt of God, giving her hands and garments to be kissed, usurping divine honor and adoration; a heretic, or at least greatly suspect of heresy. For these crimes let her be canonically and legitimately punished and corrected according to divine and canonical decrees, and all other due and appropriate ends. Jean d'Estivet, canon of the churches of Bayeux and Beauvais, promoter or prosecutor of your office, appointed and specially chosen by you, plaintiff and accuser in the name of this office, states, declares, and intends to prove and duly inform you of the things that follow against the said Joan, accused defendant. The promoter nonetheless declares that he feels no obligation to prove unnecessary claims, but only those which are, can be, and should be sufficient to accomplish his purpose, in whole or in part. He affirms the other pleas that are customarily made in such actions, and he otherwise reserves to himself the right to add, correct, change, interpret, and to perform everything else whatsoever, both of law and deed.[8]

ARTICLE 1

First, both by divine and by canon and civil law, it belongs to you—one as ordinary judge, the other as inquisitor of the faith—to expel, destroy, and utterly eradicate from your diocese and from all the kingdom of France the heresies, sorceries, superstitions, and other crimes declared above; to punish, correct, and reclaim heretics, those who set forth, declare, or make public anything or act in any way against our catholic faith; also sorcerers, diviners, invokers of demons, those who think erroneously in the faith, and such criminals and malefactors and their supporters who have been seized in this diocese and jurisdiction, even if they have committed their crimes elsewhere—just as other competent judges can and ought to do in their dioceses, limits, and jurisdictions. And for this purpose, you should be accounted, esteemed, and reckoned as competent judges, even toward a layperson of whatever status, gender, condition, or eminence.

To the first article, Joan answers that she very well believes that our lord the Roman pope and the bishops and the other members of the clergy exist to preserve the catholic faith and to punish those who fall short in it. But for herself and her actions, she will submit only to the Church in heaven, that is to God, the Virgin Mary, and the saints in paradise. And she firmly believes that she has not failed in the faith, nor would she wish to.

ARTICLE 2

The accused has performed, composed, participated in, and enacted numerous sorceries and superstitions not only this year, but from childhood, and not only in your diocese and jurisdiction, but far and wide throughout this kingdom. She prophesied the future and let herself be worshipped and adored. She invoked demons and evil spirits, took counsel with and visited them, concluded pacts and had discussions and assemblies with them, and was familiar with them. She also bestowed counsel, aid, and favor upon others so doing, and seduced them to do so, by saying, believing, affirming, and maintaining that to do so and to believe in and perform such sorceries, prophecies, and superstitious acts was not sinful, nor even forbidden, but permissible, praiseworthy, and approved, as she claimed, thus leading numerous persons of various estates and of both sexes into those errors and evil acts, and imprinting such things on their hearts. And while carrying out these crimes, the said Joan was taken and seized within your diocese of Beauvais.

To this second article Joan said that she denies the sorceries, the superstitious works, and the prophecies; as to the adoration, if some people kissed her hands or garments, it was not by her request or wish; she has guarded against this and resisted it as best she could. She denies the rest of the article.

Summary: earlier testimony introduced. March 3: the question whether she knew the thoughts of her party. March 10: the sally from Compiègne and the crossing of the bridge.[9]

ARTICLE 3

The accused has fallen into errors of the worst kind, smacking of heretical wickedness; she has stated, loudly proclaimed, made known, asserted, publicized, and impressed upon the hearts of simple people false and lying statements smacking of heresy and in fact heretical, outside and opposed to our catholic faith and its articles, the word of the Gospels, statutes made and approved in general councils, and divine, canon, and civil law—statements that were scandalous, sacrilegious, against good morals and offensive to pious ears; and she has counseled and aided those who stated, dogmatically affirmed, made known, asserted, and promulgated such statements.

Joan denies this article and asserts that she has supported the Church to the best of her ability.

ARTICLE 4

And to inform you, my reverend judges, better and more particularly of these offenses, excesses, crimes, and faults of the accused, in this diocese and many other places, as reported above: the accused is from the town of Greux; her father is Jacques d'Arc and her mother Isabelle, his wife; she [Joan] was reared to the age of eighteen or so in the village of Domrémy on the Meuse, in the diocese of Toul, the bailiwick of Chaumont en Bassigny and the jurisdiction of Monteclaire and Andelot. In childhood this Joan was not taught or instructed in the faith or its basic principles. Instead, she learned through custom and the training of certain old women to practice sorcery, divination, and other superstitions or magic arts. Many inhabitants of these towns have long been known to practice these evil spells. Joan herself said that from many of them, and especially from her godmother, she had heard much about visions and appearances of fairies or fairy spirits, *fées* in French; and still others taught her and initiated her into evil and wicked errors about these spirits, such that she confessed to you at trial that even then she did not know whether fairies were evil spirits.

With regard to this article, Joan said she acknowledges the first part, about her father and mother and her birthplace; as to the fairies, she does not understand. But regarding her instruction, she learned her faith and was well and duly taught to behave as a good child should. For her godmother, she refers to what she said elsewhere.

Asked to recite her creed, she answered: "You can ask my confessor—I said it to him."

ARTICLE 5

Near the town of Domrémy stands a large, thick, ancient tree, which common people call *l'arbre charmine fée de Bourlémont* [the charmed fairy-tree of Bourlémont], and near this tree is a spring. Evil spirits called fairies, *fées* in French, are said to gather near there, and those who cast spells are accustomed to dance with them at night around the tree and spring.

With regard to this article on the tree and the spring, she refers to the answer she made about them; she denies the rest.

Summary: *earlier testimony introduced. February 24: the tree and fountain near her village. March 1: her conversation with the saints at the fountain. March 17:*

her godmother; the question whether fairies are evil spirits; those who consort with the fairies.

ARTICLE 6

Joan used to visit the spring and tree, mostly at night but sometimes during the day, especially when the divine office was being celebrated in church, in order to be alone. Then, while dancing around the spring and tree, she would hang garlands she had made from herbs and flowers on the branches. Beforehand and afterward, she would utter certain incantations and sing songs with invocations, sorcery, and other evil spells. The next morning, these garlands would no longer be there.

With regard to this article, on Tuesday, March 27, she said that she refers to the answer she made elsewhere, and she denies the rest.

Summary: earlier testimony introduced. February 24: the tree.

ARTICLE 7

Joan would sometimes carry a mandrake in her bosom, hoping thereby to have good luck with money and temporal possessions, and claiming that mandrake like this has potency and effect.

This article on the mandrake she completely denies.

Summary: earlier testimony introduced. March 1: the mandrake.

ARTICLE 8

At around twenty years of age,[10] of her own will and without leave from her father and mother, Joan left for Neufchâteau in Lorraine, where for a time she served a woman named La Rousse, an innkeeper; many dissolute young women lived there, and the lodgers were mostly soldiers. While staying at this inn, Joan would sometimes keep to the women, but sometimes she would take the sheep to the fields and lead the horses to water, and to meadows and pastures. And there she learned to ride and gained knowledge of arms.

With regard to this article, Joan says she refers to her previous answers. She denies the rest.

Summary: earlier testimony introduced. February 22: the departure from her father's house and her time spent at Neufchâteau. February 24: interrogation on whether she took the animals to meadows.

ARTICLE 9

While in this employ, Joan dragged a young man before the magistrate in Toul for breach of promise. In pursuit of this case, she went to Toul often, and spent nearly all she had. The young man, knowing she had lived with the said women, refused to marry her and died while the case was pending. For this reason, out of a grudge, Joan left her employ.

With regard to this article, the case of matrimony, Joan says she has answered this elsewhere and refers to her answer. She denies the rest.

Summary: earlier testimony introduced. March 12: the man from Toul and the action for marriage.

ARTICLE 10

After leaving the service of La Rousse, Joan said that for five years she has had and still has visions and appearances of Saint Michael, Saint Catherine, and Saint Margaret, and that they expressly revealed to her from God that she would raise the siege of Orléans and would have Charles, whom she calls her king, crowned and would drive all his enemies from the kingdom of France. Against the wishes of her mother and father she left them and of her own accord went to Robert de Baudricourt, captain of Vaucouleurs. As commanded by Saint Michael, Saint Margaret, and Saint Catherine, she told this Robert of the visions and revelations made to her by God, as she claims. And she asked Robert to find a way for her to fulfill her revelations. Having been spurned twice by Robert and having returned home, Joan was ordered by revelation to return, and the third time Robert welcomed and received her.

In response to this article, she refers to what she has answered elsewhere.

Summary: earlier testimony introduced. February 22: the voice. February 24: the time the previous day when she heard the voice. February 27: assertion that the saints have guided her for seven years; which voice first came to her; interrogation on whether she saw Saint Michael and the angels bodily and in reality and whether there was light with the voices. March 1: interrogation on whether she had spoken with the saints since last Tuesday. March 12: interrogation on whether she had asked her voices if she should tell her father and mother of her leaving, on the dreams her father had, and on whether her father had these thoughts after she had her visions.

ARTICLE 11

Joan, Robert's intimate friend, boasted to him that once she had arranged and accomplished all that she had been commanded by God through revelation, she would have three sons: the first would be pope, the second emperor, and the third king. Hearing this, the captain said: "Then I'd like to give you one of them! Since they'll be such powerful men, I'll be better off." She answered: "No, no, gentle Robert, there's no time; the Holy Ghost will work it out." These things Robert affirmed, stated, and made public in various places, before prelates, great lords, and notable persons.

With regard to this article, Joan says she refers to her answers elsewhere. And she said she never boasted about having three children.

Summary: earlier testimony introduced. March 12: interrogation on whether her voices called her "daughter of God" or "daughter great-hearted."

ARTICLE 12

In order to begin her mission with greater success and fanfare, Joan asked the captain to have a man's costume made for her, with arms to match. Although he was appalled and resisted doing so, he eventually agreed to Joan's request and carried it out. After the clothing and arms were sewn and crafted, Joan cast aside all women's clothing and had her hair cut round [in a bowl shape], like a young man's. Then she put on a shirt, breeches, a doublet, and hose fastened together by twenty loops, high-laced shoes, a short, knee-length robe, a close-cut hood, tight-fitting boots, long spurs, a sword, dagger, cuirass, lance, and other armor befitting a man-at-arms.[11] And with these she practiced feats of arms, claiming that she was fulfilling God's commands to her, divulged through revelations, and that she was acting on God's behalf.

With regard to this article, Joan says she refers to answers she gave elsewhere.

Asked subsequently whether she had taken her clothing, arms, and other battle gear at God's command, she said that, as before, she refers to her other answers.

Summary: earlier testimony introduced. February 22: going to Robert of Baudricourt for soldiers; her statement "that when she went to her king, she was wearing men's clothing";[12] the duke of Lorraine's sending for her; her leaving Vaucouleurs wearing men's clothing and her journey; her counsel advising her well to take men's clothing; reaching her king without hindrance. February 27: interrogation on whether her voice commanded her to wear men's clothing, whether she did so at the order of Robert de Baudricourt, whether she did well in doing so; the sword she took at Vaucouleurs. March 12: interrogation on whether she wore men's clothing at the request of Robert de Baudricourt and whether the voice instructed her to take men's garb. March 17: what promise or help she expected from the Lord for wearing men's clothes.

ARTICLE 13

Joan attributes to God, to his angels, and to his saints orders that are injurious to the honor of women, prohibited by divine law, abominable to God and man, and forbidden by ecclesiastical ordinances under pain of anathema—such as wearing short, tight, and immodest men's clothing, undergarments and hose as well as other articles. Following their orders, she often wore extravagant and magnificent clothing made of precious fabrics and cloth of gold, with fur lining. She wore not only short tunics, but sleeveless coats and robes slit on the sides. And her crimes were notorious, for she was captured wearing a cape of gold cloth, completely open, a cap, and her hair cut round like a man's. In general, casting aside all feminine modesty, flouting not only womanly decency but even the conduct of virtuous men, she enjoyed all the ornamentation and attire of the most dissipated men, and even carried weapons of attack. To attribute this to the command of God, holy angels, and even holy virgins, is to blaspheme God and his saints, to overturn God's law, to violate canons, to offend the female sex and its honor, to pervert all decency of outward attire, and to approve and encourage utterly depraved behavior.

With regard to this article, Joan says she did not blaspheme God or his saints.

<And when it was explained to her that according to holy canons and Holy Scripture, for women to take men's clothing or men to take women's is an abomination to God, and she was asked whether she took these clothes by God's command, she answered: "You've had enough answers about this; if you want more answers from me, give me a delay and I'll answer."

Asked whether she would like to take women's clothes to receive her Savior this Easter, she said that she would not give up her clothes to receive [him] or for any other reason. She sees no difference between men's and women's clothes for receiving her Savior, and they should not refuse her on account of this attire.>[13]

Summary: earlier testimony introduced. February 27: interrogation on whether the command to take men's attire was lawful and whether she thought she had done well to do so. March 3: interrogation on whether, when she first approached her king, he asked if her revelation ordered her to change clothing; interrogation on whether she would sin mortally in taking women's attire.

ARTICLE 14

Joan claims to be doing right in wearing such garments and immodest men's clothing; and she will continue doing so, saying that she will remove them only if she receives clear permission from God by revelation—thus insulting God, his angels, and his saints.

With regard to this article, Joan says she is not doing evil by serving God, and tomorrow she will answer the charges in the article.

The same day, asked by one of the assessors whether she had received a revelation or instruction to wear men's clothing, she said she has answered this elsewhere and she refers to that answer. Then she said that she would answer tomorrow. And she added that she knows full well who ordered her to wear men's clothes; but she does not know how to reveal this.

Summary: earlier testimony introduced. February 24: question whether she wanted a woman's dress. March 12: interrogation on whether she did not think she was doing wrong in taking men's attire. March 17: question why she asks for a woman's gown in her final hour.

ARTICLE 15

When Joan frequently asked permission to hear Mass, she was advised to abandon men's clothing and to return to women's attire. In this, the judges gave her some hope of hearing Mass and taking communion if she would set aside men's clothes entirely and put on women's clothes, befitting the modesty of her sex. But she refused and preferred to forgo the sacraments and divine offices rather than abandon such apparel, pretending that to do so would displease God. In this she reveals her obstinacy and hardness of heart, her lack of charity, her disobedience to the Church, and her contempt for holy sacraments.

To this article, on this Tuesday, March 27, Joan replies that she would much rather die than retract what she has done by God's command.

The same day, asked whether she would abandon men's clothes to hear Mass, she said she would not yet remove them, and it was not up to her to give a time when she will do so.

That day, she said that if the judges refuse to let her hear Mass, it is well within our Lord's power to let her hear it when he pleases, in spite of them.

As to the rest of the article, she said she acknowledges that she has been advised to wear women's attire; but she denies irreverence and the other accusations.

Summary: earlier testimony introduced. March 15: wearing women's clothing to hear Mass. March 17: wearing women's clothing to hear Mass; interrogation on whether her saying that she would take women's attire if they let her go was pleasing to God.

ARTICLE 16

After her capture in the castle of Beaurevoir and at Arras, Joan was charitably advised many times by nobles and distinguished persons, men and women, to abandon men's attire and to wear clothes that are seemly and befitting her sex. But she absolutely refused and, as stated, steadfastly refuses to carry out other tasks proper to her sex, in all things behaving more like a man than a woman.

With regard to this article, Joan says that she was in fact advised to wear women's clothes at Arras and in the castle of Beaurevoir; she refused then and still does. As for the other womanly tasks, she says there are enough other women to do them.

Summary: earlier testimony introduced. March 3: interrogation on whether the masters who examined her in the other obedience asked her about changing her attire and whether she was asked to do so at Beaurevoir.

ARTICLE 17

When Joan came thus clothed and armed before Charles, she promised him three things, among others: first, that she would lift the siege of Orléans; second, that she would have him crowned at Reims; and third, that she would avenge him against his enemies and would either kill them or drive them from the kingdom by her art, all the English and Burgundians. Joan frequently and publicly boasted of these promises in many places. And to inspire greater confidence in her words and deeds, from that time forward she practiced frequent divination, uncovering the behavior, manners, and secret actions of those who came to her, whom she had never seen or heard of before. And she boasted that she knew these things by revelation.

With regard to this article, Joan says she bore news to her king from God, that our Lord would restore his kingdom, have him crowned at Reims, and drive out his enemies. And she was God's messenger in this, to tell him to set her boldly to the task and she would raise the siege at Orléans. She spoke of the whole kingdom, she said; and if the lord of Burgundy and the king's other subjects would not return to obedience, her king would make them do so by force. As to the end of the article, about recognizing Robert de Baudricourt and her king, she referred to what she has already said.

Summary: earlier testimony introduced. February 22: that when she reached Vaucouleurs, she recognized Robert de Baudricourt, though she had never seen him before; that when she met her king, she recognized him thanks to her voices. March 13: the priest with a concubine and the lost cup.

ARTICLE 18

As long as she stayed with Charles, Joan discouraged him and his advisers with all her might from attempting any peace agreement with his enemies. She always inflamed them to murder and to spill blood, claiming that peace was possible only at the edge of the lance and the sword. So God had disposed, she insisted, for otherwise the king's enemies would not relinquish their holdings in the kingdom. So to conquer them would be a great blessing to all Christendom, as she put it.

With regard to this article, Joan says that she entreated the duke of Burgundy through letters and ambassadors to make peace with her king. But as for the English, the only possible peace would be their return to England.

She has answered the rest of the article elsewhere, to which answer she refers.

Summary: earlier testimony introduced. February 27: the treaty with the captain of Jargeau.

ARTICLE 19

Through traffic with demons and through divination, Joan sent for a certain sword hidden in the church of Sainte-Catherine de Fierbois—or which she wickedly, deceitfully, and craftily hid there herself or had hidden there to seduce princes, nobles, clergy, and common people into believing more readily that she knew by revelation that the sword was there. So by this and similar means, she hoped they would find it easier to put absolute faith in what she said.

With regard to this article, on Tuesday, March 27, she says she refers to the answer she gave elsewhere and denies the rest.

Summary: earlier testimony introduced. February 27: interrogation on whether she had been to Sainte-Catherine de Fierbois and how how she knew of the sword there. March 17: the five crosses on the sword.

ARTICLE 20

Joan cast a spell on her ring, banner, and certain pieces of cloth and pennons that she often carried or had her men carry, and even upon the sword discovered by revelation, as she says, at Sainte-Catherine de Fierbois, claiming that they were blessed with good fortune. And she uttered many curses and incantations over them in various places, and publicly claimed that by their power she would perform great feats and achieve victory over her enemies; nothing bad, she said, would happen to her soldiers who carried these pennons in battle, nor would they suffer any misfortune. She proclaimed this openly and publicly at Compiègne, in particular, the eve of her attack against the duke of Burgundy, when many of her men were wounded, killed, or captured and she was caught and taken prisoner. She announced the same thing at Saint-Denis, when she incited her troops to attack Paris.

With regard to this article, on Tuesday, March 27, she said she refers to her previous answers, adding that there was no sorcery or any black art in anything she did. But as to the good fortune of her standard, she is referring to the fortune that our Lord placed in it.

Summary: earlier testimony introduced. February 27: interrogation on whether she had her sword when she was captured. March 1: interrogation on who gave her the ring that the Burgundians have. March 3: the pennons. March 17: her ring with the words "Jesus, Mary"; her touching Saint Catherine.

ARTICLE 21

Driven by rashness and presumption, Joan had letters drafted bearing the names Jesus, Mary at the head, divided by the sign of the cross, and sent them on her behalf to our lord the king, to the duke of Bedford, then regent of France, and to the lords and captains besieging Orléans. These letters, whose tenor follows, contained many evil and wicked things, hardly in keeping with the catholic faith.

With regard to this article, this Tuesday, March 27, she says she did not produce the letters out of arrogance or presumption, but by our Lord's command. And she freely acknowledges the content of the letters, except for three words.

Summary: earlier testimony introduced. February 22: the letter she sent to the English at Orléans that bears the superscription + Jesus Mary +. March 3: interrogation on whether the members of her own party firmly believe she has been sent by God.

ARTICLE 22

+ Jesus Mary +

King of England, and you, duke of Bedford, who call yourself regent of France; you, William de la Pole, count of Suffolk;[14] Sir John Talbot, and you, Sir Thomas Scales,[15] who call yourselves lieutenants of the duke of Bedford: do right by the King of Heaven and surrender to the Maid[16] sent by God, the King of Heaven, the keys of all the good towns you have taken and violated in France. She has come in God's name to proclaim the blood royal, wholly ready for peace if you wish to do right by her, to abandon France and pay for what you have taken. And all you before the town of Orléans, archers, companions-at-arms, you of gentle birth, and others, depart in God's name for your own country. If you do not, wait for word from the Maid, who will come see you shortly, to your great dismay. King of England, if you refuse this, I am a captain of war,[17] and wherever I find your men in France, I will force them to leave, whether they wish to or not. If they refuse to obey, I will have them all killed. I am sent by God, the King of Heaven, to chase you one and all[18] from France. If they obey, I shall have mercy on them. Do not think otherwise, for you shall never rule the kingdom of France, by God the King of Heaven, holy Mary's son, but Charles the true heir will rule it. God wills it, and has revealed it to him through the Maid, and he will enter Paris with a goodly company. If you refuse to believe these tidings from God and the Maid, when we find you, we shall strike you and make a greater uproar[19] than France has heard for a thousand years, if you fail to do right by us. And know full well that the King of Heaven will send the Maid more strength than you could muster in all your assaults against her and her good men-at-arms. We shall let blows determine who has the better claim from the God of heaven. Duke of Bedford, the Maid prays and requests you not to destroy yourselves. If you do right, you can still come join her company, where the French will perform the finest action ever seen in Christian lands. Answer, if you wish to make peace in the city of Orléans. If you do not, prepare yourselves soon for a great loss. Written Tuesday of Holy Week.[20]

With regard to this article, the above letter, Joan says that the English would have been wise to believe her letters. Before seven years have passed, they will fully understand what she wrote. And she refers to her other reply to this.

ARTICLE 23

From these letters it clearly appears that evil spirits have made sport of Joan, and that she often consulted them about what to do; or to mislead people, she falsely and harmfully fabricated these stories.

In answer to this article, she denies the end of it, which states that she acted by the counsel of evil spirits.

Summary: earlier testimony introduced. February 27: that she would rather be torn asunder by horses than have come to France without God's permission.

ARTICLE 24

Joan abused the names Jesus, Mary, separated by the sign of the cross, as a sign to some of her party that, when they should find these words with the cross in her letters, they should believe and do the opposite of what she wrote.

To this article, Tuesday, March 27, Joan replies that she refers to her answer elsewhere.

Summary: earlier testimony introduced. March 17: the purpose of the sign in her letters and the names Jesus, Mary.

ARTICLE 25

Usurping the office of angels, Joan stated and claimed that she was sent by God, even in matters directly involving the use of force and the spilling of human blood. Such a claim is entirely incompatible with true holiness, and shocking and abhorrent to every pious soul.

To this article, on Tuesday, March 27, Joan responds that she first sued for peace, and when peace proved impossible, she was ready to fight.

Summary: earlier testimony introduced. February 24: that she came from God and has no business here. March 17: that God sent her to help the king of France.

ARTICLE 26

When Joan was at Compiègne in August 1429, she received a letter from the count of Armagnac, the tenor of which is given below.

With regard to this article, on March 27, Joan says she refers to her answer elsewhere on this subject.

Summary: earlier testimony introduced. March 1: question of the letter from the count of Armagnac.

ARTICLE 27

My very dear lady, I commend myself humbly to you and beseech you in God's name, given the present division in the holy universal Church on the matter of the popes. For there are three contenders for the papacy: one dwells at Rome and is called Martin V, whom all Christian kings obey; the other dwells at Peñiscola, in the kingdom of Valencia, and is called Clement VIII; the third, whose whereabouts no one knows except the cardinal of Saint-Etienne and a few others with him, is called Benedict XIV. The first, called Pope Martin, was elected at Constance by the consent of all Christian nations. The one called Clement was chosen at Peñiscola, after the death of Pope Benedict XIII, by three of his cardinals. The third, called Pope Benedict XIV, was secretly elected at Peñiscola by the cardinal of Saint-Etienne. Please entreat our Lord Jesus Christ by his infinite mercy to reveal through you which of these three is the true pope, and which he would have us obey henceforth—the one called Martin, the one called Clement, or the one called Benedict, and whether we should believe secretly and employing some pretense, or publicly and openly. For we are wholly prepared to do the will and pleasure of our Lord Jesus Christ.

Entirely yours, the count of Armagnac

ARTICLE 28

Joan answered the count of Armagnac in a letter signed by her own hand, as follows:

ARTICLE 29

Jesus + Mary

Count of Armagnac, my very dear and good friend, Joan the Maid wants you to know that your message reached me, stating that you sent to learn from me which of the three popes that you mention you should believe. I cannot very well tell you the truth at present, not until I reach Paris or somewhere else at rest, for right now I am too pressed by the conduct of war. But when you know me to be at Paris, send me a message and I will tell you in all truth which one you should believe, what I have learned by the counsel of my just and sovereign Lord, the King of all the world, and as far as I can tell, what you should do. I commend you to God; may God keep you. Written at Compiègne, August 22.

ARTICLE 30

And so as stated above, asked by the count of Armagnac which of the three should be considered true pope and which he should believe, Joan not only cast doubt on who it was (when there is only one unquestioned pope), but she presumed too much for herself, little regarding the authority of the universal Church, and setting her words above the authority of the whole Church: she claimed that within a certain time, she would tell him which one to believe in accordance with what she learned by the counsel of God, as her letter makes clear.

As to articles 27, 28, 29, and 30, which were explained to her word for word, she refers to the answer she made elsewhere, in response to article 26.

<*Wednesday after Palm Sunday, March 28.* First, asked to take an oath, she said she would gladly speak the truth about matters touching the trial; and so she swore.

To the article concerning her attire, she said that she wore the clothes and the arms by God's leave, the men's clothing as well as arms.

When asked to set aside her clothing, she said she would not without leave of our Lord, even were they to cut off her head; but if it pleases our Lord, she will do so at once.

She added that without leave of our Lord, she would not take women's attire.>

ARTICLE 31

[*Wednesday, March 28.*] From her childhood onward, Joan boasted, and she boasts daily, that she had and has many revelations and visions. And though she was charitably warned and duly and legally asked about them under oath, she would not and will not swear, or explain them clearly by word or by sign; but she did and does delay, deny, and refuse. And formally denying her oath, she stated and affirmed many times in court and elsewhere that she would not make known her revelations and visions to you even if her head were cut off or her body dismembered, and that no one could drag from her the sign that God showed her, and which proved that she came from God.

With regard to this article, she says that as for revealing the sign and the other contents of the article, she may well have said she would not reveal it. She adds that the confession she made earlier should state that without our Lord's permission, she would not reveal the sign.

Summary: earlier testimony introduced: February 22: that not a day passes when she does not hear the voice. February 24: that the voice told her many things for the good of her king, which she wished her king to know; that she would not drink wine until Easter, for then he would dine more happily. February 27: that she told her king all that had been revealed to her; that she sent a letter to her king asking to enter the town where he was. March 1: interrogation on the shape of Saint Michael and whether he was naked. March 15: her attempted escape from Beaulieu; the height and bearing of the angel; interrogation on whether she knew of any crime for which she could die if she confessed it. March 17: the age and garments of Saint Catherine and Saint Margaret.

ARTICLE 32

In these matters, you absolutely can and should conclude that the revelations and visions, if Joan had them, proceeded from lying, evil spirits rather than from good; and everyone should treat them as such, especially considering her cruelty, pride, haughtiness, actions, lies, and contradictions apparent here and in many other articles; such things in fact are and should be considered indisputable presumption.

With regard to this article, on the Wednesday after Palm Sunday, March 28, she says she denies it. She acted by revelation from Saint Catherine and Saint Margaret and will maintain this until death.

Also that day, she said she had been advised by certain members of her party to put "Jesus, Mary" on her letters; she put them on some and not others. She also said that where it reads: "Whatever she did is by the counsel of our Lord," it should read instead: "All the good that I have done."

Asked that day whether she had done good or evil in going to La Charité, she said that if she did evil, she will confess it.

Asked whether she did right in going to Paris, she said that the French noblemen wished to go, and in doing so, she thinks they did their duty of opposing their enemies.

ARTICLE 33

Joan presumptuously and rashly boasted and boasts that she knows the future, and that she foretold past events, and present events that are secret or hidden. Thus she attributes to herself—a simple and untaught creature—what belongs only to divinity.

To this article, Wednesday, March 28, she answered: "It is our Lord's pleasure to reveal things to whom he pleases." As for the sword and the other future events that she mentioned, she knew them by revelation.

Summary: earlier testimony introduced. February 24: that the Burgundians will have war unless they do what they ought. February 27: interrogation on whether she told her troops at Orléans that she would receive all arrows, crossbolts, and stones; the fort to which she ordered her men to retreat; interrogation on whether she knew in advance that she would be wounded. March 1: that before seven years have passed, the English will lose a greater stake than they did at Orléans and suffer a greater loss than they ever did in France; the manner in which she knows this and the year in which it will happen; the question whether it would happen before Martinmas; what she told John Grey, who told her it would happen, and what promises Saint Catherine and Saint Margaret made to her; that she knows that her king will regain the kingdom of France. March 3: interrogation on whether the voices told her anything about her escape in a general way. March 10: interrogation on whether she ordered the sally from Compiègne at the command of her voices and whether since Melun her voices have told her that she would be captured; that when she was to leave to go see her king, her voices told her to go boldly. March 12: the manner in which she would have freed the duke of Orléans; interrogation on whether Saint Catherine and Saint Margaret told her how she would do so. March 14: the peril or danger threatening the bishop and clerks; interrogation on what the peril is.

ARTICLE 34

Persisting in her rashness and presumption, Joan stated, loudly proclaimed, and broadcast that she knows and recognizes the voices of archangels, angels, and saints of God, by claiming that she can distinguish them from human voices.

To this article, on Wednesday, March 28, she replied that she abides by her earlier answer to this. As to rashness and the end of the article, she trusts to God, her judge.

Summary: earlier testimony introduced. February 27: interrogation on whether the voice was an angel, a saint, or a messenger direct from God and how she knows one saint from the other. March 1: complete interrogation on the appearance and speech of the apparitions. March 15: interrogation on whether she has any other sign that they are good spirits, how she knew it was Saint Michael, how she knew it was the speech of angels, how she would know it was a good or an evil angel if the devil took the shape of an angel, how she eventually knew that it was Saint Michael, and what doctrine he taught her.

ARTICLE 35

Joan boasted and claimed that she could tell whom God loves or hates.

To this article, on Wednesday, March 28, she answered: "I stand by my previous answer about the king and the duke of Orléans"; she knows nothing about others. She said that she knows very well that God loves her king and the duke of Orléans more than her, for their comfort, and that she knows this by revelation.

Summary: earlier testimony introduced. February 22: her love for the duke of Orléans and her revelations about him. February 24: interrogation on whether she could make the voice take a message to her king and why the voice no longer speaks to her king as it did when Joan was in his presence. March 17: interrogation on whether she knows that Saint Catherine and Saint Margaret hate the English, whether God hates the English, and whether God favored the English when they were prospering in France.

ARTICLE 36

Joan did and does state, claim, and boast every day that not only she herself but other persons at her prompting have truly known and recognized a certain voice that came to her, which she calls her own; yet by its nature, such a voice as she described and describes should have been invisible to humans.

With regard to this article, she says she stands by her former answer on this.

Summary: earlier testimony introduced. February 22: that members of her party knew that the voice was sent by God; that her king and others heard and saw the voices.

ARTICLE 37

Joan acknowledges that she often did the opposite of what she was instructed and commanded by the revelations that she boasts she has from God, such as when she left Saint-Denis after the attack on Paris or when she jumped from the tower at Beaurevoir, and on other occasions. In such cases it is clear either that she has not had revelations from God or that she has spurned the commands and revelations which she claims completely govern her conduct. Further, she said that when she was commanded not to leap from the tower, she was tempted to do the opposite and could not do otherwise. Here she seems to misunderstand free will, and to fall into the error of those who argue that it is determined by the ordering of fate or something similar.

To this article, on Wednesday, March 28, she answered: "I stand by what I said earlier to this." Yet she added that she had permission to leave Saint-Denis.

Asked whether she does not believe she committed a mortal sin in acting against the command of her voices, she answered: "I've already answered this and I rest upon that answer." As to the conclusion of the article, she trusts to God.

Summary: earlier testimony introduced. February 22: that her voice told her to stay at Saint-Denis, but the lords took her away. March 10: interrogation on whether she would have gone if her voices had ordered her to attack from Compiègne. March 15: interrogation on whether she has ever done anything against the command and will of her voices and whether she does not believe it is a great sin to displease Saint Catherine and Saint Margaret.

ARTICLE 38

Although from childhood Joan said, did, and committed countless evils, crimes, sins, and offenses, shameful, cruel, scandalous, disgraceful, and inappropriate for her sex, she nonetheless states and affirms that she has done everything at God's bidding and according to his will, and that she has done nothing that does not proceed from God, through the revelations of holy angels and the holy virgins Catherine and Margaret.

With regard to this article, she says she refers to what she said elsewhere about this.

Summary: earlier testimony introduced. February 24: that if not for the grace of God she could do nothing; interrogation on whether the villagers of Domrémy took the side of the Burgundians or the other side and whether, when she was young, the voice told her to hate the Burgundians. March 15: interrogation on whether she has done anything in battle without counsel from her voices and whether she has ever done anything against their command and will.

ARTICLE 39

Although "the just man falls seven times a day,"[21] Joan yet stated and spread abroad that she had never committed a mortal sin, at least not to her knowledge, and even though in fact she has performed all the acts common to fighting men, and some worse still, as stated in some of the preceding and following articles.

To this article, on Wednesday, March 28, she answered: "I've already answered, and I refer to what I said before."

Summary: earlier testimony introduced. February 24: interrogation on whether she knows she is in the grace of God. March 1: her great joy when she sees her voice and the confession she receives from Saint Catherine and Saint Margaret; interrogation on whether, when she confesses, she believes she is in mortal sin. March 14: interrogation on whether it is a mortal sin to take someone for ransom and put him to death; Franquet d'Arras; her attack on Paris on a feast day; the bishop's horse; the leap from the tower of Beaurevoir; wearing men's clothing.

ARTICLE 40

Thoughtless of her salvation and incited by the devil, Joan did and does not hesitate, time and again in many different places, to receive, in immodest men's clothing that she was forbidden to wear by God and the Church, the body of Christ.

With regard to this article, she says she has already answered it, and she refers to what she said then; as for the conclusion, she trusts to God.

Summary: earlier testimony introduced. March 3: interrogation on whether she often received the Eucharist and penance at the good towns when she went through the country and whether she took the sacraments in men's attire.

ARTICLE 41

In complete despair, out of hatred and contempt for the English, and because she had heard that the destruction of Compiègne was at hand, Joan tried to throw herself from the top of a high tower and, incited by the devil, purposed in her heart to do this, and attempted and did what she could toward that end. In so casting herself down, she was also driven and led by diabolical suggestion, thus attempting to free the body rather than the soul—her own and those of many others. For she often boasted that she would kill herself rather than fall into the hands of the English.

With regard to this article, she says she refers to what she said elsewhere on the subject.

Summary: earlier testimony introduced. March 3: her stay in the tower of Beaurevoir; interrogation on whether she said that she would rather die than fall into the hands of the English. March 14: why she leaped from the tower of Beaurevoir; interrogation on whether she leaped by the counsel of her voices; that she had no desire to eat following her leap from the tower; question whether, when her speech returned, she denied God and his saints.

ARTICLE 42

Joan stated and let it be known that Saint Catherine, Saint Margaret, and Saint Michael have body parts, including head, eyes, face, hair, and suchlike. She said further that she touched Saint Catherine and Saint Margaret with her hands, and embraced and kissed them.

With regard to this article, she says she has answered this elsewhere, and she refers to what she said then.

Summary: earlier testimony introduced. March 17: interrogation on whether she ever kissed or embraced Saint Catherine and Saint Margaret, whether she felt warmth, and what part she embraced.

ARTICLE 43

Joan stated and announced that saints, angels, and archangels speak French and not English, because they are not on the English side but on the French. The saints in glory, she claims to their reproach, look with mortal hatred upon a catholic realm and a people who show devotion to all the saints, according to the decree of the Church.

To this article, explained word for word, she replied only that she trusts to God and to what she said elsewhere on this subject.

Summary: *earlier testimony introduced. March 1: that the voice is lovely, pleasant, and low; that it speaks French; question whether Saint Margaret speaks English.*

ARTICLE 44

Joan has boasted and proclaimed that Saint Catherine and Saint Margaret promised to lead her to paradise, and assured her of blessedness if she kept her virginity; and she is certain of this.

With regard to this article, she says she trusts to our Lord on this matter, and to what she has already said.

Summary: *earlier testimony introduced. February 22: that she never asked the voice for any last reward but the salvation of her soul. March 14: interrogation on whether, since her voices told her that in the end she will come to heaven, she believes herself assured of salvation; response on being told that this answer had great consequence; the certainty of her salvation, regarding her virginity; interrogation on whether after this revelation she believes she cannot commit a mortal sin and whether she need confess, since she believes from a revelation of her voices that she will be saved. March 1: that her saints promised to bring her to paradise.*

ARTICLE 45

Although the judgments of God are impenetrable, especially to our eyes, nonetheless Joan stated, declared, recounted, and proclaimed that she knew and knows who are saints, archangels, angels, and elect of God, and that she can distinguish between them.

With regard to this article, she says she refers to what she has already said about this.

Summary: *earlier testimony introduced. February 27: interrogation on how she knows it is the two saints Catherine and Margaret who appeared to her and how she knew one from the other. March 1: interrogation on whether the saints always* *appear to her in the same garb. March 3: that she knew Saint Catherine and Saint Margaret were saints of paradise.*

ARTICLE 46

She said that before she jumped, she passionately interceded with Saint Catherine and Saint Margaret for the citizens of Compiègne, saying among other things, in complaint: "How can God allow the people of Compiègne to die so wretchedly, who are so loyal to him?" In this appears her impatience and irreverence toward God and the saints.

With regard to this article, she says she refers to what she has already said on the subject.

Summary: earlier testimony introduced. March 3: that after she had leaped from the tower of Beaurevoir, Saint Catherine told her to be of good cheer and she would recover, and the people of Compiègne would lend her aid.

ARTICLE 47

In an evil mood because of the wounds she received from her fall or leap from the tower of Beaurevoir, and because her plan had failed, Joan blasphemed God and the saints, denied them in abusive terms, and utterly scorned them, to the horror of those present. Moreover, since arriving at the castle of Rouen, she has often blasphemed and denied God, the Blessed Virgin, and the saints, finding it unbearable and cursing that she has to appear on trial before the clergy and be judged there.

With regard to this article, she says she trusts to our Lord and to her previous answer.

Summary: earlier testimony introduced. March 3: interrogation on whether after leaping from the tower, she was angry and blasphemed God; Soissons and the captain who surrendered the town. March 14: interrogation on whether she has denied or cursed God since arriving in prison.

ARTICLE 48

Joan stated that she believed and believes that the spirits that visit her are angels, archangels, and saints of God, as certainly as she believes the Christian faith and its articles; yet she offers no sign sufficient to know this, nor has she consulted any bishop, priest, or Church prelate, or any cleric at all, to know whether to believe in these spirits. What is more, she said that the voices forbade her to reveal them to anyone, except first to a captain of soldiers, and then to Charles and to other purely secular persons. In these instances she admits to believing rashly and to erring on the articles of faith and their permanence, and even to having suspicious revelations that she wished to hide from prelates and clergy, and to reveal instead to laypersons.

With regard to this article, she says she has already answered it, and she refers to what is recorded above. But as to the signs, she cannot help it if those who ask for them are unworthy. For this reason, she often prayed that God might choose to reveal them to certain members of her party. She said further that as for believing in her revelations, she did not ask advice from any bishop or priest or anyone else. She said she believes it was Saint Michael who appeared to her, because of the good doctrine he revealed to her.

Asked whether Saint Michael told her he was Saint Michael, she answered: "I've already answered this"; and as for the end of the article, "I trust to our Lord." She said she believes that our Lord sent Saint Michael, Saint Gabriel, Saint Catherine, and Saint Margaret to comfort and advise her, as firmly as she believes our Lord Jesus Christ died for us and redeemed us from the pains of hell.

Summary: earlier testimony introduced. February 24: her firm belief that the voice comes from God. March 3: the heads of Saint Michael and Saint Gabriel. March 13: interrogation on whether she spoke of her visions to her priest or any other clergyman and whether she did well in leaving without her parents' permission.

ARTICLE 49

Trusting solely to her imagination, Joan adored these spirits, kissing the ground she said they passed over, kneeling to them, embracing and kissing them and paying them other reverence, thanking them with her hands clasped, encouraging their familiarity, even though she did not know whether they were good spirits; when instead, considering the circumstances, she should have judged them as they seemed to be, as evil spirits rather than good. These devotions and observances seem to tend toward idolatry and toward a pact with demons.

To this article, Wednesday, March 28, she replied, as to the beginning: "I've already answered"; and as to the end: "I trust to our Lord."

Summary: earlier testimony introduced. February 24: interrogation on whether she thanked the voice and genuflected. March 10: interrogation on what reverence she made to the sign when it came to her king and whether she and her king paid reverence to the angel when he brought the sign. March 12: interrogation on whether she spoke to God when she promised to keep her virginity; that the first time she heard the voice, she vowed to keep her virginity; question whether she made reverence to Saint Michael and the angels when she saw them. March 15: interrogation on whether she does reverence to her voice as a saint and whether she has offered candles to her saints; placing candles before the image of Saint Catherine. March 17:

the garlands she gave to her saints and hung on the tree; the question whether she made reverence to the saints when they came to her.

ARTICLE 50

Frequently and daily Joan calls on these spirits, consulting them about her future actions, such as how to answer at the trial and other matters. This seems to and does involve the invocation of demons.

With regard to this article, on Wednesday, March 28, she said: "I've answered this," and she will call those voices to her aid as long as she lives.

Asked how she calls on them, she answered: "I cry out to God and our Lord to send me counsel and strength, and then they send it to me."

Asked what words she uses when calling to them, she said she asks like this, in French: "Sweetest God, in honor of your holy Passion, I pray you, if you love me, show me how to answer these churchmen. I know well at whose command I took this clothing; but I don't know how I should leave it off. Please instruct me on this." And then they come at once.

The same day, she said she often has news from her voices for us, the bishop of Beauvais.

Asked what they say about us, she answered: "I'll tell you privately." That day, she said, they visited her three times.

Asked whether they were in her room, she answered: "I've already answered this; regardless, I clearly heard them." She said Saint Catherine and Saint Margaret told her how to answer about her attire.

Summary: earlier testimony introduced. February 24: that the voice told her to answer boldly; that she asked the voice to counsel her how to answer; the question whether the voice said anything to her before she asked it. February 27: interrogation on what the voice told her, whether the voice had given her counsel on certain points, and how she knows what questions to answer. March 12: interrogation on whether the angel failed her with respect to her good fortune and in the blessings of grace, whether she calls out to Saint Catherine and Saint Margaret or whether they come without being summoned, whether the saints did not come when summoned. March 13: interrogation on whether she had spoken with Saint Catherine since yesterday. March 14: interrogation on whether her voices ask for a delay before answering and whether there is a light with the saints.

ARTICLE 51

Joan did not hesitate to boast that Saint Michael, the archangel of God, came to her at Chinon with a mighty host of angels, and in the house of a certain woman walked with her, held her hand, and walked together up the castle steps to her king's chamber. There, joined by angels (some crowned, others with wings), the archangel made reverence to the king, bowing before him. To say such things about archangels and holy angels must be deemed presumptuous, rash, and fabricated, especially since we never read of angels and archangels making such reverence or bowing to any righteous person, not even to the Blessed Virgin, the Mother of God. Further, Joan often said that the holy archangel Gabriel came to her with Blessed Michael and a thousand thousand angels. She also boasts that at her prayer, the angel brought with him among that league of angels a most precious crown to her king, to place on his head. This crown is now stored in the king's treasury. Had the king waited a few days, Joan claims, he would have been crowned with it at Reims. But owing to the haste of his coronation, he took another. Such things as these, rather than being revealed by God, were imagined by Joan at the devil's prompting, or revealed to her by a demon in lying apparitions, to the mockery of her curiosity, because she meddled in matters too exalted for her, things beyond her nature to comprehend.

To this fifty-first article, on Wednesday, March 28, she says she has already answered about the angel who brought the sign. As to the promoter's statement about the thousand thousand angels, she says she does not remember saying that, that is a specific number. But she did indeed say that whenever she was wounded, she had great encouragement and aid from God and Saint Catherine and Saint Margaret.

As for the crown, she said she has already answered. As to the end of the article, which the promoter introduces in a way contrary to her actual deeds, she trusts to God. And as to where the crown was made and fashioned, she trusts to God.

Summary: earlier testimony introduced. February 27: interrogation on whether there was an angel over the head of her king the first time she saw him, whether there was a light, and how her king put faith in her words; that the clergy on her side believed that there was only good in her mission. March 1: interrogation on whether her king had a crown at Reims; the richer crown. March 10: interrogation on what the sign was that came to her king, why she has no desire to explain or reveal the sign, whether the sign still exists, and whether it was gold, silver, a precious stone, or a crown; that an angel of God gave her king a sign; the question whether the churchmen of her party saw the sign. March 12: interrogation on whether the angel spoke who brought the sign, whether this was the same angel which first appeared to her, and what the sign was that she gave her king. March 13: interrogation on what the sign was that she gave her king and whether she had promised Saint Catherine not to speak of it; that the sign was that an angel brought her king a crown and assured him that he would have the kingdom of France; the crown and the angel that brought it.

ARTICLE 52

Through her inventions, Joan led Christian people so far astray that in her presence many worshipped her as a saint and still do in her absence, establishing masses in her honor and prayers in church. What is more, they say she is greater than all God's saints after the Blessed Virgin; they set up her images in churches of the saints and carry images of lead and other metals, like those of canonized saints; and they publicly preach that she is God's messenger, an angel rather than a woman. Such things are destructive to the Christian religion, scandalous, and harmful to the salvation of souls.

To this article, on Wednesday, March 28, she replied that she has already answered the beginning of the article; as to the end, she trusts to God.

Summary: earlier testimony introduced. March 3: Friar Richard; interrogation on whether she has seen or has had made any images or paintings of herself; the painting in her host's house at Orléans; interrogation on whether she knows of services or masses performed for her, what honor the citizens of Troyes paid her, and whether Brother Richard preached a sermon when she arrived.

ARTICLE 53

Against the commands of God and the saints, Joan presumptuously and arrogantly took command over men, making herself leader and commander of an army sometimes numbering sixteen thousand men—including princes, barons, and many other nobles—all of whom she made serve under herself as commander in chief.

To this article, on Wednesday, March 28, she replies that as to being a war commander, she has answered elsewhere. If she was a war commander, it was to beat the English. As to the end of the article, she trusts to our Lord.

Summary: earlier testimony introduced. February 27: the number of forces her king gave her.

ARTICLE 54

Without shame, Joan traveled with men, refusing the company and attendance of women and relying only on men, whom she had assist her in the privacy of her quarters and in her secret affairs. Such a thing has never been seen or heard of in any modest and pious woman.

With regard to this article, she said that the men directed her. But as for lodging and sleeping at night, she usually had a woman stay with her. When she was fighting, she slept clothed and armed when she could not find a woman. As for the end of the article, she trusts to the Lord.

ARTICLE 55

Joan misused the revelations and prophecies she claims to have from God, turning them into worldly gain and profit. For by these revelations she acquired riches in great abundance, many furnishings, and high estate: officers, horses, ornaments, and even great revenues for her brothers and parents. In this, she resembles false prophets who, for worldly gain or favors from lords, would pretend they had divine revelations about things they knew would gratify princes, thus abusing divine oracles and attributing their lies to God.

With regard to this article, she said she has already answered it. As to the gifts to her brothers, what the king gave her was given freely, without Joan asking. But as to the accusation the promoter made at the end of the article, she trusts to our Lord.

Summary: earlier testimony introduced. March 10: interrogation on whether she had other riches from her king besides horses, whether she had a treasury, what horse she was riding when she was captured, and who gave it to her.

ARTICLE 56

Joan often boasted of having two counselors she calls Counselors of the Fountain, who came to her after her capture, as shown in the confession of Catherine de la Rochelle before the official at Paris. Catherine said that Joan would escape from prison with the devil's help if she were not well guarded.

With regard to this article, Joan said she stands by her previous answer on this. As to the Counselors of the Fountain, she does not know what that means. But she truly believes she once heard Saint Catherine and Saint Margaret there. As to the end of the article, she denies it and affirms under oath that she would not wish the devil to drag her from prison.

Summary: earlier testimony introduced. March 3: Catherine de la Rochelle.

ARTICLE 57

On the feast of the Nativity of Blessed Mary, Joan gathered all the soldiers from Charles's army to attack Paris, and led them to the city, promising them they would enter it that day—so she knew by revelation—and ordering every possible preparation for the assault. And yet she did not hesitate to deny this in court, before you. In many places, such as at La Charité-sur-Loire, at Pont-l'Evêque, and at Compiègne, where she attacked the army of the duke of Burgundy, she made many promises and prophesied the future, claiming she knew things by revelation; yet they never came to pass, and instead the opposite happened. And in your presence she denied making these promises and predictions, given that things did not turn out as she had said; yet many reliable witnesses report that she stated and publicized them. At the attack on Paris, moreover, she said that a thousand thousand angels were ready to take her to paradise should she die. Yet when asked why there had been no entry into Paris, contrary to her promise, but instead many of her soldiers and she herself had been seriously injured, some even killed, she reportedly answered that Jesus had failed her in his promise.

With regard to this article, on Wednesday, March 28, she says she has answered the beginning of the article elsewhere. "And if I'm further advised on this, I'll happily tell you about it." As to the end of the article, that Jesus failed her, she denies it.

Summary: earlier testimony introduced. March 3: La Charité. March 13: going to Paris, to La Charité, and to Pont-l'Evêque; attacking Paris on the Nativity of Blessed Mary.

ARTICLE 58

Joan had painted on her banner two angels next to God holding the world in his hand, with the words "Jesus, Mary" and other images. She said she did this by command of God, who revealed it to her through angels and saints. And she placed it in the cathedral of Reims near the altar when Charles was crowned, in her pride and vainglory wishing the banner to be specially honored by the others. She also had her coat of arms painted with two gold lilies on a field of azure, between the lilies a silver sword with a gold hilt and guard, the point ending in a golden crown. Such things seem to tend toward pride and vanity, not religion or piety; and to attribute such vanities to God and the angels shows no respect for God and his saints.

To this article, this Wednesday, March 28, she answered: "I've answered this." And to the suggestion of the promoter:[22] "I trust to or wait upon our Lord."

Summary: earlier testimony introduced. February 27: her banner at Orléans. March 3: that her standard was in the church at Reims, near the altar. March 10: the design on her banner; interrogation on whether she had a shield and arms. March 17: complete interrogation about the banner.

ARTICLE 59

At Saint-Denis in France, Joan offered and set up in a high place of the church the arms she carried when she was wounded in the attack on Paris, that they might be honored by the people as relics. And in the same town she had candles burned and poured the melted wax on the heads of children, telling their fortunes and prophesying their future through this sorcery.

To this article, Wednesday, March 28, she answered as to the arms, "I've already answered"; as to the melted candles and dripping wax, she denies it.

Summary: earlier testimony introduced. March 17: the arms she offered in the church of Saint-Denis.

ARTICLE 60

Scorning the teachings and decrees of the Church, Joan refused many times to swear to tell the truth, thereby rendering herself suspect of doing or saying things concerning the faith and revelations that she dares not reveal to the ecclesiastical judges for fear of a well-deserved punishment. She herself seems to acknowledge as much by the proverb, "People are sometimes hanged for telling the truth." And she often says: "You won't learn everything"; and "I'd rather have my head cut off than tell you everything."

With regard to this article, Wednesday, March 28, she says she requested an adjournment only in order to answer questions more certainly. As for the end of the article, she had doubts about answering and therefore requested an adjournment to learn whether she should answer the question. She said that since her king's counsel does not concern the trial, she does not wish to reveal it. She revealed the sign to her king because the churchmen forced her to tell it.

Summary: earlier testimony introduced. February 22: interrogation on whether there was any light or an angel when the voice revealed the king to her, and on what kind of revelations her king had. February 24: attempts to persuade Joan to take the oath; interrogation on whether the voice forbade her to tell everything, whether the voice forbade her to tell her revelations, whether this was forbidden her, whether she believes that telling the truth displeases God, whether her counsel revealed that she would escape from prison, whether that night the voice counseled her what to answer, whether any light appeared on the last two days she heard voices, whether she sees anything else with the voices, and whether the voice had vision. February 27: attempts to persuade Joan to take the oath; interrogation on whether Saint Catherine and Saint Margaret are dressed in the same cloth, whether they are of the same age, whether they speak together or one after the other, which one first appeared to her, what shape Saint Michael took, what he said to her on that first occasion, whether Saint Michael and the other saints told her not to reveal their appearance to her without their leave, what sign she gives to show that the revelation comes from God, and what revelations her king had. March 1: interrogation on what promises the saints made to her, whether they promised her anything beyond that they would lead her to paradise, whether the saints told her that she would be freed from prison in three months, whether her counsel told her that she would be freed from prison, whether the voices forbade her to tell the truth, what sign she gave to her king that she was from God, whether she knew the sign, to whom she promised this, and whether anyone else was present when she showed the sign to the king. March 3: interrogation on whether God created Saint Michael and Saint Gabriel in the same manner and shape in which she sees them, whether she knew by revelation that she would escape, whether her voices told her anything about it, and whether when

God told her to change her clothing, it was by the voice of the saints. March 12: interrogation on whether she had received letters from Saint Michael or her voices.

ARTICLE 61

Admonished to submit all her words and deeds to the judgment of the Church militant, and told the difference between the Church militant and the Church triumphant, Joan said she submits to the Church triumphant, while refusing to submit to the Church militant, and thereby demonstrating that she misunderstands the article of the creed, "One holy Church," etc., and errs on this point. She says she is subject directly to God, and leaves her actions to him and to the saints, not to the judgment of the Church.

With regard to this article, she says she would do honor and reverence to the Church militant as much as she can. But as for referring her actions to the Church militant, she answered: "I must trust to the Lord God who had me do this."

Asked whether she refers her actions to the Church militant, she answered: "Send the clerk to me on Saturday and I'll answer you then."

Summary: earlier testimony introduced. March 15: the difference between the Church triumphant and the Church militant; warnings and requests to Joan to yield to the Church; interrogation on whether she would submit what she has said and done to the decision of the Church. March 17: interrogation on whether she thought she would have to tell the truth to the pope about everything they asked her touching the faith. March 31: complete interrogation over the Church militant and the Church triumphant. April 18: that the more she feared for her life because of her illness, the more should she amend her life; interrogation on whether she would submit to the Church, given that she requested that the Church administer the Eucharist to her.[23]

ARTICLE 62

Joan strives to shock the people, persuading them to put absolute trust in all she says and will say. So she takes upon herself the authority of God and the angels, and raises herself above all ecclesiastical power to lead people into error, as the false prophets used to do when they founded sects of error and damnation and set themselves apart from the one body of the Church. This is destructive of the Christian religion and, if prelates of the Church took no action, could overturn all ecclesiastical authority. Men and women will rise up on every hand, pretend to have revelations from God and the angels, and sow lies and errors, as we have seen now these many times after this woman lifted herself up and began scandalizing Christian people and spreading her deceits abroad.

With regard to this article, Wednesday, March 28, she said she would answer it Saturday.

ARTICLE 63

At the trial, in violation of her oath, Joan does not hesitate to lie, claiming many contradictory and inconsistent things about her revelations; she breathes curses upon lords, distinguished persons, and an entire nation; and without shame she makes many frivolous and ridiculous statements unbefitting a holy woman, which show that she is guided and governed in her actions by evil spirits and not by the counsel of God and the angels, as she herself boasts. As Christ says of false prophets: "By their fruits you shall know them."[24]

With regard to this article, Wednesday, March 28, she said she refers to what she said before on this, and for the conclusion, she trusts to God.

Summary: earlier testimony introduced. February 27: the sword that she took from Lagny to Compiègne. March 1: that she would have died but for the revelation that comforts her each day; the hair of Saint Michael.

ARTICLE 64

Joan boasts that she knows she has been forgiven for the sin she committed in desperation, when she was incited by an evil spirit and cast herself from a high tower of the castle of Beaurevoir. Yet Scripture says that no one knows if he is worthy of love or hatred, and thus whether he has been purged from sin or justified.[25]

To this article, on Wednesday, March 28, she answers: "I've given you a sufficient answer on this, and I refer to that answer." And for the end of the article, she trusts to God.

ARTICLE 65

Joan has stated many times that she asked God to send her a clear revelation, through the angels and Saint Catherine and Saint Margaret, for her conduct—for instance, whether she should answer truthfully at the trial on certain points and personal details. This is to tempt God and to ask forbidden things of him needlessly, and before conducting all possible human inquiry and investigation. And especially in the leap from the tower, she clearly seems to have tempted God.

With regard to this article, on Wednesday, March 28, she said she has already answered this, and does not wish to declare what has been revealed to her without God's permission. She does not ask God about the article unless it is necessary. She wishes he would send more revelations, so that it might be clearer that she has come from God—that is to say, that he sent her.

ARTICLE 66

Some of these matters depart from divine, evangelical, canon, and civil law, and are contrary to decrees approved in general councils; they contain spells, divinations, and superstitions; they smack of heresy, some formally, others by causation or otherwise; many lead to errors in the faith and encourage heresy; some are seditious, some disturb or hinder the peace; some urge the shedding of human blood; some are even curses and blasphemies against God and the saints, offending the ears of the pious. Through her foolhardiness, and incited by the devil, the accused in these instances has offended God and his holy Church, has sinned and transgressed against the Church. For these crimes she is a cause of scandal and has been notoriously denounced, and therefore must be corrected and reformed by you.

With regard to this article, Joan said she is a good Christian. As for all the other accusations in the article, she trusts to the Lord.

ARTICLE 67

Each and every one of these things the accused has committed, performed, stated, pronounced, declared, dogmatically affirmed, spread abroad, and accomplished in this jurisdiction and elsewhere, in many different places of this kingdom, not once but many different times, days, and hours. She has relapsed into her offenses and given counsel, aid, and approval to others committing them.

Joan denies this article.

ARTICLE 68

After a loud report struck your ears not once but many times, and you learned of the public notoriety of these matters and gathered evidence on them, you found the accused to be gravely suspect and denounced. You therefore decided to establish an inquiry against her, to be conducted by you or one of you, and to summon her to answer these questions, as has been done.

Joan said that this article concerns the judges.

ARTICLE 69

With regard to these accusations, the accused was and is gravely suspected, accused of scandal, and publicly denounced by many good and respectable persons. Yet she has neither corrected herself nor reformed in any way, but rather has delayed and refused to correct and reform herself and has persisted in these errors, even though you and several other notable clerics and honorable persons have, charitably and otherwise, duly and sufficiently warned, summoned, and requested her to do so.

With regard to this article, she said she did not commit the crimes alleged by the promoter against her. For the rest, she trusts to the Lord. As for the crimes alleged against her, she does not believe she has done anything against the Christian faith.

Asked whether she would submit to the Church and to those charged with the task of correction if she had done anything contrary to the Christian faith, she said she would answer Saturday after dinner.

ARTICLE 70

Each and every one of these things is true, widely known, and evident, and public opinion and report have been preoccupied with them and remain so; and on many occasions, the accused has sufficiently acknowledged and admitted to upright and reliable persons, both in and out of court, that they are true.

Joan denies this article, except for the things she has admitted.

The plaintiff requests you to examine the accused on these and other points that you will supply, correct, and improve. Now that the facts in the case have been established in whole or in part, sufficient for the purpose, the plaintiff concludes that you may sentence the accused for each and every reason mentioned above, and that you may speak and judge further according to law and reason. He humbly beseeches your attention to these matters.

Saturday, March 31. The following Saturday, the last day of March, the vigil of Easter, the year of our Lord 1431.

We the judges, presiding in Joan's prison at the castle of Rouen, assisted by reverend masters Jean Beaupère, Jacques de Touraine, Nicolas Midi, Pierre Maurice, Gérard Feuillet, doctors; Guillaume Haiton and Thomas de Courcelles, bachelors of theology; with Guillaume Mouton and John Grey, witnesses.

Joan was examined on certain questions that she had delayed answering until today, when she would reply to the articles, as stated above.

First, she was asked whether she would submit to the judgment of the Church on earth all she has said and done, whether good or evil, especially the errors, crimes, and faults of which she is accused, and everything that touches her trial. She said that in all they ask, she submits to the Church militant, as long as it does not order her to do something impossible. She deems "impossible" that she should retract what she has done and said: the visions and revelations she claims to have from God, as stated in the trial record. She will not retract them for anything. As for what God had her do, and what he commands now and in the future, she will not stop doing these things for anyone living. It would be impossible for her to retract them. Should the Church command her to do something against the command she claims to have from God, she would not do it for anything.

Asked whether she would submit to the Church if it were to tell her that her revelations are deceptions or the work of the devil, she said she always trusts to God on this, whose commandment she will always keep. She knows full well that everything mentioned in her trial record comes by God's command. What she claims to have done by God's command she could not have done otherwise. Should the Church command her to do the opposite, she would not submit to anyone in the world but God, and she would always obey his good commands.

Asked whether she believes she is subject to God's Church on earth, that is to our father the pope, the cardinals, archbishops, bishops, and other prelates of the Church, she said yes, God being first served.

Asked whether her voices commanded her not to submit to the Church militant on earth or to its judgment, she said she does not answer the first thing that comes into her head. Her answers come from the command of her voices. They do not tell her to disobey the Church, God being first served.

Asked whether she had any files while at the castle of Beaurevoir, in Arras, or anywhere else, she answered: "If they were found on me, I have nothing else to say about it."[26]

After these questions, we departed, to continue in this matter of faith later on.

Monday, April 2. The following Monday after Easter, April 2, the year of our Lord 1431, and the following Tuesday and Wednesday, we the judges and the other reverend masters assembled by us examined the articles transcribed above, the questions, and the answers of Joan, and reduced them to certain statements and propositions in the form of twelve articles that embrace many of Joan's statements in brief and summary form. We have concluded by sending these assertions to doctors and experts in canon and civil law, requesting their advice and consideration for the good of the faith.

Thursday, April 5. The following Thursday, April 5, we sent our schedule of indictment with the statements, in the following form, to the doctors and experts we knew were in the town:

Schedule of Indictment Containing the Twelve Articles

We, Pierre, by divine mercy bishop of Beauvais, and Jean Le Maistre, vice-inquisitor, pray and request you, for the good of the faith, that by next Tuesday you submit to us your salutary counsel, sealed and in writing, on the statements below; that is, whether on being seen, considered, and compared, all or some of them are against the true faith or are suspected of being opposed to sacred Scripture, the Holy Roman Church, or its approved doctors and canonical decrees; whether they are scandalous, rash, threatening to the state, damaging, criminal, against good morals, or offensive in any way—or whether anything should be said about them at trial.

Written on Thursday after Easter, April 5, the year of our Lord 1431.

The Contents of the Assertions

ARTICLE 1

First, a certain woman states and affirms that when she was around thirteen years old, she saw with her bodily eyes Saint Michael, who would comfort her, and sometimes Saint Gabriel, and they appeared in the body. Sometimes she also saw a great host of angels; and then Saint Catherine and Saint Margaret appeared to her in the body. She also sees them each day and hears their voices, and sometimes embraces and kisses them, materially and bodily touching them. She has seen the heads of these angels and saints, but will say nothing of the rest of their bodies or clothing. Sometimes Saint Catherine and Saint Margaret spoke to her by a certain fountain, near a tall tree commonly called the fairies' tree. It is widely reported that fairies gather at the fountain and tree, and that many who are sick with the fever visit the fountain and tree to recover their health, even though it is an unholy place. There and elsewhere, she has often worshipped them [the saints] and shown them reverence.

She also says that Saint Catherine and Saint Margaret revealed themselves to her, wearing beautiful and precious crowns. From that time, and many times thereafter, they told her that God had commanded her to go to a certain prince of this world, and to promise him that with her help and labors, he would recover great worldly realms and glory through force of arms and would conquer his enemies; and that this same prince would welcome her and give her weapons and an army of soldiers to accomplish these things.

Again, Saint Catherine and Saint Margaret instructed her in God's name to wear men's clothes, which she has worn and still wears, steadfastly obeying this command to such an extent that she said she would rather die than set aside this clothing. She stated this openly at various times, adding on other occasions: "except by God's command." She also chose not to attend Mass, and to forgo the holy Eucharist during the time designated by the Church for the faithful to receive this sacrament, rather than take women's clothes and leave off men's. These women also encouraged her in this, that without the knowledge of her parents and against their will, when she was around seventeen she left her father's house and joined a company of soldiers, living with them day and night, and rarely if ever having another woman with her.

These saints told and commanded her many other things, on account of which she claims to be sent by the God of heaven and the Church victorious of saints now in blessedness, to whom she submits all she has done for good. But she delays and refuses to submit herself or her words and deeds to the Church militant. Though asked and admonished many times on this point, she says she cannot do otherwise than what she claimed in her trial to do by God's command. In these matters she does not submit to the decision or judgment of any living person, only to the judgment of God. And she says these saints have revealed to her that if she preserves her virginity, as she vowed to do the first time she saw and heard them, she will enter into the glory of the blessed and her soul will be saved. By reason of this revelation, she claims to be as sure of her salvation as if she were present even now in the kingdom of heaven.

ARTICLE 2

This woman says that the sign that convinced the prince to whom she had been sent to believe in her revelations and to allow her to go to battle was that Saint Michael came to the prince, accompanied by a host of angels, some wearing crowns, others with wings, Saint Catherine and Saint Margaret among them. The angel and this woman took a long walk together on the ground, along the road, up the steps, and into the chamber, escorted by other angels and these saints. And one angel gave a rich crown of purest gold to the prince and bowed before him, showing him reverence. Once, she stated that when her prince received this sign, she thought he was alone, but there were many others nearby; yet another time she said that she thought an archbishop took the sign of the crown and gave it to the prince, in the presence and view of many temporal lords.

ARTICLE 3

This woman knew and is sure that the one who visits her is Saint Michael, because of the wise counsel, encouragement, and teaching Saint Michael gave her and because he said his name, that he was Michael. Likewise, she can clearly recognize Saint Catherine and Saint Margaret and tell them apart, because they say their names and greet her. This is why she believes it is Saint Michael himself who visits her and that his words and deeds are good and true, just as firmly as she believes that our Lord Jesus suffered and died for our redemption.

ARTICLE 4

This woman states and affirms that she is as sure that certain future events, which are purely contingent, will happen as she is of the things she sees in front of her.[27] And she boasts that through the verbal revelations of Saint Catherine and Saint Margaret she has and did have knowledge of hidden things; for instance, that she will be freed from prison, and that in her company, the French will perform an action finer than any seen in Christian lands. She also claims that without anyone's help, through revelation, she has recognized people she never saw before, and that she uncovered and revealed a sword hidden in the ground.

ARTICLE 5

This woman states and affirms that by God's command and at his good pleasure, she took and wore men's attire, and still does. She says further that because God commanded her to wear men's clothes, she has to wear a short tunic, a hood and doublet, breeches, and hose with many points and to have her hair cut round above her ears, leaving nothing about her to indicate the female sex except what nature gave to distinguish her sex. She says she has often received the Eucharist in these clothes. She refused, and still does, to put women's clothes back on; and though she has been asked and warned kindly on this point many times, she says she would rather die than abandon men's clothes, sometimes stating this simply, other times adding "except by God's command." And she says that if she found herself in men's clothes among those for whom she formerly fought, and if she could do as she did before her capture and imprisonment, it would be one of the greatest blessings that could ever come to the whole kingdom of France. She added that not for anything in the world would she swear to abandon men's clothes and to give up arms. And in all these matters, she says she has done and does well, and that she has obeyed God and his commands.

ARTICLE 6

This woman acknowledges and claims that she ordered many letters written with the names Jesus, Mary and the sign of the cross at the beginning. Sometimes she put a cross to signify that what was commanded in the letter should not be done. But in others, she ordered it to be written that she would have those who disobeyed her letters and warnings killed, and that blows would determine who has the better claim from the God of heaven. And she often says that she has done nothing except by revelation and by the command of God.

ARTICLE 7

This woman says and acknowledges that when she was around seventeen years old, on her own and by revelation, as she says, she went to a certain squire she had never seen before, leaving her father's house against the will of her parents, who nearly went out of their minds once they realized she was gone. This woman asked the squire to lead her or have her led to the prince mentioned above. Then this man of war, a captain, gave the woman men's clothing and a sword, at her request. And he chose one knight, a squire, and four servants to lead her. When they had come to the prince, the woman told him she wished to conduct the war against his enemies and promised him that she would put him in great dominion and would overcome his enemies, and that the God of heaven had sent her to do this. In these matters she says she has done right, by the command of God and by revelation.

ARTICLE 8

This woman says and acknowledges that without anyone's inciting or pushing her, she threw herself from a high tower, preferring death to captivity among her enemies or to life after the destruction of Compiègne. She adds that she could not help falling, yet Saint Catherine and Saint Margaret forbade her to throw herself down, and she says that to offend them is a grave sin. But she knows full well that this sin was forgiven after she confessed it. She says she had a revelation about this.

ARTICLE 9

This woman says that Saint Catherine and Saint Margaret promised to take her to paradise if she kept the virginity she pledged to them, both in body and in soul. She says she is as certain of this as if she were among the blessed in glory even now. She does not believe she has committed any mortal sins; for if she were in mortal sin, she supposes Saint Catherine and Saint Margaret would not visit her each day, as they do.

ARTICLE 10

This woman says and affirms that God loves certain persons she has identified and named, still wayfarers in this world, and that he loves them more than he does her. She knows this by the revelation of Saint Catherine and Saint Margaret, who often speak to her in French, not English, since they are not on that side. Once she understood through revelation that the voices favored the prince mentioned above, she had no love for the Burgundians.

ARTICLE 11

This woman says and acknowledges that she has often shown reverence to these voices and spirits that she calls Michael, Gabriel, Catherine, and Margaret, so baring her head, kneeling, kissing the ground they walk on, pledging her virginity to them, and sometimes embracing and kissing Catherine and Margaret. She has touched them bodily and materially, and asked for their advice and help, sometimes summoning them, although they often visit her unbidden. And she assents to and obeys their counsels and commands and has from the beginning, without asking advice of anyone, as of her father or mother, a priest, a prelate, or any clergyman whatsoever. Nonetheless, she firmly believes that the voices and revelations she has had through these saints come from God and at his bidding; she believes this as firmly as she believes the Christian faith and that our Lord Jesus Christ died for us. If an evil spirit were to appear to her pretending to be Saint Michael, she could easily tell whether it was he. This woman also says that at her own request, without being forced or asked, she swore to Saint Catherine and Saint Margaret not to reveal the sign of the crown that was to be given to the prince to whom she was sent. And at last she says, unless she has permission to reveal it.

ARTICLE 12

This woman says and acknowledges that if the Church wished her to do something against the command she claims to have from God, she would not do it for anything, but she asserts she is certain that the things stated in the record were done at God's command, and that she could not have done the contrary. She will not submit to the judgment of the Church militant or to any person in the world, only to our Lord God, whose commands she will always keep, especially the revelations and the things she claims to have done in obedience to them. She has never answered, here or elsewhere, by trusting to her own judgment but has answered at the command of her voices and revelations. Yet the judges and others present have often reminded her of the article of faith "One holy catholic Church" and explained that every faithful pilgrim in this world must obey and submit his words and actions to the Church militant, particularly in matters of faith and those which concern holy doctrine and ecclesiastical decrees.

Here follow the deliberations on these assertions, received on various days following.

First, sixteen doctors deliberated, licentiates and bachelors of theology, as contained in a notarized statement addressed to this question, whose tenor follows.

Notarized Statement Presenting the Opinion of Sixteen Theologians

In the name of the Lord, amen. Be it clearly apparent and known to all by this notarized statement that in the year of our Lord 1431, the ninth indiction, Thursday, April 12, the fourteenth year of the pontificate of our holy father and lord in Christ reverend Martin V, pope by divine providence,[28] in the presence of us, the undersigned notaries public and witnesses, there appeared in person reverend fathers and lords, esteemed and wise men, reverend masters: Erard Emengart, presiding; Jean Beaupère, Guillaume le Boucher, Jacques de Touraine, Nicolas Midi, Pierre de Miget, prior of Longueville, Maurice du Quesnay, Jean de Nibat, Pierre de Houdenc, Jean le Fèvre, Pierre Maurice, the reverend abbot of Mortemer, Gérard Feuillet, Richard Praty, and Jean Charpentier, professors of theology; William Haiton, bachelor of theology; Raoul le Sauvage, licentiate of theology; as well as Nicolas Couppequesne, Ysambard de la Pierre, and Thomas de Courcelles, also bachelors of theology, and Nicolas Loiselleur, master of arts.

They have stated that the reverend father in Christ the lord bishop of Beauvais and Brother Jean Le Maistre, vicar of the honorable doctor Master Jean Graverent, inquisitor of heresy in the kingdom of France, both judges in a certain cause of faith submitted to them, have called upon each of these doctors and masters in the matter of a certain schedule that begins "We, Pierre," etc., followed by the articles that begin "A certain woman," etc.[29] These doctors and masters received the schedule of indictment in due form and examined its contents diligently and repeatedly, in full, mature deliberation. They have considered, they said, that every professor of theology is legally bound to give profitable counsel in matters of doctrine, for the good of the faith, whenever asked to do so by prelates of the Church and inquisitors of heresy. And therefore, as bound by their profession, they wish, according to their ability and duty before God, to obey the reverend judges and their request. First, since the reverend judges have often and earnestly entreated them in writing and in speech, they have declared that, for the good of the faith and in order to satisfy this request, they intend to make a doctrinal pronouncement in this matter, which will be in harmony with Holy Scripture, the teachings of the saints, and ecclesiastical ordinances; and they will take into account nothing but the will of God and the truth of the faith. Second, they have declared that, both in this matter and in all others, they submit everything they say and decide to the examination, correction, and full judgment of the Holy Roman Church and to all those entrusted with this task now and in the future. Here they affirm the other pleas customarily made in such cases, in the best manner and form used for such pleas.

With these pleas formulated, the doctors and masters deliberated as follows:

> After having carefully examined, compared, and considered the rank of this person, her words, her actions, and the manner of her apparitions and revelations and their purpose, substance, and circumstances, and all the things included in the articles and in the process, we say that one must conclude that the apparitions and revelations of which she boasts, and which she claims she had from God through angels and saints, were not so, but were instead humanly fabricated stories, or they proceeded from an evil spirit, and this woman did not have sufficient signs to believe and know this. These articles contain lying fabrications—some having no semblance of truth, yet she believed them quite readily—also superstitious divinations, scandalous and impious behavior, rash, presumptuous, and boastful words, blasphemy against God and the saints, disrespect toward her parents, acts inconsistent with love of one's neighbor, idolatry or at least deceitful inventions, actions fracturing the unity, authority, and power of the Church, misunderstandings, and grave suspicion of heresy. And since she believes that Saint Michael, Saint Catherine, and Saint Margaret appear to her and that their words and deeds are good, just as staunchly as she believes the Christian faith, she must be held suspect of error in the faith. For if she thinks that the articles of faith should be believed no more firmly than that those who she says have appeared to her are Saint Michael, Saint Catherine, and Saint Margaret, and that their words and deeds are good, she errs in the faith. Further, to say that she has done well all that is contained in the fifth article, besides what is stated in the first article about not receiving the sacrament of Eucharist in the time designated by the Church, and to say that she has done all these things by God's command—these are blasphemies against God and errors in the faith.

The doctors and masters have asked us, the notaries public, for a notarized statement about the preceding matters and have desired that we convey it to the reverend judges.

Done in the chapel of the manor of the archbishop of Rouen, in the year, indiction, month, day, and pontificate mentioned above, in the presence of wise men, the reverend Jean de la Haye and Jean Bareton, beneficed priests in Rouen Cathedral, witnesses summoned and requested on these matters.

Signed as follows:

And I, Guillaume Manchon, priest of the diocese of Rouen, notary public sworn by apostolic and imperial authority, and of the archbishop's court of Rouen, was present and saw and heard done each and every one of these things as they were said, acted, and done, together with the notary below and the witnesses above. Therefore in faith and witness of these things, I have signed below and placed my accustomed seal, together with the seal and signature of the other notary public, on this present notarized statement, faithfully written in my own hand. G. Manchon.

And I, Guillaume Colles, also called Boisguillaume, priest of the diocese of Rouen, notary public by apostolic authority, and of the archbishop's court of Rouen, scribe sworn in the case, was present and saw and heard each and every one of these things done when they were said, acted, and done, together with the above witnesses and notary. Therefore in faith and witness of the truth of these things, I have signed with my accustomed seal and name this present notarized statement, faithfully produced, yet written in a different hand. Colles.

Summary. *In the days following, the judges solicited opinions from other assessors regarding the twelve articles and the decision of the theologians. Many of their responses restate the accusations against Joan, and most find her in violation; many defer to the decision of the theologians on April 12. The opinions are summarized here.*

Opinions of the Assessors

Summary. *Denis Gastinel: If Joan does not abjure her crimes, she should be handed over to the secular arm. If she does, she should be sentenced to prison.*

Jean Basset: He has "little or nothing" to say in such a difficult matter. Her revelations are "possible with God," but unconfirmed. She errs in taking men's clothing, in not taking the Eucharist at least once a year, and in refusing to submit to the Church militant. His judgment, however, assumes that her revelations are not from God. On this point he defers to the theologians.

Gilles, abbot of Fécamp (dated April 21, Fécamp): He adheres to the decision of the theologians. Jacques Guesdon, Jean Maugier, Jean Bruillot, Nicolas de Venderès, Nicolas Caval, Jean Hulot de Châtillon, and Jean Guérin deliver similar opinions.

Gilles Deschamps (dated May 3): Unless she corrects her statements or a "more wholesome" interpretation of them is given, her assertions are suspect in the faith.

Robert Le Barbier: He defers to the decision of the theologians but thinks that their decision should be sent to the faculties of law and theology at Paris for their opinion.

Jean Alespée: He defers to the decision of the theologians, but if the faculties of theology and law at Paris are consulted, he submits to their decision and to that of the Church and the general council.

Jean de Bouesgue, doctor of theology and almoner of Fécamp: Joan is schismatic and a heretic, and should be punished according to the law.

The cathedral chapter of Rouen (May 4): Considering the importance of the matter, they delayed responding to consider the decision of the faculties at Paris. Following the assembly of May 2, and seeing that Joan refused to heed warnings and submit to the Church, they agree with the decision of the theologians.

Aubert Morel and Jean Duchemin (one document): They repeat, sometimes in the exact same language, the decision of Jean Basset.

Eleven advocates of the court of Rouen[30] (one document, April 30): They also repeat the decision of Jean Basset.

Philibert de Montjeu, bishop of Coutances (dated May 5, Coutances): Joan is "moved by a subtle spirit, prone to evil, incited by a devilish instinct, and barren of the grace of the Holy Spirit." Justice should not be postponed. She must revoke her errors or be treated as an obstinate offender.

Zanon de Castiglione, bishop of Lisieux (dated May 14, Lisieux): No clear sign of holiness appears in Joan to validate her revelations. Considering her mean estate, her foolish statements, and the form and manner of her visions, he concludes that her revelations are not from God, but are either the illusions of devils or human lies. She must submit to the Church or be judged schismatic.

The following masters gave earlier opinions (not included in the trial record) that the judges deemed insufficient.

Nicolas, abbot of Jumièges, and Guillaume, abbot of Cormeilles (one document, April 29): Earlier, they responded that the entire trial should be submitted to the

University of Paris, but "you were not satisfied with this response." Their present response is that Joan should be publicly admonished, and if she persists in evil, she must be deemed suspect in the faith. Her revelations and men's attire are not supported by holiness of life or miracles. As to whether she is guilty of mortal sin, God alone knows. They cannot judge hidden things, and they defer to the theologians.

Raoul Roussel (dated April 30): He can say nothing further except that he believes Joan and her supporters are lying to help their cause. He defers to the theologians.

Pierre Minier, Jean Pigache, and Richard de Grouchet (one document): They insist as before that a formal answer would require certainty about the origin of the alleged revelations, a knowledge that is impossible to attain. If the revelations proceed from an evil spirit or are imagined, many of the statements are suspect. But if they come from God, which is not apparent, they could not be interpreted as evil.

Raoul le Sauvage: He finds her in error in most of the articles. As for the claim to see Saint Michael and the sign given to Charles VII, they cannot be certainly known, but he fears she is lying. He concludes that the propositions should be repeated to her in French, and she should be warned to amend herself. To remain above suspicion, the articles should be sent to the Holy See.

Wednesday, April 18. Wednesday, April 18, 1431: We the judges know from the reports and deliberations of many—doctors of theology, doctors and licentiates of canon law, and other graduates in these faculties—the serious and grave shortcomings in Joan's answers and statements; and we know that should she refuse to correct them, she would expose herself to grave dangers. We have therefore exhorted and warned her in love and kindness, and have had many good and learned men, doctors and others, warn her, to return to the way of truth and to the profession of our faith. To this end, we have entered Joan's prison on this day, attended by Guillaume le Boucher, Jacques de Touraine, Maurice du Quesnay, Nicolas Midi, Guillaume Adelie, and Gérard Feuillet, doctors; and Guillaume Haiton, bachelor of theology.

In their presence, we the bishop spoke to Joan, who said she was sick. We told her that these doctors and masters had come to her in love and friendship to visit her in her sickness, to comfort and encourage her. Then we related to her that over many days, she had been in-terrogated on great and difficult matters concerning the faith, before many wise men, and that she had given many different answers. When these learned and knowledgeable men had studied these answers and diligently considered them, they found that many of the things she has said and confessed are a danger to the faith. But since she was an unlearned woman, ignorant of the Scriptures, we offered to choose learned and knowledgeable men, honest and kind, who could duly in-struct her. We encouraged the doctors and masters there by every trust binding them to true doctrine in the faith to give fruitful counsel to Joan for the salvation of her soul and body. If Joan knew others suited for this task, we offered to find them for her, so that they could advise and instruct her what to do, hold, and believe.[31] We added that we were men of the Church, called to this task, willing, ready, and able to attend to the salvation of body and soul by all possible means, just as we would do for our neighbors and for our own selves. Every day, we would find these men for her due instruction, and in general we were ready to do everything that the Church customarily does in such cases, for she does not close her heart to any who return. Finally, we told Joan to consider well this wholesome warning and to pay full heed to it. For if she were to oppose it, relying upon her own judgment and in-experience, we would have to abandon her. Then she might consider the peril awaiting her, which we tried to avoid with all our might and our love.

Joan answered that she was grateful for the concern shown for her salvation, and she stated further: "I believe I'm in serious danger of dying from this illness. If God should so please I ask you for confes-sion and the Eucharist, and to be buried in holy ground."

Then she was told that if she wished for the sacraments of the Church, she had to confess as a good catholic, and submit to the Church; but if she still refused to submit to the Church, she could not receive the sacraments she asked for, except for penance, which we were always ready to give.

But she answered: "I don't know what else to tell you."

Then she was told that the more she feared for her life because of her illness, the more she should amend her life. She would not receive the rites of the Church as a catholic if she refused to submit to the Church.

She answered: "If my body dies in prison, I trust you will bury me in holy ground. If you don't, I trust in God."

She was told that she had said earlier in her trial that if she had done or said anything against the Christian faith, she would not persist in it.

She answered: "I refer to the answer I made on this, and to the Lord."

Because she said she has many revelations from God through Saint Michael, and through Saint Catherine and Saint Margaret, she was asked whether she would believe any good creature who claimed to have a revelation from God about Joan's mission. She answered that no Christian in the world could come and claim to have a revelation without her knowing very well whether or not he spoke the truth; she would know this through Saint Catherine and Saint Margaret.

Asked whether she did not suppose that God could reveal something to any good creature that Joan might not know, she said it is a good thing to know he could. "But I would not believe any man or woman," she said, "unless I had a sign."

Asked whether she believes that Holy Scripture is revealed by God, she answered: "You know this very well, and it's good to know it is."

Then she was summoned, exhorted, and requested to take good advice from the clergy and famous doctors, and to believe it for the salvation of her soul.

Asked again whether she would submit her words and actions to the Church militant, she answered for the last time: "Whatever happens to me, I will not say or do anything different from what I said earlier in the trial."

Hearing this, the esteemed doctors exhorted Joan as urgently as possible to submit herself and her actions to the Church militant, citing and explaining many passages of Holy Scripture to her, with many examples. One of the doctors advising her <Master Nicolas Midi> quoted Matthew 18: "If your brother offends you," etc.; and the passage following: "If he will not hear the Church, treat him as a gentile and tax collector."[32] He explained these passages to Joan in French, telling her at last that if she would not obey the Church, she would have to be abandoned as a heathen.

Joan answered that she was a good Christian and had been baptized, and that she would die as a good Christian.

She was asked whether she would submit to the Church militant, given that she requested that the Church administer the Eucharist to her; for if so, then they would administer the sacrament to her. She said that as for submission, she will answer nothing different from her previous answers. She loves God, serves him, and is a good Christian. She would like to help and support the Church with all her power.

Asked whether she would like a lovely and memorable procession to bring her back into good standing, if she is not at present, she said she wishes for the Church and catholics to pray for her.

Wednesday, May 2. On Wednesday, May 2, the year of our Lord 1431, we the judges presided in the room near the great hall of the castle of Rouen, assisted by reverend fathers, lords, and masters, summoned by our command:[33] Nicolas of Jumièges and Guillaume de Cormeilles, abbots and doctors of canon law; the abbot of Saint-Ouen, the prior of Saint-Lô, Pierre, prior of Longueville, Jean de Nibat, Jacques Guesdon, Jean Fouchier, Maurice du Quesnay, Jean le Fèvre, Guillaume le Boucher, Pierre Houdenc, Jean de Châtillon, Erard Emengart, Richard Praty, Jean Charpentier, Pierre Maurice, doctors of theology; Nicolas Couppequesne, Guillaume Haiton, Thomas de Courcelles, Richard de Grouchet, Pierre Minier, Raoul le Sauvage, Jean Pigache, Jean Maugier, and Jean Eude, bachelors of theology; Raoul Roussel, treasurer of Rouen Cathedral, doctor of canon and civil law, and Jean Guérin, doctor of canon law; Robert Le Barbier, Denis Gastinel, and Jean le Doux, licenciates of canon and civil law; Nicolas de Venderès, archdeacon of Eu, Jean Pinchon, archdeacon of Josas, Jean Bruillot, cantor of Rouen Cathedral, Richard des Saulx, Laurent du Busc, Aubert Morel, Jean Duchemin, Jean Colombel, Raoul Anguy, Jean le Tavernier, Guérould Poustel, licentiates of canon law; André Marguerie, archdeacon of Petit-Caux, Jean Alespée, Chancellor Gilles Deschamps, Nicolas Caval, canons of Rouen Cathedral; Guillaume de Livet, Pierre Carrel, Geoffroi du Crotay, Bureau de Cormeilles, licentiates of civil law; Guillaume Desjardins and Jean Tiphaine, doctors of medicine; Guillaume de la Chambre, licentiate of medicine; Brother Ysambard de la Pierre, Guillaume Legrant, Jean de Rosay, curate of Duclair, Brother Jean des Bats, Eustache Cateleu, Regnault Lejeune, Jean Mahommet, Guillaume le Cauchois, Jean le Tonnelier, and Laurent Leduc, priests.

We the bishop addressed the reverend masters as follows:

After this woman was fully examined and had answered the articles that the promoter presented to her at trial, we took her confessions, summarized in the form of assertions, and sent them to doctors and experts in theology and in canon and civil law, to have their advice on them. We knew long ago that many felt that this woman appeared at fault in many respects, although we still have not ultimately decided the matter. And before we come to a final decision, many honest, conscientious, and learned men have thought it highly expedient to try by every possible means to instruct her on the points where she seems at fault, and to try as best we can to lead her back to the path and knowledge of truth. We have desired to accomplish this, and do still, with all our heart. We ought all to seek this—especially we who live in the Church and have jurisdiction over sacred matters—to show her in love the things she has said and done that depart from faith, truth, and religion, and to warn her, lovingly, to think of her salvation. This is why we tried to lead her to repent through the offices of many worthy doctors of theology whom we sent to her on various days; now some, now others gave themselves to this task with all gentleness, yet without compulsion of any kind. But the wiles of the devil have triumphed, and thus far these doctors have accomplished nothing in this matter. When we saw that a private warning of this kind bore no fruit, it seemed advisable that you—seated in solemn assembly—should warn this woman in love and kindness to repent. For perhaps your presence and an exhortation of the many will more easily bring her to humility and obedience, and instead of placing too much trust in her own judgment, she will trust the council of honest and wise men, learned in divine and human laws, and will not expose herself to grave perils that could endanger her body and soul.

To deliver this warning, we have appointed a very learned old master of theology, an expert in these affairs, Master Jean de Châtillon, archdeacon of Evreux, who, if it pleases him, will now accept the task of explaining to this woman some specific points in which she seems in error, as we have learned from the counsels and deliberations of experts; and he will convince her to abandon these faults and crimes and to recognize the path of truth. For this reason, this woman will now be led here before you and admonished. And if anyone else can say or do something to move her to swifter repentance and to instruct her with profit for the salvation of her body and soul, we beg you, do not hesitate to speak to us or to the assembly.

That same day, after Joan had arrived and had been led before the judges, we the bishop advised Joan on behalf of ourselves and the other judge to follow the advice and warnings that the reverend archdeacon, professor of theology, would give her, for he would tell her many things useful for the salvation of her body and soul. But if she refused to do so, she would be putting her body and soul in great danger. And he would explain many things to Joan according to the schedule below.[34]

Then we the judges asked the reverend archdeacon to proceed charitably to the admonitions. Obeying our request, he began to teach and instruct Joan. First, he explained to her that all the faithful in Christ are required to believe and maintain the Christian faith and its articles. And he advised and asked her, by way of a general admonition, to correct and amend herself, her words and deeds, according to the counsel of the esteemed doctors and masters, experts in divine, canon, and civil law.

To this general admonition Joan answered: "Read your book"—that is, the schedule the reverend archdeacon was holding—"and then I'll answer you. I wait on God, my creator, in everything; I love him with all my heart."

Then, when she was asked whether she had anything else to say in reply to the general admonition, she answered: "I wait upon my judge, the King of Heaven and earth."

After this, the reverend archdeacon proceeded to the specific admonitions for Joan, as contained in the following schedule, which begins as follows:

1. First, he reminded her how she had said earlier that if anything wicked was found in her words and actions, and the clergy brought it

to her attention, she would correct it. This was a good and praiseworthy thing to say, for all good Christians should be humble, always ready to obey those wiser than themselves, and to trust the judgment of good and wise men rather than their own opinion. But now the doctors and clergy have examined her words and behavior for many days, and they have found many serious faults in them. Yet if she humbly wishes to reform her ways, as a good and devout Christian should, the churchmen are ready to treat her with mercy and love, for her salvation. But if she persists in her belief out of pride and arrogance, supposing that she knows more than doctors and learned men about matters of faith, she will be putting herself in grave danger.

2. Then he explained to her, with respect to the revelations and visions she claims to have, that she refuses to submit to the Church militant or to any living person but wishes to trust her words and actions to God alone. He declared to her the nature of the Church militant, the authority it has from God, those who exercise that authority, and how every Christian must believe that there is one holy catholic Church, guided by the Holy Ghost, and that it never errs or fails. Every catholic must obey it as a son does a mother, and submit all his words and deeds to its decision. And no one, no matter what her visions or revelations, should for that reason withdraw from the Church's judgment, for even the apostles submitted their writings to the Church. All Scripture, which is revealed by God, is given to us for our belief by our mother the Church, the infallible guide to which we must conform in all things, without any schism or division whatsoever, as the apostle Paul teaches in many passages. Moreover, every revelation from God moves us to obedience and humility toward our superiors and the Church, never to the contrary. The Lord does not wish anyone to claim to be subject to God alone, or to trust her words and actions only to him. Instead, he gave and entrusted to men of the Church the power and authority to know and judge the acts of the faithful, whether good or evil; whoever despises them [men of the Church] despises God, and whoever hears them hears God. Finally, he urged her to believe that the catholic Church cannot err or pass false judgment on anyone, for whoever does not believe this errs in the article "One holy catholic Church," which had been explained to Joan at length. If

anyone stubbornly persisted in this belief, he would be considered a heretic. She was also urged to submit all her words and deeds to Holy Mother Church and to her decision, for he who does not is schismatic and shows himself to be in error concerning the holiness of the Church and its infallible guidance by the Holy Ghost. And he indicated the serious punishments that canon law inflicts upon those who stray.

3. He then explained to her how for a long time, she has insisted on wearing men's clothes in the fashion of men-at-arms, and she continually wears them for no good reason, against the honor of her sex. This is scandalous and against good and decent manners. She also has her hair cut round. All these things are against the commandment of God in Deuteronomy 22: "A woman shall not be clothed with man's apparel."[35] They are against the teaching of the Apostle, when he says that a woman should cover her head.[36] They are against the prohibitions of the Church declared in holy general councils.[37] They are against the teaching of the saints and doctors, both in theology and in canon law. And they serve as bad examples for other women. Joan is committing a particularly grievous fault in this matter, for out of a perverse desire to wear this disgraceful clothing, she chose not to receive the Eucharist during the time appointed by the Church, rather than set aside these clothes and take others in which she could receive the sacrament properly and reverently. In this, her perversity has led her to scorn the commandment of the Church, despite her having been warned about this many times, especially at Easter, when she said that she wished, that she earnestly desired, to hear Mass and receive the Eucharist. She was then told to take women's clothes, but she refused to do so, and still does. She shows in these things that she has gravely sinned. He therefore urged her to cease this behavior and to set aside her men's clothing.

4. Not satisfied with wearing such clothing under these circumstances, Joan even wished to claim that she was doing right in this, and not sinning. Now, to say that someone is doing right by contradicting the teachings of the saints and the commandments of God and the apostles and by scorning the teaching of the Church out of a perverse desire to wear unseemly and disgraceful clothing is an error in the

faith. And if someone were to defend this obstinately, she would lapse into heresy. Further, she even wanted to assign these sins to God and the saints, whom she therefore blasphemes by assigning to them what is improper. For God and the saints wish all virtue to be preserved, and sins, evil desires, and other such things to be avoided. Nor do they wish the teachings of the Church to be despised on account of such things. He therefore urged her to stop repeating such blasphemies, and to stop presuming to assign such things to God and the saints and defending them as permissible.

5. Many eminent and distinguished clerics have carefully considered and inspected Joan's public statements about her revelations and visions, and the outright lies she invented about the crown brought to Charles and the visit of the angels; and these statements have been recognized as falsehoods and fabrications both by those who joined our party afterward and by others.[38] They considered the things she said about kissing and embracing Saint Catherine and Saint Margaret, that they came to her daily, sometimes several times a day, though they had no special purpose and no clear reason to visit her so often; and they observed that saints have never been known to appear like this in such miraculous visions. They considered that she claimed to know nothing about their limbs or other personal traits, except for their heads, a claim inconsistent with such frequent visions; and they considered the many things she said they taught her about what clothing to wear and about what answers to give at the trial—teachings inconsistent with those of God and the saints, which no one should think they taught her. And the doctors and experts carefully considered many other things concerning this matter. They see and recognize that God did not send her these revelations and visions, as she boasts. And they showed her how dangerous it is to presume one is worthy of such visions and revelations and therefore to lie about things that extend even to God, falsely prophesying and telling the future: powers that God has not given her, but which she invents out of the imaginations of her own heart. The apostasy of the people could follow from this, the creation of new sects, and many other evils, to the ruin of the Church and catholic people.

How dangerous it is to explore with reckless eagerness things that are too exalted, and to believe in new things without counsel of the Church and prelates, or even to invent things that are novel and strange! For demons are known to insinuate themselves into these unwholesome desires by means of occult suggestion or open appearances, thereby transforming themselves into angels of light,[39] and under the form of godliness or some other good thing drawing souls into wicked pacts and plunging them into error; God permits these things to punish the presumption of those who pursue such investigations. He therefore urged her to cease from speaking such lies and vanities, and to return to the path of truth.

6. From this root of imagined revelations, she has rushed headlong into many other crimes; so, for example, usurping the office of God, she has dared to relate future contingencies, and to reveal things hidden, such as the sword buried in the ground. She even boasts that she is certain whom God loves and, for her own part, that she has been forgiven for the sin she committed in leaping from the tower of Beaurevoir. These things partake of divination, presumption, and rashness. She also said she worshipped strange things that appeared to her, even though she reported having insufficient proof to justify her belief in them as good spirits. Nor did she take the advice of her own priest or any other clergyman on this matter, but boasted about herself, even while verging on idolatry, and rashly believed in things when she should have been skeptical, even though some of the things she saw seem to have been imaginary. She also dared to say that she believed her visitors were Saint Catherine and Saint Margaret and angels just as firmly as she believed the Christian faith. In this she believed rashly and seemed to think that our reasons for believing the Christian faith and its articles are no better or stronger than hers for believing in new and strange things that the Church has neither determined nor investigated. What is more, Christ, the saints, and the Church have taught us not to believe in such visions idly. And she was told to consider these matters carefully.

After the archdeacon had explained these things to Joan in French, she answered as follows. First, to the first and second articles: "I have the same answer now as before."[40]

When she was told about the Church militant and was advised

to believe and accept the article "One holy catholic Church," and to submit to the Church militant, she answered: "I fully believe in the Church on earth; but as I've said before, for my words and actions, I wait upon and trust to the Lord God." And further: "I fully believe that the Church militant can neither err nor fail; but as for my words and deeds, I leave them to God and trust entirely to him, for he had me do all that I've done." She says again that she submits to God, her creator, who had her do these things; she trusts to him and to his own person.

Asked whether she means that she has no judge on earth, and that our lord the pope is not her judge, she answered: "I have nothing else to tell you. I have a good master, God, and I fully trust in him and in no other."

When she was told that if she would not believe in the Church and in the article "One holy catholic Church," she would be a heretic on that account, and be punished with fire by other judges, she answered: "I have nothing more to tell you. If I saw the fire, I would say what I'm saying to you now, and nothing else."

Asked whether, if our lord the pope, the cardinals, and other churchmen were here, she would submit to a general council, she answered: "You will get nothing more out of me on this."

Asked whether she would submit to our lord the pope, she answered: "Take me to him and I'll answer him." She would give no further answer.

Then in response to the admonitions about clothing in the third and fourth articles, she said that she would gladly wear a robe and a woman's hood to go to church and receive the Eucharist, as she said earlier, as long as right afterward she could remove them and put her present clothes back on. To the other warning that she had no reason to wear these clothes, especially in prison, she answered: "When I have finished what God sent me here to do, I'll wear women's clothes."

Asked whether she believes she is doing right to wear men's clothes, she answered: "I wait upon God."

And when she was advised about the contents of the fourth article, she said she had blasphemed neither God nor the saints.

Warned again to cease wearing men's clothes and believing that she is doing right in wearing them, and to take women's clothes, she said she would not change.

Asked whether she makes the sign of the cross every time Saint Catherine and Saint Margaret come, she said that sometimes she does, sometimes not.

To the warnings in the fifth article about revelations, she replied that as to this she trusts to her judge, that is, to God. Her revelations come directly from God.

She was asked whether, regarding the sign given to her king, she would call on the archbishop of Reims, to the lord de Boussac,[41] to Charles of Bourbon, to the lord de la Trémoille, and to Etienne, called La Hire,[42] to whom or to some of whom she claims to have shown the crown mentioned above and who, she says, were present when the angel brought the crown to her king and gave it to the archbishop, or whether she would call on others of her party who would write under their seals about what happened.

She answered: "Send a messenger, and I'll write to them about this whole trial." Otherwise she neither trusts nor calls on them.

To the warnings in the sixth article about presuming to foretell future contingencies, she said: "I trust regarding this matter to my judge, God, and to what I said earlier, which is written in the book."

Asked whether, if three or four clerks[43] of her party were sent to her here under safe conduct, she would refer to them for her apparitions and the things contained in this trial, she said let them come, and then she will answer. Otherwise she would not refer or submit to them in this trial.

Asked whether she would trust or submit to the church of Poitiers where she was examined, she answered: "Do you think you can catch me like this and draw me into your power?"

In conclusion, Joan was abundantly and freshly warned in general terms to submit to the Church under pain of being abandoned by the Church. If the Church abandoned her, her body and soul would be in grave danger, her soul of eternal fire, her body of the fire of this world, by the sentence of other judges.

She answered: "If you do what you say against me, evil will visit your bodies and souls."

Asked to give a single reason for which she does not yield to the Church, she refused to answer again.

Then many doctors and expert men of various ranks and faculties warned and pleaded with her gently and urged her to submit to the universal Church militant, to our lord the pope and to the general council,[44] explaining the dangers that threatened her soul and body unless she should submit herself and her actions to the Church militant.

She answered as before.

At last, we the bishop told Joan to take great care and to consider for herself these warnings, counsels, and kind entreaties, and to think otherwise.

Joan asked: "How much time do I have to decide?"

We told her to decide immediately and answer what she would do. And when she gave no further answer, we left and Joan was taken back to prison.

Wednesday, May 9. In the same year, Wednesday, May 9, Joan was brought before us, the judges, in the great tower of the castle of Rouen, in the presence of the reverend father the lord abbot of Saint-Corneille of Compiègne; Masters Jean de Châtillon and Guillaume Erard, doctors of theology; André Marguerie and Nicolas de Venderès, archdeacons of Rouen Cathedral; Guillaume Haiton, bachelor of theology; Aubert Morel, licentiate of canon law; Nicolas Loiselleur, canon of Rouen Cathedral; and reverend Jean Massieu.

Then Joan was requested and advised to tell the truth about many different matters in her trial that she had denied earlier or had lied about, in the face of positive information, proofs, and overwhelming presumptions. Many of these were read and explained to her, and she was told that if she would not confess the truth about them, she would be put to the torture, and she was shown the instruments ready in the tower. Officers were also present who were ready to put her to the torture, upon our order, so as to lead her back to the path and knowledge of the truth, and thereby save her soul and body, which, by her false stories, she had exposed to grave dangers.

Joan answered: "In truth, if you tear my limbs apart and separate my soul from my body, I still won't tell you anything else. And if I tell you anything, later I will say that you forced it out of me."

She said that on the last feast of Holy Cross,[45] she took comfort from Saint Gabriel; and she believes it was Saint Gabriel and knows it from her voices. She says she asked her voices for advice about whether to submit to the Church, since the churchmen were pressing her strongly to do so, and they told her that if she wants God to help her, she should wait on him for all her actions.

She says she knows full well that God was always master of all her deeds, and that the devil never had power over them.

She says further that she asked her voices whether she would be burned, and they told her to wait on the Lord, and he would help her.

Asked whether she would refer to the archbishop of Reims about the sign of the crown she claims was given to him, she answered: "Have him come here, <so that I can hear him,> and then I'll answer you. He wouldn't dare contradict what I've told you."

Seeing the hardness of her heart and the tone of her answers, we the judges feared that the instruments of torture would profit her little, and decided not to apply them until we had further counsel on the matter.

Saturday, May 12. On Saturday, May 12, in our episcopal house at Rouen, we the judges presided over the assembly of esteemed and reverend masters: Raoul Roussel, treasurer; Nicolas de Venderès and André Marguerie, archdeacons of Rouen Cathedral; Guillaume Erard, master of theology; Robert Le Barbier, Denis Gastinel, Jean le Doux, and Aubert Morel, licentiates of canon law; Thomas de Courcelles and Nicolas Couppequesne, bachelors of theology; Nicolas Loiselleur and Brother Ysambard de la Pierre.

We the bishop recalled the events of last Wednesday, and asked the assessors for advice about what to do, in particular whether it was expedient to put Joan to the torture.

<First, master Raoul Roussel said no, to keep a trial so well conducted from being maligned.

Master Nicolas de Venderès said he thought it was inexpedient for now.

Master André Marguerie said it was inexpedient at present.

Master Guillaume Erard said it was unnecessary, since they have plenty enough evidence without it.

Master Robert Le Barbier said the same. She should be charitably warned once and for all to submit to the Church; if she does not, then let the trial continue in the Lord's name.

Master Denis Gastinel said it was inexpedient.

Master Aubert Morel said he thought it was expedient to put her to the torture, to know the truth of her lies.

Master Thomas de Courcelles said he thought it was good to do so. He added that she should be interrogated about whether she wishes to submit to the judgment of the Church.

Master Nicolas Couppequesne said it was inexpedient; but let her be warned again in kindness to submit to the decision of the Church.

Master Jean le Doux said the same.

Brother Ysambard de la Pierre said the same; but let her be warned one last time to submit to the Church militant.

Master Nicolas Loiselleur said he thought that for the health of her soul, she should be put to the torture. Nonetheless, he yields to the opinions of the preceding.

Master Guillaume Haiton arrived late and said she should not.

Master Jean Le Maistre, vice-inquisitor, said she should be asked again whether she believes she ought to submit to the Church militant.>

After hearing their answers and considering what Joan had said that Wednesday, and after taking into account her attitude and will, and the circumstances of the case, we decided that it was inexpedient and unnecessary to put her to the torture, and that we would proceed to other matters.

Saturday, May 19. The following Saturday, May 19, before us the judges, seated in judgment in the chapel of the archbishop's house of Rouen, there appeared esteemed men, reverend fathers and masters: Gilles, abbot of Fécamp, and Guillaume, abbot of Mortemer,[46] doctors of theology; Nicolas, abbot of Jumièges, and Guillaume, abbot of

Cormeilles, doctors of canon law; the abbot of Préaux, the prior of Saint-Lô, the prior of Longueville, Jean de Nibat, Jacques Guesdon, Jean Fouchier, Maurice du Quesnay, Jean le Fèvre, Guillaume le Boucher, Pierre Houdenc, Jean de Châtillon, Erard Emengart, Jean Beaupère, Pierre Maurice, Nicolas Midi, doctors of theology; Guillaume Haiton, Nicolas Couppequesne, Thomas de Courcelles, Richard de Grouchet, Pierre Minier, Raoul le Sauvage, Jean Pigache, bachelors of theology; Raoul Roussel, doctor of canon and civil law; Jean Guérin, Pasquier de Vaux, doctors of canon law; Robert Le Barbier, Denis Gastinel, licentiates of canon law; André Marguerie, licentiate of civil law; Nicolas de Venderès, Jean Pinchon, licentiates of canon law; Jean Alespée, Gilles Deschamps, Nicolas Caval, licentiates of civil law; Jean Bruillot, licentiate of canon law; Nicolas Loiselleur, canon of Rouen Cathedral; Jean le Doux, Guillaume de Livet, Pierre Carrel, Geoffroi de Crotay, Richard des Saulx, Bureau de Cormeilles, Aubert Morel, Jean Duchemin, Laurent du Busc, Jean Colombel, Raoul Anguy, Guérould Poustel, licentiates, some of canon and some of civil law.

In their presence we the bishop explained how we had recently received a great many consultations and opinions from esteemed doctors and masters on the statements and confessions of Joan. On the strength of these consultations, we could have proceeded to conclude the case, for they appeared sufficient and just. But to bring honor and reverence to our mother the University of Paris, to receive a fuller and clearer explanation of the subject, to put consciences fully at rest, and to edify all those concerned, we decided to send the statements to our mother the university, in particular to the faculties of theology and canon law, and we asked for opinions from doctors and masters there, especially in the two faculties. Consumed with zeal for the faith, the university, and in particular the two faculties, held earnest, mature, and solemn deliberations on each statement, and sent us their opinions in a notarized statement. We then ordered the opinions in the document to be read word for word, openly and clearly, to all the aforesaid doctors and masters. After hearing the opinions of the university and the faculties, the masters gave and explained their own opinions, conforming to those of the faculties and the university, in addition to their earlier opinions, both on the limitations of the assertions and on how to proceed further. We have directed that these opinions and letters of the university be copied here.

First there follows the letter of the university to our king.

Letter of the University of Paris to Henry VI

Summary. Notes that the king has begun a trial against Joan; mentions good accounts of the trial from Jean Beaupère, Jacques de Touraine, and Nicolas Midi; offers the university's counsel on the articles through these masters; encourages him to conclude the matter as soon as possible. Dated May 14, 1431, Paris. Signed: "Hébert."

Here follows the letter of the University of Paris to us the bishop.

Letter of the University of Paris to Pierre Cauchon

Summary. Praises Cauchon for his diligence in prosecuting the case; notes that Joan's poison had infected nearly the entire Western world; mentions that Jean Beaupère, Jacques de Touraine, and Nicolas Midi have provided a report of the procedures thus far; further commends Cauchon for his role and praises the form of the trial; notes that all the requests of the masters have been granted; the university has taken care to put its deliberations and conclusions into writing, which the masters will show him, explaining other things in person, as well; promises further support in prosecuting the case. Dated May 14, 1431, Paris. Signed: "Hébert."

Here follow the deliberations of the University of Paris.

Reports of Deliberations at the University of Paris

Summary. Report of the University of Paris stating that on April 29, 1431, the university having assembled at St. Bernard to deliberate on the twelve articles, the decision was made to submit them to the faculties of theology and canon law for deliberation.

Summary. Report of the University of Paris stating that on May 14, 1429, the university having assembled at St. Bernard to consider the deliberations of the faculties of theology and canon law on the twelve articles, the decision of each faculty, given in writing, was presented and read.

Here follow the articles on the words and deeds of Joan, commonly called the Maid.

Summary. The text of the twelve articles of April 5 is reproduced here.

Here follow the deliberations and conclusions of the sacred faculty of theology of the University of Paris on the above articles on the words and deeds of Joan, commonly called the Maid.

Summary. In its response to the twelve articles, which it submits to the judgment of the pope and the general council, the faculty of theology condemns the statements and actions of Joan reported in each article.

Here follow the deliberations and doctrinal determination of the esteemed faculty of canon law of the University of Paris on the above twelve articles concerning the words and deeds of Joan, commonly called the Maid.

Summary. The faculty submits its doctrinal determination on the twelve articles to the pope and the general council and concludes that if Joan upheld the propositions expressed in the twelve articles, 1) she is schismatic, 2) she has erred in the faith against the article "One holy catholic Church," 3) she is apostate for cutting off her hair and rejecting women's dress, 4) she is a liar and false prophetess in saying that she is sent by God and speaks with angels and saints, 5) she errs in the faith for enduring anathema for a long time and for preferring to forgo the body of Christ and confession rather than wear women's dress, and 6) she errs in saying that she is certain that she will be taken to heaven; if she does not abjure her error, she must be abandoned to the secular judge.

After the reading of these decisions, the rector confirmed that the decisions were those each faculty had given; particular points were discussed; after further deliberation, the decisions were ratified; Jean Beaupère, Jacques de Touraine, and Nicolas Midi asked for notarized statements of these decisions.

Signed: "Jean Bourillet and Michel Hébert, public notaries."

Deliberations of the Doctors and Masters Then at Rouen

Summary. Forty-seven masters gave their opinions; most stated their support for the decision of the University of Paris, that unless Joan abjured, she should be condemned as a heretic and delivered to secular justice; some also recommended that Joan be warned one last time; some said that the case could be concluded and the sentence pronounced on the same day; some deferred to the judges for subsequent procedure.*

After thanking the reverend fathers and masters, we concluded that Joan should be warned kindly to return to the path of truth and salvation of body and soul, and that according to their good and whole-some counsel, we should proceed to the conclusion of the case. At last, we set a day for sentencing.

Wednesday, May 23. The following Wednesday, May 23, Joan was led before us, the judges, seated in judgment, in a room near her prison in the castle of Rouen. Present there were reverend fathers: the bishops of Thérouanne and of Noyon, masters Jean de Châtillon, archdeacon of Evreux, Jean Beaupère, Nicolas Midi, Guillaume Erard, Pierre Maurice, doctors of theology; André Marguerie, licentiate of laws; Nicolas de Venderès, licentiate of canon law; and archdeacons and canons of Rouen Cathedral.

In Joan's presence, we had certain points explained wherein Joan had erred and transgressed according to deliberation of the faculties of theology and canon law of the University of Paris. The faults, crimes, and errors she committed in each case were also explained to her. And we advised her to abandon these transgressions and errors, to mend her ways, and to submit to the correction and decision of our Holy Mother Church, as detailed more fully in the schedule below, which was explained to her in French by master Pierre Maurice, canon of Rouen Cathedral and renowned doctor of theology.

Here follows the tenor of the schedule:

1. First of all, Joan, you said that from the age of around thirteen you had revelations and visions of angels and Saint Catherine and Saint Margaret, and that you have seen them often with your bodily eyes; and they have spoken with you and still do often speak and have told you many things that are explained more fully in your trial record.

Now, on this point, the clerks of the University of Paris and others have considered the manner of these revelations and visions, the purpose and substance of the things revealed, and your character. Taking everything into account, they have said that these things are false, misleading, and harmful stories; or that these revelations are superstitious, and they proceed from evil and diabolical spirits.

2. You said your king had a sign proving that God sent you: Saint Michael, accompanied by a host of angels, some with wings, others with crowns, Saint Catherine and Saint Margaret among them, came to you in the town and castle of Chinon; and they climbed the castle steps with you into the chamber of your king,

before whom bowed the angel that bore the crown. One time you said that when your king received the sign, he was alone; another time you said that the crown, which you call a sign, was handed to the archbishop of Reims, who handed it to your king in the presence of many princes and lords, whom you named.

On this point, the clerks say that this is not plausible, but a presumptuous, misleading, and destructive lie, a fabricated affair that diminishes angelic honor.

3. You said you recognized the angels and saints by the good advice, comfort, and teaching they gave you, and because they told you their names and the saints greeted you. You also believe it was Saint Michael who appeared to you, and that their words and deeds are good. You believe these things just as firmly as you believe in the faith of Jesus Christ.

On this point, the clerks say that these signs are insufficient for recognizing angels and saints, and that you believed too readily and rashly. And as for the comparison you make to believing "just as firmly," and so on, you err in the faith.

4. You said you are sure of certain things to come, and that you knew things hidden; you also recognized people you never saw before, all by means of the voices of Saint Catherine and Saint Margaret.

On this point, the clerks say that this claim involves superstition and divination, that it is a presumptuous and empty boast.

5. You said that at God's command and at his good pleasure, you wore and still continually wear men's garb. And since God commanded, you took a short tunic, a doublet, and hose with many points; you wear your hair short, cut round above your ears, leaving nothing to indicate the female sex except what nature gave you; and you often received the Eucharist in this clothing. Although you have been advised many times to abandon it, you utterly refuse to do so, saying that you would rather die than abandon it, except by God's command; and that if you were still in these clothes among members of your party, it would be a great blessing for France. You also say that not for anything would you take an oath not to wear these clothes and arms. And in all these things, you claim to do right by God's command.

On this point, the clerks say that you blaspheme God and scorn him in his sacraments; you transgress divine law, Holy Scripture, and canon law; you transgress and err in the faith; you make empty boasts; you are prone to idolatry; and you worship yourself and your clothing, according to the rites of the heathen.

6. You said you often put the names Jesus, Mary and the sign of the cross in your letters, as a sign to your correspondents not to do what is stated in the letters. In other letters, you boasted that you would see killed all who would not obey you, and that blows would determine who has the better claim from the God of heaven. You often said you had done nothing except by revelation and command of the Lord.

On this point, the clerks say you are treacherous, cunning, cruel, eager to shed blood, seditious, encouraging tyranny, blaspheming God's commandments and revelations.

7. You say that following your revelations, at age seventeen you left your parents' house, against their will, thereby driving them nearly out of their minds. And you went to Robert de Baudricourt, who at your request gave you men's clothing and a sword, and an escort to take you to your king. When you met him, you told him you had come to defeat his enemies, and you promised to put him in great dominion, that he would gain victory over his enemies, and that God had sent you to him. You also say that you did right in these matters, obeying God through revelation.

On this point, the clerks say you behaved disrespectfully toward your parents, breaking God's command to honor your parents; that your behavior was scandalous, blasphemous toward God, and erring in the faith; and that you made a presumptuous and rash promise.

8. You said that of your own free will, you leaped from the tower of Beaurevoir, preferring to die rather than be handed over to the English and survive the destruction of Compiègne. And though Saint Catherine and Saint Margaret forbade you to leap, you could not help doing it. And despite your great sin in offending those saints, you knew from your voices that God had forgiven you after you had confessed.

On this point, the clerks say that you showed cowardice bordering on despair and even suicide; that you also made a rash and presumptuous claim to be forgiven of sin; and that you are in error concerning the doctrine of free will.

9. You said that Saint Catherine and Saint Margaret promised to take you to heaven as long as you kept the virginity that you pledged and promised them. You are as certain of this as if you were even now in the glory of the blessed. You do not believe you committed a mortal sin, for if you were in mortal sin, the saints would not visit you every day as they do.

On this point, the clerks say that your claim is rash and presumptuous, and a destructive lie; and it contradicts your earlier testimony. Further, you stray from the Christian faith.

10. You said that you know full well that God loves certain living persons more than you, and that you know this by revelation from Saint Catherine and Saint Margaret; that these saints speak French, not English, because they are not of that party; and that once you learned that the voices favored your king, you disliked the Burgundians.

On this point, the clerks say that this claim is rash presumption, superstitious divination, blasphemy against Saint Catherine and Saint Margaret, and a violation of the commandment to love one's neighbor.[47]

11. You said that to the ones you call Saint Michael, Saint Catherine, and Saint Margaret, you made many reverences, kneeling, removing your cap, kissing the ground they walked on, and pledging your virginity to them; that you also kissed and embraced them and invoked their names; and that you believed them the first time they visited you, without taking counsel from a priest or any other clergyman; and yet you believe these voices come from God as firmly as you believe the Christian faith and the Passion of our Lord Jesus Christ. You said further that if any evil spirit were to appear to you as Saint Michael, you could easily recognize and discern it. You also said that of your own accord you swore not to speak of the sign given to your king, adding, "except by command of God."

On this point, the clerks say that, supposing you have had the revelations and visions you boast of, the way that you say, you are an idolater and an invoker of demons, erring in the faith; and you have made rash statements and taken an unlawful oath.

12. You said that if the Church wanted you to disobey the command you claim to have from God, you would not do so for anything, and that you well know that the things recorded in your trial come from God's command and that it would be impossible for you to do otherwise. On these matters you refuse to yield to the judgment of the Church on earth or to any living person except God alone. You say further that you do not produce these answers from your own understanding, but by the command of God, even though the article of faith "One holy catholic Church" has been explained to you many times and you have been told that every Christian should submit all his words and deeds to the Church militant, especially in the area of revelations and such matters.

On this point, the clerks say that you are schismatic, you fail to understand the unity and authority of the Church, you are apostate, and you have stubbornly erred in the faith.

Then after these assertions and the opinion of the University of Paris had been told and explained to Joan, she was advised in French by the same doctor to give utmost attention to her words and actions, especially as to the last article. He addressed her:

Joan, dearest friend, now it is time at the end of your trial to think carefully about what has been said. On four occasions, and now here again, you have been diligently warned by the bishop of Beauvais, by the vice-inquisitor, and by other doctors sent on their behalf, in public and in private, for the honor and respect we owe to God, for the faith and law of Christ Jesus, for the peace of our consciences, for the avoidance of scandal, and for the salvation of your body and soul. You have been told what punishments await you, of both body and soul, unless you correct and amend your words and submit yourself and your behavior to the Church and accept its judgment. And yet thus far you have given no thought to this.

Now, although many of the judges thought the evidence against you was sufficient, they earnestly desired the salvation of your body and soul, and have sent your statements for examination to the University of Paris, the light of all knowledge and destroyer of errors. After receiving its opinion, they decided to admonish you yet again by warning you of the errors, scandals, and other sins you have committed. They beg, pray, and admonish you by the bowels of our Lord Jesus Christ, who gladly suffered cruel death to redeem the human race: correct your words and submit to the judgment of the Church, as every Christian is bound and obligated to do. Do not be separated from the Lord Jesus Christ, who created you to partake of his glory. Do not choose the path of eternal damnation with God's enemies, who work daily to trouble mankind, transforming themselves into the image of Christ, his angels and saints, whom they claim to be, as described more fully in the lives of the Fathers and in Scripture.[48] So if anything like this appears to you, do not believe it, but cast out all trust and imagination in such things, and be satisfied with the statements and opinions of the University of Paris and of the other doctors who know God's law and Holy Scripture. They think you should put no trust in such apparitions, nor in any strange vision or forbidden novelty unsupported by the authority of sacred Scripture, or by a sufficient sign or miracle. You have neither of these; yet you have believed such things carelessly, neither praying devoutly to God to give you certainty about such things nor consulting a prelate or some other learned churchman who could instruct you. And considering your status and the simplicity of your knowledge, you should have done so.

Take this example: your king has entrusted you to guard a fortress, forbidding you to admit anyone. Then someone claims to come in the king's name. But you would neither believe nor admit him unless he brought you a letter or some other positive sign. So when our Lord Jesus Christ ascended into heaven and entrusted the governance of the Church to his blessed apostle Peter and his successors, he forbade them to receive any who came in his name, unless they had sufficiently proven themselves in some form other than their own words. You certainly should not have trusted those who you say have so come, nor should we trust you, for the Lord taught the contrary.

First, Joan, consider the following. What if, when you were in your king's dominion, a knight or someone else who had been born in his domain were to have said: "I'll not obey the king anymore or submit to his officers." Would you not say he should be condemned? What do you say for yourself, then, who were begotten in the faith of Christ by the sacrament of baptism, made a daughter of the Church and bride of Christ, if you do not obey the officers of Christ—that is, the prelates of the Church? What judgment will you assign yourself? Stop saying these things, I beg you, if you love God, your creator, your beloved spouse and your salvation, and obey the Church by submitting to its judgment. You know that if you do not and if you persist in this error, your soul will be damned to eternal torments, perpetual grieving, and I greatly fear that your body will come to ruin. Do not be held back by the useless shame and the human disgrace, the fear that in doing as I say, you will lose the great honors that you once enjoyed. You should first consider God's honor and your salvation, of body and soul. All these will be lost unless you do as I say, for otherwise you divide yourself from the Church and the pledge you made in holy baptism, and you remove the authority of God from the Church, which is led, ruled, and governed by the authority of God and his Spirit. He also told the prelates of the Church: "Who hears you, hears me, and who spurns you, spurns me."[49] So when you refuse to be subject to the Church, you in fact withdraw from it; and in refusing to be subject to it, you are not subject to God and you err in the article "One holy catholic Church"—this Church that has been sufficiently explained to you, its nature and its authority, in the preceding warnings.

In view of these matters, then, on behalf of my lords the bishop of Beauvais and the vice-inquisitor, your judges, I warn, pray, and entreat you by your devotion to the Passion of your creator, and by the love you bear for the salvation of your soul and body, correct and amend all these things and come back to the path of truth by obeying the Church and by submitting to its judgment and decision. By so doing, you will save your soul and, I believe, redeem your body from death. But if you do not, and should you persist, know that your soul will be utterly damned; your body, I fear, will also be destroyed. May Jesus Christ keep you from such a fate.

After Joan had been admonished in this fashion and had heard these entreaties, she answered as follows: "As for my words and deeds mentioned in the trial, I refer to them and wish to stand by them."

Asked whether she does not believe she is bound to submit her words and deeds to the Church militant or to someone besides God, she answered: "I will maintain what I always said during the trial." She added that if she were condemned and saw the fire burning and the wood prepared, and the executioner ready to light the fire, and she were in the fire itself, still she would say nothing else and would uphold what she had said at the trial, even unto death.

Then we her judges asked the promoter and Joan whether either wished to say anything else. They said they did not. We then proceeded to the conclusion of the trial, according to the text of a schedule that we the bishop held, whose tenor follows: "As legal judges in this office, we have determined and declared ourselves competent to whatever extent necessary, and, inasmuch as you have renounced further questioning, we declare this trial ended. And we assign tomorrow as the day when you will hear us render justice and when we shall deliver our sentence and proceed further, as law and reason dictate."

Present as witnesses, Brother Ysambard de la Pierre and reverend Matthieu le Bateur, priests; and Louis Orsel, clerk, of the dioceses of Rouen, London, and Noyon.

Thursday, May 24. The first sentence. Thursday after Pentecost, May 24, 1431. We the judges arrived in the morning at a public place, the cemetery of the abbey of Saint-Ouen of Rouen, with Joan before us on a scaffold or platform.[50] First, we ordered a solemn sermon preached by master Guillaume Erard, a distinguished doctor of theology, as a wholesome admonition for Joan and for the great multitude of people gathered there.[51] We were assisted by the most reverend father in Christ, Henry, by divine favor priest of Saint Eusebius and cardinal of the Holy Roman Church, commonly called cardinal of England;[52] reverend fathers in Christ, the bishops of Thérouanne, Noyon, and Norwich; the abbots of Sainte-Trinité de Fécamp, Saint-Ouen of Rouen, Jumièges, Bec-Hellouin, Cormeilles, Saint-Michel-au-péril-de-la-mer,[53] Mortemer, and Préaux; the priors of Longueville-Giffard and

Saint-Lô of Rouen; Masters Jean de Châtillon, Jean Beaupère, Nicolas Midi, Maurice du Quesnay, Guillaume le Boucher, Jean le Fèvre, Pierre de Houdenc, Pierre Maurice, Jean Fouchier, doctors of theology; Guillaume Haiton, Nicolas Couppequesne, Thomas de Courcelles, Raoul le Sauvage, Richard de Grouchet, Pierre Minier, Jean Pigache, bachelors of theology; Raoul Roussel, doctor of canon and civil law; Jean Guérin, doctor of canon law; Nicolas de Venderès, Jean Pinchon, Jean le Doux, Robert Le Barbier, licentiates of canon law; André Marguerie, Jean Alespée, licentiates of civil law; Aubert Morel, Jean Colombel, Jean Duchemin, licentiates of canon law; and very many others.

The doctor began his sermon, taking his text from John 15: "A branch cannot bear fruit of itself, unless it remain in the vine."[54] Then he told how all catholics should remain in the true vine of Holy Mother Church, which Christ planted with his right hand, and he showed Joan that she had cut herself away from the unity of the Church by many errors and serious crimes and had often scandalized Christian people. So he admonished and urged her and all the people with wholesome doctrine.

Having concluded, the doctor spoke thus to Joan: "Here are my reverend judges, who have repeatedly summoned you and asked you to submit all your words and deeds to Holy Mother Church; they have explained to you time and again that you said and did many things that they thought were evil and erroneous."

Joan replied: "I'll answer you. As for submitting to the Church, I already answered them on this point: let everything I've said and done be reported to Rome, to our holy father the pope, to whom I yield after God. As for my words and deeds, I offered them on God's behalf." She said she blames no one for them, not her king or anyone else. If there be any fault in them, it is hers and no one else's.

Asked whether she would retract all her words and deeds that the clerks have condemned, she answered: "I yield to God and our holy father the pope."

She was then told that this was insufficient, that it was impossible to go find the pope at such a distance. The ordinaries were her judges, each for his diocese, and therefore she must trust to Holy Mother

Church and hold to what the clerks and the other experts have said and decided about her words and deeds. And we warned her three times about this.

Then, since the woman would say no more, we the bishop began to deliver our final sentence. After we had read much of the sentence, Joan began to speak, and said she wished to hold to all that the Church had decided and that we judges wished to say and declare, and she would completely obey our decision. And she repeatedly said that since the clergy had declared that her visions and revelations should not be upheld nor believed, she would not uphold them, but would submit entirely to Holy Mother Church and to the judges.

Then in the presence of the above and before a great crowd of clergy and people, she pronounced her recantation and abjuration, according to the text of a certain schedule in French that was read to her, which she pronounced and signed with her own hand, as follows:

The Abjuration of Joan (Original in French)

All who have erred and sinned in the Christian faith and by the grace of God have returned to the light of truth and unity of our Holy Mother Church should take the utmost care to keep the Enemy of hell from causing them to backslide and relapse into error and damnation.[55] For this reason, I, Joan, commonly called the Maid, a wretched sinner, do recognize the fetters of error binding me, and by God's grace do return to our Holy Mother Church; to show that I have not returned under false pretense, but with a good heart and will, I confess that I have grievously sinned: by falsely pretending that I had revelations and visions from God through his angels and Saint Catherine and Saint Margaret; by seducing others; by believing foolishly and carelessly; by practicing superstitious divination; by blaspheming God and his saints; by transgressing divine law, Holy Scripture, and canon law; by wearing immodest, shameful, and dishonorable clothing, against natural decency, and my hair cut round like a man's, against all virtue of the female sex; by presumptuously bearing arms; by cruelly desiring the shedding of human blood; by claiming that I have done all these things by command of God, his angels and saints, and that these things were good and not evil; by scorning God and his sacraments; and by encouraging sedition and committing idolatry, adoring and invoking evil spirits. I also confess that I have been schismatic and have in many ways strayed from the faith.

I abjure, detest, renounce, and utterly abandon these crimes and errors with a good heart and without pretense, by the grace of our Savior, and return to the path of truth through the holy doctrine and good counsel of you and the doctors and masters you sent me. In all these things, I submit to the correction, disposition, amendment, and entire judgment of our Holy Mother Church and of your good justice. And I vow, swear, and promise to blessed Peter, prince of apostles, to our holy father the pope in Rome, his vicar, and to his successors, and to you, my lords, the reverend bishop of Beauvais and the religious Brother Jean Le Maistre, vice-inquisitor, my judges, that never by any encouragement or other means will I return to these errors, from which it has pleased our Lord to deliver and save me. But I shall ever abide in unity with our Holy Mother Church and in obedience to our holy father the pope of Rome. And this I say, affirm, and swear by almighty God and his Holy Gospels. In proof of this, I have signed this schedule with my mark.

Thus signed: "Joan +."

Here follows the abjuration translated into Latin.

The Abjuration of Joan (in Latin)

Summary. *The same text appears in Latin.*

Sentence after the Abjuration

At length, after we the judges had accepted her recantation and abjuration as stated above, we the bishop pronounced our final sentence:

In the name of the Lord, amen. All pastors of the Church who long to shepherd the Lord's flock faithfully must strive with all their might, carefully and vigilantly, to resist the deceitful sower of errors, whose wiles and poisons threaten to infect the flock of Christ. The need is even greater in these dangerous times, as the apostle foretold, when many false prophets will come, bringing sects of perdition and error into the world.[56] And if Holy Mother Church does not repel their false devices with sound doctrine and canonical sanctions, they could seduce the faithful of Christ with strange doctrines.

You, Joan, commonly called the Maid, have been summoned in a trial of faith for many wicked crimes and have been brought before us, Pierre, by divine mercy bishop of Beauvais, and Brother Jean Le Maistre, vice-inquisitor for this city and diocese appointed to this task by the celebrated doctor Master Jean Graverent, inquisitor for heresy in France. For this reason, we have seen and carefully examined the course of your trial and all that happened, especially your responses, confessions, and assertions; we have considered the noteworthy opinion of the masters of theology and canon law at the University of Paris, and also of the entire university, besides the host of other prelates, doctors, and experts in theology and canon and civil law dwelling in this city of Rouen and elsewhere who discussed your assertions, words, and deeds; we have taken mature counsel and conferred with votaries of the Christian faith; and we have considered and examined all else that deserved consideration in this matter and that could or should instruct us or any other righteous judge.

Keeping our eyes fixed on Christ and the honor of the true faith, that our judgment may come forth from the Lord's countenance,[57] we say and determine that you have most grievously sinned by falsely pretending to revelations and holy visions, by seducing others, by believing carelessly and rashly, by practicing superstitious divination, by blaspheming God and his saints, by transgressing law, Holy Scripture, and canonical sanctions, by scorning God in his sacraments, by fomenting sedition, by apostasizing, by falling into schism, and by erring against the catholic faith in many ways. But since with God's help, after repeated warnings kindly and patiently delivered, you at last returned to the bosom of Holy Mother Church and recanted your errors with a contrite heart and unfeigned faith,[58] as we believe—errors condemned in a public sermon—and since your own lips abjured them aloud, along with all heresy, according to a form consistent with ecclesiastical laws: by this document we release you from the bonds of excommunication that enchained you, provided that you return to the Church with a true heart and unfeigned faith, and that you observe what we impose upon you now and in the future. Yet because you have rashly sinned against God and Holy Church, as stated, we condemn you in a final sentence to a salutary penance of perpetual imprisonment, with the bread of sorrow and the water of affliction, that you may weep there for your faults and henceforth do nothing that will make you weep; always reserving our grace and right to moderate this sentence.

The afternoon of the same day. The afternoon of the same day, we, Brother Jean Le Maistre, vice-inquisitor, assisted by lords and masters

Nicolas Midi, Nicolas Loiselleur, Thomas de Courcelles, and Brother Ysambard de la Pierre, with certain others, arrived at the prison where Joan was staying, and explained to her that God had shown her great favor that day, and that the clergy had been very merciful to her in receiving her back into the grace and pardon of Holy Mother Church. She should therefore humbly submit to and obey the sentence and decision of the judges and clergy, and utterly abandon her errors and old stories and never return to them. We told her that if she did return to them, the Church would not receive her again, but would abandon her altogether.[59] She was also told to set aside men's attire and take women's, as the Church had commanded.

Joan said she would gladly take women's attire and would obey and yield to the clergy in all things. Then, being offered women's clothes, she put them on at once and took off the men's garments. She also wished and allowed her hair, which had been cut short and round, to be shaved off.

3

Trial for Relapse

Joan withdraws her recantation and resumes wearing
men's clothing. Sentenced as a relapsed heretic, she is
handed over to the secular authorities for punishment.

Monday, May 28. The following Monday, May 28, the day after Holy
Trinity, we the judges arrived at Joan's prison to observe her condition.
Also present were lords and masters Nicolas de Venderès, Guillaume
Haiton, Thomas de Courcelles, Brother Ysambard de la Pierre, Jacques
Camus, Nicolas Bertin, Julien Flosquet, and John Grey.

And because Joan was wearing men's clothes, namely a short tunic,
hood, and doublet, with other men's garments that she had abandoned by our order for women's dress, we asked her when and why
she had put on men's clothing.

Joan said she had just recently resumed men's clothes and abandoned women's.

Asked why she had done so, and who had induced her to do so, she
said she had taken them of her own will, without being forced, and
that she preferred these clothes to women's.

Then she was told that she had promised and sworn never again to
wear men's clothes.

She said she never understood that she was taking such an oath.

Asked again why she had resumed men's clothing, she said that being among men, she thought that wearing men's clothes was more
lawful and appropriate than wearing women's. She added that she had

taken them because they had not kept their promise that she might go to Mass to receive the body of Christ and might be released from her chains.

Asked whether she had taken an oath earlier not to take men's clothes, she said she would rather die than be bound in fetters; but if they allow her to go to Mass and release her from the chains, and if she is given an agreeable prison <and a woman as a companion>, she will be good and do as the Church wishes.

Since we the judges heard that she still clung to the illusion of her pretended revelations, those she had formerly renounced, we asked her whether she had heard the voices of Saint Catherine and Saint Margaret since last Thursday. She said yes.

Asked what they told her, she said that through Saint Catherine and Saint Margaret, God sent her word of the great pity of her betrayal when she abjured and recanted to save her life, and that she had damned her soul to save her life. She said that before Thursday, her voices had told her what to do that day, and she did it. They told her to answer the preacher boldly when she was on the platform before the people. And Joan said that he was a false preacher and accused her of many things she had never done. If she were to say that God had not sent her, she would be damned, for God truly had sent her. Since Thursday, her voices had told her that she had done great harm by saying that what she had done was wrong. Whatever she said and recanted on Thursday, she did only from fear of the flames.

Asked whether she believes that her voices are Saint Catherine and Saint Margaret, she said yes, and they are from God.

Asked to tell the truth about the crown, she answered: "Everything I told you in the trial was the truth, as best I knew it."

Then she was told that when she abjured on the scaffold, before judges and people, she admitted that she had falsely boasted that the voices were Saint Catherine and Saint Margaret.

She said that she did not intend to do so. She did not deny or intend to deny her visions, that is, that they were Saint Catherine and Saint Margaret; she did everything out of fear of the flames, and her entire recantation was untrue. She prefers to do her penance once and for all by dying, rather than endure the torment of prison any longer. She never did anything against God or the faith, despite her recantation, and she understood nothing in the formula of abjuration. <At that moment [that is, at the abjuration]> She did not intend to recant anything unless it pleased God. If the judges wish, she will take women's clothes; for the rest, she will do nothing else.

Hearing these things, we left her, to proceed further according to law and reason.

Tuesday, May 29. The next day, Tuesday after Trinity Sunday, May 29, in the chapel of the archbishop's residence in Rouen, we the judges assembled doctors and experts in theology and canon and civil law: reverend fathers in Christ, the abbots of Holy Trinity of Fécamp, Saint-Ouen of Rouen, and Mortemer; reverend masters Pierre, prior of Longueville-Giffard, Jean de Châtillon, Erard Emengart, Guillaume Erard, Guillaume le Boucher, Jean de Nibat, Jean le Fèvre, Jacques Guesdon, Pierre Maurice, doctors of theology; Jean Guérin and Pasquier de Vaux, doctors of canon law; André Marguerie, Nicolas de Venderès, archdeacons of Rouen Cathedral; Guillaume Haiton, Nicolas Couppequesne, Guillaume de Baudribosc, Richard de Grouchet, Thomas de Courcelles, bachelors in theology; Jean Pinchon, Jean Alespée, Denis Gastinel, Jean Maugier, Nicolas Caval, Nicolas Loiselleur, Guillaume Desjardins, canons of Rouen Cathedral, some masters and others licentiates of canon and civil law and of medicine; Jean Tiphaine, Guillaume de la Chambre, Guillaume de Livet, Geoffroi du Crotay, Jean le Doux, Jean Colombel, Aubert Morel, Pierre Carrel, licentiates of canon or civil law, or masters or licentiates of medicine; Martin Lavenu, Brother Ysambard de la Pierre, and reverend Guillaume du Désert, canon of Rouen Cathedral.

In their presence, we the bishop explained that after the last public session here on the vigil of Pentecost, following their advice, we had directed that Joan be warned and instructed on the specific points wherein the University of Paris believed she had transgressed and erred, and we had urged her to abandon these errors and return to the path of truth. And since she would neither agree nor speak further, and since the promoter likewise had nothing further to say or bring against her, we had ended the trial and assigned the following Thursday for the parties to hear us render justice.

Then we reminded them what had happened on that Thursday, how after a solemn sermon and admonitions, Joan had recanted and abjured her errors and signed the abjuration with her own hand; and how, after dinner, we the vice-inquisitor and our assistants had kindly urged Joan to persist in her good intention and to beware of relapse; then how, in obedience to the commands of the Church, she had given up men's clothing and accepted women's; but that led by the devil, she had stated once again before many witnesses that her voices and spirits had come and told her many things; and how casting off women's dress, Joan again took men's clothing. Having heard this, we visited and examined her.

Then we ordered Joan's last confessions and assertions to be read, those she made to us yesterday, and we asked for counsel and advice from those present. They pronounced as follows:

Summary. All twenty-seven masters considered her a relapsed heretic, though many recommended further reading and explanation of the abjuration to her and preaching. Most recommended that in handing her over to the secular authority, there should be a plea to treat her with leniency (this a standard formula); however, Denis Gastinel and Pasquier de Vaux advised against such a plea.

After hearing the opinions of each one, we thanked them and concluded that the trial should continue against Joan as a relapsed heretic, according to law and reason.

Wednesday, May 30. The last day of the trial. The next day, Wednesday, May 30, we summoned Joan to hear justice pronounced by the appointed officer, as appears more fully from our letter and from the officer's report. Here follows the letter:

The Summons of Pierre Cauchon for Joan's Appearance

Summary. Pierre Cauchon, writing to all public priests appointed as rectors of churches in the city and diocese of Rouen, notes that Joan has relapsed, and therefore commands each one to summon Joan to appear the next day to hear the sentence of condemnation. Dated Tuesday, May 29, 1431.

Here follows the executor's letter executing the summons:

The Execution of the Summons

Summary. Jean Massieu, writing to Pierre Cauchon, Jean Le Maistre, and Jean Graverent, informs them that the summons has been executed. Dated Wednesday, May 30. 1431, at seven o'clock in the morning.

Around nine o'clock in the morning that same day, we the judges arrived at the Old Market of Rouen near the Church of Saint-Sauveur, assisted by reverend fathers in Christ the bishops of Thérouanne and Noyon; masters Jean de Châtillon, André Marguerie, Nicolas de Venderès, Raoul Roussel, Denis Gastinel, Guillaume le Boucher, Jean Alespée, Pierre de Houdenc, Guillaume Haiton, the prior of Longueville, Pierre Maurice, and many other lords, masters, and clergymen. Then Joan was led before us, within view of a great multitude of people assembled there, and she was placed upon a scaffold. For her wholesome admonition and the people's edification, master Nicolas Midi, a distinguished doctor of theology, preached a solemn sermon, taking his text from the Apostle, the first letter to the Corinthians, chapter twelve: "If one member suffer, the others suffer with it."[1]

After the sermon, we again warned Joan to be mindful of her soul's salvation and to think of her sins, to repent in honest sorrow. We urged her to believe the clergy and the worthy men who taught her about salvation, and especially to listen to the two venerable preaching friars standing near her, whom we had directed to instruct her constantly and earnestly with wholesome admonitions and counsels.

Finally, we the bishop and the vice-inquisitor, taking into account all these matters, concluded that this woman, moved by a stubborn rashness, had never truly renounced her errors and wicked crimes, but that the devilish malice of her stubbornness was revealed in her false and deceitful sham of contrition, repentance, and amelioration, and in her perjury of God's holy name and in her blasphemy of his unutterable majesty, and that it had shown her to be many times more damnable than before, and therewith obstinate, incorrigible, and a relapsed heretic, utterly unworthy of the grace and communion that we had mercifully offered her in our previous sentence. And after considering each point of the matter and after mature deliberation and counsel with many experts, we proceeded to our final sentence, as follows:

In the name of the Lord, amen. Whenever the deadly poison of heresy infects a member of the Church, who is then transformed into a member of Satan, utmost care must be taken to keep the contagion of the disease from spreading to other parts of the mystical body of Christ. The holy fathers also set down that hardened heretics should be removed from the company of the just, rather than allowing such poisonous vipers to be nourished in the bosom of Holy Mother Church, gravely endangering the other faithful.

Therefore we, Pierre, by divine mercy bishop of Beauvais, and brother Jean Le Maistre, vicar of the distinguished doctor Master Jean Graverent, inquisitor of heresy, both competent judges in this office, have declared a just verdict that you Joan, commonly called the Maid, have fallen into various errors and crimes such as schism, idolatry, invocation of demons, and many others. And yet since the Church never closes her bosom to any who return, we supposed that you had returned from these errors and crimes with a pure mind and sincere faith when on a certain day you renounced them and publicly swore, vowed, and promised never to return to those errors or to any heresy, no matter who persuaded you, but instead to remain continually in the unity of the catholic Church and in fellowship with the Roman pontiff, as stated in greater detail in a schedule signed by your own hand. But after you recanted your errors, the author of schism and heresy attacked and seduced your heart, and—alas!—you fell into the same errors and crimes, like a dog returning to its vomit,[2] as appears sufficiently and plainly from your willing confessions and statements. And we concluded that it was plainly evident that earlier you denied your false stories merely in word, and with a false heart, rather than a sincere and honest soul.

We therefore declare that you have fallen again under sentence of excommunication and into your original errors, and we declare you a relapsed heretic. Seated in judgment, we do make known and pronounce in writing by this our sentence that you are a corrupt member, and that to prevent you from infecting other members, you should be driven from the unity of the Church, divided from its body, and handed over to the secular power; we cast you out, separate, and deliver you, praying the secular power to be lenient in its judgment toward you with respect to the death and mutilation of the body.[3] And if true signs of repentance should appear in you, you may receive the sacrament of penance.

This sentence was pronounced in part before the abjuration.

In the name of the Lord, amen. All pastors . . . righteous judge.[4]

Keeping our eyes fixed on Christ and the honor of the true faith, that our judgment may come forth from the Lord's countenance,[5] we say and determine that you have falsely imagined revelations and divine apparitions, that you are a pernicious temptress, presumptuous, credulous, rash, superstitious, a false prophetess, a blasphemer against God and his saints, scornful of God in his sacraments, a transgressor of divine law, sacred doctrine, and ecclesiastical decrees; that you are seditious, cruel, apostate, schismatic, straying in many ways from our faith; and that in these ways you have rashly sinned against God and his Church. Moreover, we ourselves and certain learned and expert doctors and masters who were concerned for the salvation of your soul have often warned you on our behalf, duly and sufficiently, to correct and amend yourself in these matters and to submit to the guidance, judgment, and correction of Holy Mother Church. Yet you would not do so, nor did you concern yourself with it, but in your hard-heartedness and stubbornness you positively denied the accusations and repeatedly refused to submit to our lord the pope and to the holy general council. We therefore lawfully declare you an excommunicate and heretic, as one obstinate and confirmed in these sins, faults, and errors. And now that your errors have been condemned in a public sermon, we declare that, as a limb of Satan cut off from the Church, infected with the leprosy of heresy, you are to be abandoned to secular justice, lest you infect other limbs of Christ, and we do so abandon you; and we pray the secular power to be moderate in its judgment upon you, short of death and mutilation. And if you show true signs of repentance, you may receive the sacrament of penance.

I, Guillaume Colles, also called Boisguillaume, priest and notary named above, do attest that collation was duly made with the original register; and therefore I have signed this present copy containing 158 folios with my manual sign.[6] Here I sign with my own hand, followed by the two other notaries below.

Boisguillaume.

And I, Guillaume Manchon, priest of the diocese of Rouen, notary public by apostolic and imperial authority, do attest that I was present with the other notaries at the collation of the trial proceedings, and that collation was duly made with the original register of the proceedings. Therefore with the other notaries in this trial I have signed below with my own hand and have affixed my manual sign, as requested.

G. Manchon.

And I, Nicolas Taquel, priest of the diocese of Rouen, notary public sworn by imperial authority and by the archbishop's court of Rouen and summoned to a part of this trial, do attest that with the above notaries I witnessed and heard the collation of this trial record with the original register of the trial and that the collation was duly performed. Therefore with the other notaries, I have signed this copy of the record below with my own hand, and affixed my manual sign, as requested.

N. Taquel.[7]

4

Aftermath

The authorities deliver their assessments after the death of Joan.

June 7: Report of the Events of May 30 in Joan's Cell

Information recorded after the execution about many things that Joan said at her end and on the point of death.

On Thursday, June 7, of the same year, 1431, by virtue of our office, we the judges gathered information about some of the things that Joan had said in the presence of reliable witnesses when she was still in prison, before she was led to judgment.

First, the venerable and prudent Master Nicolas de Venderès, licentiate of canon law, archdeacon of Eu at Rouen Cathedral, around fifty-two years old, being produced, sworn, received, and examined this day as witness, stated under oath that on Wednesday, May 30, the eve of Corpus Christi,[1] while Joan was still in prison in the castle of Rouen, she said that considering that her voices had promised her deliverance from prison and that she now saw the contrary, she understood and knew that they had deceived her.

Joan said and confessed that she had seen and heard with her very eyes and ears the voices and apparitions mentioned at the trial. And there were witnesses present at this, namely, we the judges, and Masters Pierre Maurice, Thomas de Courcelles, Nicolas Loiselleur, Brother Martin Lavenu, Jean Toutmouillé, and reverend Jacques le Camus, with a few others.

Brother Martin Lavenu, priest, of the Order of Friars Preachers, around thirty-three years old, produced, received, sworn, and examined as witness, stated and set down that on the morning of the day Joan was sentenced, before she was led to judgment, in the presence of Masters Pierre Maurice, Nicolas Loiselleur, and the said Toutmouillé, companion of the speaker, she stated and confessed that she knew and realized that her voices and apparitions had deceived her, for they had promised her deliverance and release from prison, and she clearly saw the contrary.

Asked who moved Joan to say this, the speaker said that he himself, and Masters Pierre Maurice and Nicolas Loiselleur, urged her for her soul's salvation and asked her whether it was true that she had received voices and apparitions. And she said yes, and persisted in this belief to the last. She did not clearly describe their appearance, except, as he recalls, that they came in great numbers yet in the slightest dimension. Then he heard Joan say and confess that because the churchmen believed that any spirits she had came from evil spirits, she also believed as much, nor would she put any more faith in those spirits. And he believed that Joan was then of sound mind.

He added that the same day he heard Joan say and confess that although in her statements and answers she had boasted that an angel of God had brought a crown to the one she calls her king, and that she herself had accompanied the angel when he brought the crown to him, along with many other things described at greater length in the record, she nonetheless stated and confessed willingly and uncoerced that regardless of what she had said and boasted about the angel, no angel had brought a crown; rather, she herself was the angel who told and promised her king that if he would set her to the task, she would see him crowned at Reims. Nor was there any other crown sent by God, no matter what she had said and claimed in the course of the trial about the crown or sign given to her king.

The esteemed and wise Master Pierre Maurice, professor of theology and canon of Rouen [Cathedral], about thirty-eight years old, produced, received, sworn, and examined as witness this day, stated that he visited Joan on the morning of the day she was sentenced, while she was still in prison, to urge her to save her soul. And while he was exhorting her and asking her about the angel who she said brought the crown to the one she calls her king, she said that she herself was the angel.

Asked about the crown she promised him, and the host of angels who accompanied her, she said it was true, they appeared to her as the tiniest of creatures.[2]

And finally, when the speaker asked her whether this apparition was real, she said yes, whether they were good or evil spirits, they had really appeared to her, saying in French: "Soit bons, soit mauvais esprits, ils me sont apparus."[3] Joan also said that she usually heard the voices at compline when the bells rang, and when they rang in the morning as well. He said it seemed clear that they were evil spirits who promised her freedom, and that she had been deceived. Joan replied that it was true, she had been deceived. He also heard her say that she yielded to the churchmen to say whether they were good or evil spirits. And he believes that Joan was of sound mind and understanding when she said these things.

Brother Jean Toutmouillé, priest of the Order of Friars Preachers, about twenty-four years old, produced, received, sworn, and examined as witness this day, declared under oath that on the day Joan was sentenced, Wednesday, the eve of Corpus Christi, he accompanied Brother Martin Lavenu of the same order to visit Joan that morning, to urge her to save her soul; and he heard from Master Pierre Maurice, who was already there, that she had stated and confessed that the crown was nothing but a fiction, and that she herself was the angel; and the master reported this in Latin.

Then Joan was questioned about her voices and apparitions. She said that she had really heard the voices, particularly when the bells rang at compline and matins, although Master Pierre told her that sometimes people hear the bells and think they can hear or understand certain words.

Joan also said and confessed that her apparitions had sometimes come to her in a great multitude and in the smallest dimension, or as the tiniest things, but she did not otherwise specify their shape or appearance.

He said that when they arrived that day in the room where Joan was held, we the bishop told Joan in French in the presence of the vice-inquisitor: "Now, see here, Joan, you have always told us that your voices promised that you would be freed, and now you see how they have deceived you. Now tell us the truth." Then Joan answered: "In truth, I see very well that they've deceived me."

He heard her say nothing more at that time, except that at first, before we, the judges, came to her prison, Joan was asked whether she believed that her voices and apparitions proceeded from good or evil spirits. She answered: "I don't know; I yield to my mother the Church," or "to you who are men of the Church." And it seemed to him that Joan was of sound mind; and he heard Joan confess this too, that she was of sound mind.

Reverend Jacques le Camus, priest, canon of Reims [Cathedral], around fifty-four years old, produced, sworn, and examined as witness that day, declared under oath that on Wednesday morning, the eve of Corpus Christi, he accompanied us the bishop to the room where Joan was held in the castle of Rouen and heard what Joan said and confessed publicly and in a loud voice audible to all those present— namely, that she, Joan, had seen apparitions come to her and heard voices promising that she would be freed from prison. And she clearly understood that she had been deceived, and she believed, therefore, that they were not good voices or good things.

A little later, she confessed her sins to Brother Martin of the Order of Preachers; and after receiving confession and penance, when the brother wanted to administer the Eucharist to Joan and held the consecrated host in his hands, he asked her: "Do you believe that this is the body of Christ?" Joan answered: "Yes, and this alone can free me; I ask you to administer it to me." And then the brother said to Joan: "Do you still believe in these voices?" Joan answered: "I believe in God alone, and I no longer put any faith in those voices, because they have deceived me."[4]

Master Thomas de Courcelles, master of arts and bachelor of theology, around thirty years old, produced, received, sworn, and examined as witness this day, said and declared under oath that on Wednesday, the eve of Corpus Christi, he was with us the bishop in the room where Joan was held in the castle of Rouen, and he heard and understood us ask Joan whether her voices had told her that she would be freed. She said they had told her she would be freed and that she should be of good cheer. And Joan added, he thought, upon reflection:

"I see clearly that I've been deceived." Then we the bishop, as he recalls, told Joan that she could very well see that these voices were not good spirits and did not come from God; for if they had, they would never have said something false or lied.

Master Nicolas Loiselleur, master of arts, canon of Rouen and Chartres Cathedrals, around forty years old, produced, received, sworn, and examined this day as witness, said and declared under oath that on Wednesday morning, the eve of Corpus Christi, he accompanied the esteemed Master Pierre Maurice, professor of theology, to the prison where Joan, commonly called the Maid, was held, to urge and warn her to save her soul. When she was asked to tell the truth about the angel who, as she said at her trial, brought a precious crown of purest gold to the one she calls her king, and to conceal the truth no longer, considering that her only thought now was the salvation of her soul, he heard Joan say that it was she who had announced to her king the crown in question, and she was the only angel.

Then she was asked whether a crown had really been sent to her king. She said that this was nothing but the promise of coronation she made to him, her promise that he would be crowned.

The witness added that he had heard Joan say many times to Master Pierre and to the two Dominicans and to us the bishop, and to many others as well, that she really had had revelations and apparitions of spirits, and that she had been deceived in these revelations; and she clearly understood and saw this, for these revelations had promised to free her from prison, whereas she now perceives the contrary. And as to whether the spirits were good or evil, she deferred to the clergy; but she no longer had any faith in the spirits, nor would she.

The speaker said that he urged her to remove the error she had sown in the people, to confess publicly that she had been tricked and that she had tricked the people by crediting these revelations and by urging the people to believe them, and to ask humbly for pardon. Joan said she would gladly do this, but she feared she would forget when the time came—that is, when she was led to judgment before the people; she prayed her confessor to remind her of this and of other things concerning the salvation of her soul.

From this and from many other proofs, the speaker believed that Joan was then of sound mind and showed clear signs of sorrow and repentance for her crimes. Both in prison to many witnesses and at the public judgment, he heard her ask for forgiveness from the English and Burgundians with great sorrow of heart; for as she admitted, she had caused them to be killed and put to flight and had injured them in many other ways.

Letter of Henry VI to the Emperor, Kings, Dukes, and Other Christian Princes

Here follows the letter that our lord the king [Henry VI] wrote to the emperor, kings, dukes, and other Christian princes.[5]

Your imperial highness, most serene king and our dear brother, you have demonstrated zealous affection toward the honor of the catholic faith and the glory of Christ's name; you have engaged to defend the faithful and to attack wicked heretics through great endeavors and tireless labors; and your spirits rejoice with great joy whenever you hear that the holy faith has been exalted and pestilent errors overthrown. This consideration has moved us to write in full to your serenity regarding the just punishment that a certain false prophetess, raised up for a short time in our kingdom of France, suffered for her faults.

With wondrous presumption, this woman whom the common people called the Maid rose up against natural decency, clothed in men's attire and armed as a soldier, and dared to mingle in the slaughter of men in fierce combat, and to take part in battles. She even presumed to boast that she was sent by God to wage war, and that Michael, Gabriel, and a great host of other angels, along with the holy virgins Catherine and Margaret, visibly appeared to her. For almost a full year she inveigled the people, until a great part of them turned away from hearing the truth, being turned aside unto fables[6] about the exploits of this superstitious woman, which common report spread to almost the entire world. At last, seeing his people thrust too readily toward new and dangerous beliefs before it was proved whether the spirit was from God,[7] divine mercy took compassion on them and delivered the woman into our hands and power.

Although she had inflicted great damage upon our nation and brought many troubles to our kingdom, and we could therefore have sentenced her to heavy and swift punishments, yet our intention was not at all to avenge the injury in this way or to hand her over at once to secular justice for punishment. We were asked by the bishop in whose diocese she had been captured to surrender her for judgment to the jurisdiction of the Church, for she was said to have committed serious and scandalous crimes against the true faith and the Christian religion. Therefore, as befits a Christian king honoring ecclesiastical authority with a son's affection, we immediately delivered this woman to the judgment of Holy Mother Church and to the bishop's jurisdiction. And assuredly, with the vice-inquisitor of heresy he conducted a most worthy trial in the matter, with great solemnity and suitable dignity, to the honor of God and the wholesome edification of the people.

In fact, after the judges had interrogated this woman many days, they submitted her confessions and statements to doctors and masters of the University of Paris, and to many other learned men. From these deliberations, they considered the woman to be a superstitious person, a diviner, an idolater, a summoner of demons, a blasphemer of God and the saints, a schismastic straying in many ways from the faith of Christ. Now, in order for this wretched sinner to be cleansed of such wicked crimes and for her soul to be healed of its extreme diseases,[8] she was warned repeatedly for many days with kind entreaties to cast off all error, to enter the straight path of truth, and to beware the grave danger to her body and soul. But the spirit of pride had so filled her heart that sound doctrines and wholesome counsels could in no way soften her iron heart. Rather, she constantly boasted that she had done everything by the command of God and holy virgins who visibly appeared to her; and worst of all, she acknowledged no earthly judge and would submit to no one but God alone and the blessed souls triumphant in heaven, so scorning the judgment of our supreme pontiff, the general council, and the universal Church militant. Seeing the hardness of her heart, the judges brought the woman before the people and proclaimed her errors in a public sermon, gave her the final warnings, and at last began reading their sentence of condemnation. But before the reading was concluded, she changed her mind and cried out that she would say better things. When the judges understood this, their hearts were cheered, and, hoping to redeem her body and soul from destruction, they listened favorably to her words. Then she submitted to the rule of the Church and with full voice recanted and abjured her errors and ruinous crimes, signing the schedule of this recantation and abjuration with her own hand. So Holy Mother Church, rejoicing over the sinner that does penance and the lost sheep, which had wandered through the wilderness, brought back to the fold, committed her to prison to do wholesome penance.[9]

But the fire of her pride, which had seemed quenched, was revived by demonic winds and enkindled into destructive flames, and the miserable woman returned to her errors and lying follies that she had earlier vomited forth.[10] Finally, as ecclesiastical sanctions dictate, to prevent her from infecting other members of Christ, she was handed over to the judgment of secular authority, which determined that her body should be consumed by fire. Seeing her end near, the wretched woman openly acknowledged and plainly confessed that the spirits that she often claimed had appeared to her visibly were evil, lying spirits; they had falsely promised to free her from prison, and she admitted that she had been tricked and deceived.

Such was the outcome and the end, most serene king, that we have thought good to make known to you, that your royal highness may know for certain the matter itself and inform others of this woman's death. For we consider one thing altogether necessary to faithful people, that your serenity and other ecclesiastical and secular princes may diligently dissuade catholic people from presuming to believe lightly in superstitions and idle fancies, especially in these latter days when we see many false prophets and sowers of error go out into different lands.[11] Rising up against Holy Mother Church with shameless audacity, they would perhaps have infected all the people of Christ, if heavenly mercy and its faithful ministers had not applied themselves with ready diligence to drive back and punish the efforts of the wicked.

Most serene king, may Jesus Christ keep your highness to guard his Church and the Christian religion through long days, in prosperity and in fulfillment of your wishes.

Given at Rouen, June 8, 1431.

Letter of Henry VI to Prelates, Dukes, Counts, and Nobles in France

Here follows the letter that Henry VI wrote to prelates of the Church, dukes, counts, and other nobles, and to the cities of France.

Summary. Most of this letter is a translation of the previous letter into French, but this version also urges that sermons be preached against Joan. Dated June 28, 1431, Rouen.[12]

Recantation and Sentence of a Friar Who Spoke Evil of Joan's Judges

Here follows the recantation of a certain friar who spoke evil of the judges who tried this woman.

Reverend father in Christ, and you, religious master, vicar of the religious Jean Graverent, distinguished professor of theology and inquisitor of heresy for all France, specially appointed by the Holy Apostolic See: I, Brother Pierre Bosquier of the Order of Friars Preachers, wretched sinner and your subject, do desire as a good and true catholic to obey in all things my holy mother the Church and you my judges in this case, with all humility and devotion, and do confess myself bound to this. By evidence gathered on your order you have found me guilty of the following: that on May 30, the eve of Corpus Christi, I said that you and those who had judged this woman Joan, commonly called the Maid, had done, and were doing, an evil thing. But since Joan was brought before you judges to be tried on a matter of faith, these words are foolish and seem to declare support for heresy. And since it has been found that I spoke these words, so help me God, in truth I spoke them without thinking and inadvertently, and in my cups. I confess that I have gravely sinned in this matter, and I ask pardon of our Holy Mother Church and of you, my judges and dread lords, on my knees and with joined hands, most humbly submitting myself to your amendment, correction, and punishment and humbly praying the Church to set aside its rigor and to grant me mercy.

Here follows the sentence.

In the name of the Lord, amen. We, Pierre, by divine mercy bishop of Beauvais, and Brother Jean Le Maistre, specially appointed to this city and diocese of Rouen and to the following case by the celebrated doctor Jean Graverent, inquisitor of heresy for all the kingdom of France by apostolic authority, considering the facts of an accusation of faith brought and pending before us against the religious Brother Pierre Bosquier, and having seen clear evidence gathered at our command and reported to us about the accusations against him, and seeing that the accused accepts this evidence, we consider it legitimately established that soon after our final sentence whereby we abandoned the woman Joan, commonly called the Maid, to secular jurisdiction as a heretic, the accused stated and pronounced in a certain place before a few witnesses that we had done evil and that all those who had judged her had done evil. These words seem to declare support for this Joan, and he has thereby gravely sinned and erred. Nonetheless, because this Brother Pierre has expressed his desire as a good and true catholic to obey our Holy Mother Church and us, his judges in this case, with all humility and devotion and in all things, and because he has entirely submitted to our correction and is eager to obey our commands—preferring a merciful to a strict judgment, and especially considering his position and that he made his remarks in his cups, as he says and asserts—we do absolve him from his former sentences, we reunite him to the catholic flock, and we restore him to his good reputation, if need be. Nevertheless, until next Easter we condemn him to prison on bread and water in the house of the Dominicans in Rouen, in this final sentence pronounced by us, seated in judgment, always reserving our grace and right of moderation.

Given at Rouen, August 8, 1431.

Letter of the University of Paris to the Pope, the Emperor, and the College of Cardinals

Copy of the letter sent by the University of Paris to the pope, the emperor, and the College of Cardinals.

Summary. *Observes that great efforts are needed to preserve the Church in these latter days, when false prophets will rise up; praises the bishop of Beauvais for his diligence in the case of Joan, whose trial is described; notes her relapse into heresy following her abjuration, and then her confession at the end "that she had been tricked and deceived" by her spirits, and that she "asked pardon of all"; laments the ready belief accorded her and considers this a sign of the times. Undated.*

Appendix

The "Poitiers Conclusions"

For several weeks in March and April 1429, Joan was examined by a group of masters in Chinon and in Poitiers. The following document, often called the Poitiers Conclusions, is the only vestige of opinion from theologians or canon lawyers who participated in these examinations.[1]

Given his own needs and those of his kingdom, and considering the continual prayers of his poor people to God and to all others who love peace and justice, the king should neither reject nor resist the Maid, who says she is sent by God to give him aid, notwithstanding that these promises may concern only human works. Nor should he believe in her at once and without reflection. But following Holy Scripture, he should test her in two ways: through human caution, examining her life, behavior, and intention, as Saint Paul the Apostle says: "Try the spirits if they be of God";[2] and through earnest prayer, seeking a sign of some divine work or hope that might allow him to determine that she is come by the will of God. So God commanded Ahaz to ask for a sign when God promised him victory, telling him: "Ask for a sign from the Lord";[3] and so did Gideon, who asked for a sign,[4] and several others, etc.

Since the coming of the Maid, the king has observed and regarded her in these two ways: that is, trial by human caution and by prayer, asking God for a sign. As to the first, human caution, he has had the Maid tested concerning her life, her birth, her conduct, and her intent and has kept her with him for six weeks, presenting her to everyone, whether clerks, clergymen, pious persons, soldiers, women, widows, or others. She has talked with everyone publicly and privately. Yet no evil has been found in her, only goodness, humility, virginity, piety, honesty, and simplicity; and wonderful things about her birth and life are reported as true.

As to the second manner of trial, the king asked her for a sign, and she answered that she would reveal it before the town of Orléans, and nowhere else: for so she has been ordered by God.

Given that the Maid was tried as completely as the king had it in his power to do, and given that no evil was found in her, and considering her reply, which is to show a divine sign before Orléans—seeing her constancy and perseverance in her intention, and her pressing requests to go to Orléans to show the sign of divine aid—the king should not forbid her to go to Orléans with his soldiers, but should have her taken there honorably, while trusting in God. For to doubt or abandon her in the absence of any appearance of evil would be to resist the Holy Ghost, and to be rendered unworthy of God's aid, as Gamaliel said in a council of Jews with regard to the apostles.[5]

Chronology

1412?   Joan's birth

1425?   First time Joan hears voices

1428   *May.* First meeting with Robert de Baudricourt
July. Joan at Neufchâteau
Case at Toul for breach of promise

1429   Second meeting with Robert de Baudricourt at Vaucouleurs
Meeting with Charles, duke of Lorraine
February. Departure from Vaucouleurs
Early March. Arrival at Chinon
March. Examination at Poitiers
April. Departure from Chinon for Tours
April 29. Arrival at Orléans
May 8. Siege of Orléans lifted
July 17. Coronation of Charles VII at Reims Cathedral
September. Joan at Saint-Denis and Paris
November. Joan at La Charité

1430   *May 23.* Capture of Joan at Compiègne

May–June/July. Joan at Beaulieu
June/July–September/November. Joan at Beaurevoir
September or November. Joan at Arras
December 23. Arrival at Rouen

1431 *January 9.* Beginning of trial
February 21. Joan's first appearance in court
March 10. Beginning of sessions in prison
March 26. Beginning of ordinary trial
May 23. Formal charges against Joan, and warning
May 24. Joan's abjuration and sentence to life in prison
May 28. Joan's withdrawal of her abjuration
May 29. Decision to deliver Joan to the secular arm
May 30. Burning of Joan of Arc at the stake as a heretic

1450 Royal inquest into the original trial

1452 Renewed investigation by Guillaume d'Estouteville

1455 Authorization of formal retrial by Pope Calixtus III

1456 *July 7.* Nullification of original trial verdict

Major Participants in the Trial

For further information on the judges and assessors, and on other persons mentioned in the trial, see Régine Pernoud and Marie-Véronique Clin, *Joan of Arc: Her Story*, trans. and rev. Jeremy duQuesnay Adams (New York, 1998), 167–217; Pierre Tisset, *Procès de condamnation de Jeanne d'Arc* (Paris, 1960–1971), 2:383–425; and W. P. Barrett, *The Trial of Jeanne d'Arc* (New York, 1932), 389–473, which is a translation of the dramatis personae in Pierre Champion, *Procès de condamnation de Jeanne d'Arc* (Paris, 1920–1921).

ROYALTY AND NOBILITY

Charles VII. King of France from 1422 to 1461. Crowned at Reims Cathedral on July 17, 1429, with Joan in attendance.

Henry VI. King of England from the age of nine months. He reigned from 1422 to 1461 and from 1470 to 1471. All the trial documents written in his name were the work of his ministers.

Jean de Luxembourg. Lord of Beaurevoir and count of Ligny (d. 1440), loyal supporter of the duke of Burgundy. One of Luxembourg's vassals captured Joan and delivered her to him.

Philip the Good. Duke of Burgundy from 1419 to 1467. Came to power following the assassination in 1419 of his father, John the Fearless, and made an alliance with England in 1420 that lasted until 1435.

Guillaume Colles. One of two notaries (with Guillaume Manchon) appointed by Cauchon for the trial.

Guillaume Manchon. One of two notaries (with Guillaume Colles) appointed by Cauchon for the trial.

Jean d'Estivet. Promoter, or prosecutor, who introduced the articles of accusation against Joan on March 27–28. Later vilified by the scribes Colles and Manchon for his hatred and mistreatment of Joan.

Jean de la Fontaine. Counselor and examiner who interrogated Joan at several sessions. According to testimony at the nullification trial, he fled Rouen after counseling Joan. He does not appear in the record after March 28.

Jean Graverent. Dominican inquisitor of France, who did not attend the trial (he was engaged at another trial) but instead appointed Jean Le Maistre as his deputy.

Jean Le Maistre. Dominican "vice-inquisitor" for Jean Graverent. Nominally a judge coequal in authority to Bishop Cauchon, Le Maistre in fact played only a small role.

Jean Massieu. "Usher," or executor of writs, at the trial.

Pierre Cauchon. Bishop of Beauvais and supporter of the Anglo-Burgundian regime. Because Joan was captured in his diocese, he had jurisdiction over her trial. The trial was moved to Rouen because his territory had been lost to the French. He was responsible for having the Latin trial record drawn up.

Thomas de Courcelles. Theologian who translated the trial from French into Latin in the months following the trial. Courcelles also read the articles of accusation against Joan on March 27–28.

Notes

INTRODUCTION

1. I quote from the excerpts in Jules Quicherat, ed., *Procès de condamnation et de réhabilitation de Jeanne d'Arc dite la Pucelle* (Paris, 1841–1849), 4:503.

2. *A Parisian Journal, 1405–1449*, trans. Janet Shirley (Oxford, 1968), 264–265.

3. Germain Lefèvre-Pontalis and Léon Dorez, eds., *Chronique d'Antonio Morosini* (Paris, 1901), 3:348–357. The editor dates this section of the chronicle between July 8 and July 14, 1431.

4. Nicolas Lami, who was present on March 3, left immediately for the council and informed Nider about Joan. See Quicherat, *Procès*, 4:504. Jean Beaupère, one of the primary interrogators, departed on May 28, two days before Joan's execution. On Joan's judges and assessors at the council, see Heinz Thomas, "Jeanne la Pucelle, das Basler Konzil und die 'Kleinen' der Reformatio Sigismundi," *Francia* 11 (1983): 327–331.

5. Reginald Hyatte, ed., *Laughter for the Devil: The Trials of Gilles de Rais, Companion-in-Arms of Joan of Arc, 1440* (Cranbury, N.J., 1984).

6. On other trials, see Pierre Tisset, *Procès de condamnation de Jeanne d'Arc* (Paris, 1960–1971), 3:61 n. 1; and Karen Sullivan, *The Interrogation of Joan of Arc* (Minneapolis, 1999), xiii. On the manuscripts, see Tisset, *Procès*, 1:xix–xxx.

7. Pierre Duparc, "La délivrance d'Orléans et la mission de Jeanne d'Arc," in *Jeanne d'Arc: Une époque, un rayonnement* (Paris, 1982), 153–158.

8. On attitudes in Paris, see *A Parisian Journal.*

9. See here Marina Belozerskaya, *Rethinking the Renaissance: Burgundian Arts across Europe* (Cambridge, 2002). On Cauchon's support for the house of Burgundy, see François Neveux, *L'évêque Pierre Cauchon* (Paris, 1987), 43–45.

10. Neveux, *L'évêque Pierre Cauchon*, 74–77.

11. For more on the function of the promoter, see the section later in the introduction under the heading "Inquisitorial Procedure."

12. An early sixteenth-century map of the Old Market is reproduced as plate 3 in Tisset, *Procès*, vol. 3, following p. 234.

13. W. S. Scott, *The Trial of Joan of Arc, Being the Verbatim Report of the Proceedings from the Orléans Manuscript* (London, 1956), 16–17. Scott's discussion of the manuscripts is quite tendentious and in some cases misleading, though widely cited in the literature.

14. Tisset, *Procès*, 3:29; Salomon Reinach, "Observation sur le texte du Procès de condamnation de Jeanne d'Arc," *Revue historique* 148 (1925): 201.

15. Caterina Bruschi, "'Magna diligentia est habenda per inquisitorem': Precautions before Reading Doat 21–26," in *Texts and the Repression of Medieval Heresy*, ed. Caterina Bruschi and Peter Biller (Woodbridge, England, 2003), 107 and n. 86. On the uses made of inquisitorial registers, see James Given, *Inquisition and Medieval Society* (Ithaca, N.Y., 1997), 28–42, esp. 39–42.

16. Tisset, *Procès*, 3:11–12 n. 6. For a good general overview of the investigations leading to the nullification trial, see Malcolm Vale, *Charles VII* (Berkeley, Calif., 1974), 60–69. See also Régine Pernoud and Marie-Véronique Clin, *Joan of Arc: Her Story*, trans. and rev. Jeremy duQuesnay Adams (New York, 1998), 139–158.

17. P. Doncoeur and Y. Lanhers, eds., *L'enquête ordonnée par Charles VII en 1450 et le codicille de Guillaume Bouillé* (Paris, 1956), 10–12.

18. The edition is P. Doncoeur and Y. Lanhers, *L'enquête du cardinal d'Estouteville en 1452* (Paris, 1958).

19. The edition is Marie-Joseph Belon and François Balme, *Jean Bréhal, grand inquisiteur de France, et la réhabilitation de Jeanne d'Arc* (Paris, 1893), 28–46. For an English translation of the twenty-seven articles, see Pernoud and Clin, *Joan of Arc*, 152–155.

20. Vale, *Charles VII*, 68.

21. Doncoeur and Lanhers, *L'enquête ordonnée par Charles VII*, 50.

22. See the discussion, with references, in Tisset, *Procès*, 3:17–29. On the Latin translation, see Pierre Duparc, ed., *Procès en nullité de la condamnation de Jeanne d'Arc* (Paris, 1977–1988), 1:217.

23. Duparc, *Procès en nullité*, 98–100.

24. A good number of other manuscripts survive that were copied from the five original manuscripts. See Tisset, *Procès*, 1:xxvii–xxx; Nadia Margolis, *Joan of Arc in History, Literature, and Film* (New York, 1990), 13–16.

25. These final pages are reproduced in plates 2–4 in Tisset, *Procès*, vol. 1, following p. 436. For a complete facsimile of one of the three manuscripts, see

Le procès de condamnation de Jeanne d'Arc: Reproduction en fac-similé du manuscrit authentique . . . (Paris, 1955). The most recent description of these manuscripts, to my knowledge, is Jean Fraikin, "La date de la rédaction latine du procès de Jeanne d'Arc," *Quaerendo* 3 (1973): 40–45.

26. Duparc, *Procès en nullité*, 1:416.

27. Fraikin, "La date de la rédaction latine," 39–66. The same article was reprinted without footnotes in *Bulletin de l'Association des Amis du Centre Jeanne d'Arc* 8 (1985): 11–23. The article is summarized in English in Pernoud and Clin, *Joan of Arc*, 236–237.

28. See, for example, Susan Schibanoff, "True Lies: Transvestism and Idolatry in the Trial of Joan of Arc," in *Fresh Verdicts on Joan of Arc*, ed. Bonnie Wheeler and Charles T. Wood (New York, 1996), 33. This is also the clear assumption in Henry Ansgar Kelly, "The Right to Remain Silent: Before and after Joan of Arc," in *Inquisitions and Other Trial Procedures in the Medieval West* (Aldershot, England, 2001), 1013 n. 103, originally published in *Speculum* 68 (1993): 992–1026, and Charles T. Wood, *Joan of Arc and Richard III* (New York, 1988), 235 n. 8.

29. Scott, *The Trial of Joan of Arc*, 19. The specific passage in question here was the "formula of abjuration" that Joan signed at Saint-Ouen on May 24. For further discussion, see the note to the abjuration in the translation.

30. For a complete list of pieces included in and omitted from the official translation, see Paul Doncoeur, *La minute française des interrogatoires de Jeanne la Pucelle* (Melun, France, 1952), 15–18.

31. Régine Pernoud is thus misleading and incorrect in saying (*Joan of Arc*, 140) that Courcelles took advantage of his position "to remove his name from the list of those who had voted for torture"; Courcelles suppressed the entire list, not just his own name. Even so, during testimony at the retrial, Courcelles did deny that he had supported the use of torture. Duparc, *Procès en nullité*, 1:356.

32. Tisset, *Procès*, 1:xxv.

33. For the discussion that follows of the interview on May 30, see Tisset, *Procès*, 3:41–45; Neveux, *L'évêque Pierre Cauchon*, 185–189, 256–259.

34. Neveux, *L'évêque Pierre Cauchon*, 188.

35. On this point, see Sullivan, *The Interrogation of Joan of Arc*, esp. xvi–xviii; see also John H. Arnold, "Inquisition, Texts and Discourse," in *Texts and the Repression of Medieval Heresy*, 63.

36. See also Susan Crane, "Clothing and Gender Definition: Joan of Arc," in *Inscribing the Hundred Years' War in French and English Cultures*, ed. Denise N. Baker (Albany, N.Y., 2000), 197–199.

37. Exceptions include: Tisset, *Procès*, vol. 3; Neveux, *L'évêque Pierre*

Cauchon, 129–191; and Kelly, "The Right to Remain Silent." Also occasionally relevant is Duparc, *Procès en nullité*, vol. 5 (Paris, 1988).

38. See the general remarks of Stephan Kuttner, "The Code of Canon Law in Historical Perspective," *Jurist* 28 (1968): 141–146.

39. The older study is Antoine Dondaine, "Le manuel de l'inquisiteur (1230–1330)," *Archivum fratrum praedicatorum* 17 (1947): 85–194. See also the work of R. Parmeggiani, cited in *Texts and the Repression of Medieval Heresy*, xv–xvi, 13 n. 27; Christine Caldwell, "Doctor of Souls: Inquisition and the Dominican Order, 1231–1331" (Ph.D. diss., University of Notre Dame, 2002), 32–38.

40. Kelly, "The Right to Remain Silent," 1001; on Gui's complaints about the "inconveniences" resulting from Clement V's legislation on torture, see Caldwell, "Doctor of Souls," 167–168, 171.

41. Caldwell, "Doctor of Souls," 51–52.

42. Nicolas Eymeric, *Directorium inquisitorum* (Rome, 1578), 379–380; Tisset, *Procès*, 3:58–59.

43. On torture generally, see Caldwell, "Doctor of Souls," 161–176.

44. Dondaine, "Le manuel de l'inquisiteur (1230–1330)," 86.

45. John Van Engen, "The Church in the Fifteenth Century," in *Handbook of European History, 1400–1600*, vol. 1, *Structures and Assertions*, ed. T. A. Brady, H. A. Oberman, and J. D. Tracy (Grand Rapids, Mich., 1994), 311.

46. For a different view, see Kelly, "The Right to Remain Silent," 992–1026. The quotation is from p. 1011 n. 91.

47. Edward Peters, "Inquisition," in *The New Catholic Encyclopedia* (2002), 7:489.

48. This view is so commonplace as not to require references. For a more nuanced view, see Neveux, *L'évêque Pierre Cauchon*.

49. Mark Twain, *Personal Recollections of Joan of Arc* (New York, 1996 [1896]), 335.

50. Régine Pernoud, *Jeanne devant les Cauchons* (Paris, 1970), 36.

51. In general on this point, see Neveux, *L'évêque Pierre Cauchon*, 138–139, on which I have relied heavily in this paragraph.

52. R. A. Griffiths, *The Reign of King Henry VI* (Thrupp, England, 1998), 189–194; Neveux, *L'évêque Pierre Cauchon*, 88–89.

53. See, for example, Eymeric, *Directorium inquisitorum*, 284, 287.

54. Enguerrand de Monstrelet, *Chronicles*, trans. Peter E. Thompson (London, 1966), 312.

55. In any case, as Kelly has emphasized, Boniface VIII included laws in his *Liber sextus* (1298) that allowed judges to omit the establishing of notoriety if the accused did not object. For further discussion and references to the litera-

ture, see Kelly, "The Right to Remain Silent," 996–997, 1021–1022; Tisset, *Procès*, 3:72–73.

56. Tisset, *Procès*, 3:32–33.

57. Fredric L. Cheyette, "Inquest, Canonical and French," *Dictionary of the Middle Ages* (New York, 1985), 6:479.

58. Tisset, *Procès*, 1:184: "Incipit processus ordinarius post processum factum ex officio." The distinction is repeated on the same page.

59. Tisset, *Procès*, 3:57–63, esp. 60–61. Tisset was following a distinction laid down by R. Naz on the inquisition *cum promovente*. Naz, "Inquisition," in *Dictionnaire de droit canonique* (Paris, 1935–), 5:1421–1422. Tisset's lead has been followed by Pierre Duparc, *Procès en nullité*, 5:10–11; Jean Fraikin, "La date de la rédaction latine," 27; François Neveux, *L'évêque Pierre Cauchon*, 140. See also Cheyette, "Inquest, Canonical and French," 479.

60. Doncoeur and Lanhers, *L'enquête ordonnée par Charles VII*, 48–49.

61. Kelly, "The Right to Remain Silent," 1019–1020, 1020 n. 143.

62. Tisset, *Procès*, 3:131, citing the text in Quicherat's edition.

63. Neveux, *L'évêque Pierre Cauchon*, 178–179.

64. On this point, see Tisset, *Procès*, 3:130–133; Neveux, *L'évêque Pierre Cauchon*, 176–180. My interpretation here owes much to both authors.

65. I have relied here on Tisset, *Procès*, 3:151–159; Neveux, *L'évêque Pierre Cauchon*, 180–183.

66. Kelly, "The Right to Remain Silent," 1024.

67. Twain, *Personal Recollections*, vii–viii.

68. The best point of entry here is Howard Kaminsky, "From Lateness to Waning to Crisis: The Burden of the Later Middle Ages," *Journal of Early Modern History* 4 (2000): 85–125. For France, with an emphasis on social and economic factors, see James L. Goldsmith, "The Crisis of the Late Middle Ages: The Case of France," *French History* 9 (1995): 417–450.

69. Pernoud and Clin, *Joan of Arc*, 49–50. This idea is developed further in Pernoud's essay "Joan of Arc or the Survival of a People," in *Fresh Verdicts on Joan of Arc*, 289–293.

70. Hélène Millet, "Ecoute et usage des prophéties par les prélats pendant le Grand Schisme d'Occident," *Mélanges de l'Ecole française de Rome, Moyen Âge* 102 (1990): 438–441.

71. Noël Valois, "Jeanne d'Arc et la prophétie de Marie Robine," in *Mélanges Paul Fabre* (Geneva, 1902), 465–466.

72. For a full discussion of the three visionaries treated here, see André Vauchez, "Jeanne d'Arc et le prophétisme féminin des XIVe et XVe siècles," in *Jeanne d'Arc: Une époque, un rayonnement* (Paris, 1982), 159–168.

73. For an English translation of one of these works, Jean Gerson's *De distinctione verarum revelationum a falsis* (c. 1402), see Brian Patrick McGuire, *Jean Gerson: Early Works* (New York, 1998), 334–364, 455–460.

74. *A Parisian Journal*, 253–254; Vauchez, "Jeanne d'Arc et le prophétisme féminin," 166.

75. She is mentioned in his *Formicarius* (Cologne, 1480 [reprint Graz, 1971]), 223 (bk. 5, chap. 8). Compare Pernoud and Clin, *Joan of Arc*, 234.

76. The best starting point here is Francis Rapp, "Jeanne d'Arc, témoin de la vie religieuse en France au XVe siècle," in *Jeanne d'Arc: Une époque, un rayonnement* (Paris, 1982), 169–179. See also the essays in Ann W. Astell and Bonnie Wheeler, eds., *Joan of Arc and Spirituality* (New York, 2003); in particular, on Joan's devotion to Mary, the article in that volume by Ann Astell, "The Virgin Mary and the 'Voices' of Joan of Arc," 37–60.

77. Adrien Harmand, *Jeanne d'Arc, ses costumes, son armure: Essai de re-constitution* (Paris, 1929), 14; Duparc, *Procès en nullité*, 1:476–477.

78. For contemporary references and in general on Joan's clothing, see Harmand, *Jeanne d'Arc, ses costumes, son armure*, 9–19, esp. 15–17.

79. Kelly DeVries, "A Woman as Leader of Men: Joan of Arc's Military Career," in *Fresh Verdicts on Joan of Arc*, 9.

80. Quicherat, *Procès de condamnation*, 5:150–153.

81. See, for example, the reference to "the hardness of her heart and the tone *[modis]* of her answers" at the end of the interrogation on May 9.

82. The phrase is from the subtitle of Marina Warner's book *Joan of Arc: The Image of Female Heroism* (New York, 1981).

83. See Van Engen, "Church in the Fifteenth Century," 309–323.

PREPARATORY TRIAL

1. The formal title of the Dominican order.

2. Heb. 12:2.

3. Joan was captured at Compiègne by Guillaume Vandonne, a vassal of Luxembourg. Vandonne delivered her to Luxembourg, who took Joan to his castle at Beaulieu, and from there to Beaurevoir.

4. Henry VI. The claim of the kings of England to rule France was a root cause of the Hundred Years' War.

5. The vacancy of the archbishopric of Rouen lasted from December 8, 1429, to April 12, 1432. *Fasti ecclesiae gallicanae* (Turnhout, Belgium, 1996–) 2:121–123.

6. Indictions were fifteen-year cycles, instituted by Constantine and used

to count the years starting from AD 312–13. The "ninth indiction" means the ninth year in the present indiction.

7. The bachelor of theology is the equivalent of the licentiate of canon law or medicine. In either case, the individual might or might not go on to become a doctor. The Latin text of the trial includes the names of the "assessors" who attended each session and advised the judges on questions of law, doctrine, and procedure. For further information on these individuals, see the sources listed in "Major Participants in the Trial," preceding the Notes.

8. The promoter fulfilled the office of prosecutor against the defendant.

9. The names of the scribes who copied the letter.

10. Guillaume Vandonne, a vassal of Philip, duke of Burgundy.

11. The previous letter does not contain five readily distinguishable articles.

12. The rector of the University of Paris at the time was Thomas de Courcelles. The rector was the chief representative of the university, one of whose functions was to execute university decrees, as here.

13. This letter and the following letters appointing the notaries, the counselor, and the executor are dated from the house of one Jean Rubé, canon of Rouen Cathedral. Several meetings of the judges and assessors took place there.

14. In the house of Jean Rubé.

15. In this gesture, the person taking the oath put his clasped hands between the hands of the one accepting the oath, as in the ceremony of homage.

16. Cauchon is questioning Joan here.

17. *Joan swore*   French text: "she swore to tell the truth about everything to be asked of her concerning matters of faith, but she refused to tell anyone about her revelations."

18. Domrémy, situated in the Meuse Valley, lay in a region between the kingdom of France and the Holy Roman Empire.

19. Joan's father was a person of some distinction in Domrémy. He attended the sacring of Charles VII at Reims. Her mother was from the nearby town of Vouthon, part of the duchy of Bar, which belonged to the king of France.

20. A problematic passage, since in fact most of the assessors at the trial were French.

21. Neufchâteau was a town a short distance south of Domrémy, loyal to Charles VII. Joan went to Neufchâteau with her entire family.

22. *at her father's house*   French text and D'Estivet: "in this house she attended to household chores and did not go to the fields to watch the sheep

or other animals." In the French text and D'Estivet, this sentence thus refers (more plausibly) to the stay of Joan at Neufchâteau.

23. *and the voice came around noon*   French text: "And the voice came at noon in the summer, while she was in her father's garden, on a fast day."

24. *that her father knew*   D'Estivet has, instead, "that her father must know nothing of her departure." This translation of D'Estivet seems to fit better with the sense of the passage.

25. Robert de Baudricourt (d. 1454), knight and captain of Vaucouleurs, was loyal to Charles VII.

26. Durand Laxart, actually the husband of her first cousin. He led Joan to Robert de Baudricourt and was present at the sacring at Reims.

27. Charles II, duke of Lorraine (1365–1431), formerly a Burgundian supporter and considered to be completely self-interested. Joan went to the duke's residence at Nancy before leaving for Chinon.

28. The cathedral of Auxerre.

29. The French text and D'Estivet omit "with the one mentioned above."

30. Charles, duke of Orléans (1394–1465): the assassination of Charles's father, Louis, by agents of John the Fearless on November 23, 1407, led to civil war. Charles was captured at Agincourt in 1415 and taken to England, where he remained until 1440. He made a name as one of the greatest French poets of the fifteenth century. Joan later expressed a desire to liberate the duke.

31. This statement ("as recorded . . . Rouen") is probably a gloss inserted by the translator, not part of the original French minute.

32. The text of this letter constitutes Article 22 in the testimony of March 27.

33. The date was March 4.

34. Charles of Bourbon (1401–1456), count of Clermont, was duke of Bourbon in 1434. He led an army to Orléans and participated in the military campaign that followed the lifting of the siege.

35. Joan was at Saint-Denis near Paris in late August and early September 1429.

36. This occurred on September 8.

37. *adding that all the clergy*   French text: "and I think that all the clergy of Rouen and Paris wouldn't know how to compel me, save in error."

38. D'Estivet also adds this text.

39. D'Estivet: "She does not know whether or not she should tell all the things that have been revealed to her." This passage is missing from the French minute.

40. *she said that the light comes*   French text: "she said that the light comes before the voice." The French text seems preferable here.

41. This response echoes contemporary prayers, though Joan's reworking is more forceful. See Pierre Tisset, *Procès de condamnation de Jeanne d'Arc* (Paris, 1960–1971), 2:63 n. 63.

42. *when the first voice*   French text: "when the voice first came to her."

43. No such answer is recorded.

44. D'Estivet adds, "and she herself drank from it." The French text omits this clause.

45. Probably a construction of flowers assembled in May to mark the beginning of summer.

46. St. Catherine of Alexandria, according to tradition, was martyred in the fourth century. She was a popular saint in France during the Middle Ages and the patroness of young women. St. Margaret of Antioch is supposed to have been martyred under Diocletian. She is invoked by women in childbirth. The parish church of Domrémy has a statue of St. Margaret that may have existed in Joan's day.

47. Joan was examined at Chinon and at Poitiers in March 1429 by theologians and canon lawyers sympathetic to Charles VII. The record of the Poitiers examination is lost. A short document circulated by Charles VII and expressing a favorable opinion on Joan does survive: see Appendix.

48. D'Estivet has "daily," rather than "always."

49. *she had received comfort*   French text: "she had received counsel from Saint Michael." St. Michael the archangel was popular in the Lorraine region where Joan lived, and Charles VII saw St. Michael as the protector of the kingdom.

50. A variant in two of the Latin manuscripts might be translated as a more pungent reply: "She further told the interrogator that he was not the only one to receive light."

51. According to one chronicler, this town surrendered to Joan in June 1429.

52. The brothers are Jean and Pierre d'Arc. Jean accompanied Joan to Chinon, and both Jean and Pierre fought at Orléans. Ecus were French gold coins issued from 1388 to 1475.

53. The essential study on Joan's clothing, armor, and banners, with drawings, is Adrien Harmand, *Jeanne d'Arc, ses costumes, son armure: Essai de reconstitution* (Paris, 1929); on her banner, see 284–309.

54. The fortress at the bridge was Tourelles, which was south of the Loire. The fortress of Saint-Loup lay to the east on the opposite bank, facing the

island of Saint-Loup. See the map of Orléans in Régine Pernoud and Marie-Véronique Clin, *Joan of Arc: Her Story*, trans. and rev. Jeremy duQuesnay Adams (New York, 1998), 278–279. The number of men the king actually provided is disputed (one historian suggested instead 3,500), but the number Joan gives continues to be cited in the literature. See, most recently, Kelly DeVries, *Joan of Arc: A Military Leader* (Stroud, England, 1999), 53.

55. Sir Henry Biset, who was killed in the fighting. The successful attack on Jargeau took place on June 11–12, 1429.

56. Jean IV of Armagnac. Martin V, chosen pope at the Council of Constance in 1417, was almost universally accepted as pope at this time. But the Avignonese pope Benedict XIII had defied the Council and moved to Peñiscola in Spain, where he died in 1424. He had two successors, Clement VIII and Benedict XIV, each claiming to be the one true successor. Jean IV adhered to the Avignon line of popes because of his loyalty to the king of Castille, and was excommunicated as a result in March 1429. See Tisset, *Procès*, 3:115–117.

57. Presumably this sentence was added by the translator, Thomas de Courcelles.

58. John of Lancaster (1389–1435), duke of Bedford, regent of France after the death of Henry V on August 31, 1422. He married Anne of Burgundy, Philip's sister.

59. The feast of St. John the Baptist is June 24.

60. Martinmas is celebrated November 11.

61. This statement suggests that Cauchon is not the one questioning Joan here.

62. A plant thought to have magical properties because its root was shaped like a man.

63. Where the Burgundians delivered Joan to the English in November 1430.

64. Used to weigh souls, a part of the iconography of St. Michael.

65. The French text, which is slightly different here, says that Jean Beaupère is questioning Joan, by order of Pierre Cauchon.

66. This earlier testimony was apparently omitted.

67. *natural heads*   French text: "heads naturally" *(testes naturellement)*; D'Estivet: "material heads."

68. *in the same manner and shape*   French text: "with the same heads," repeating the idea from the previous paragraph. This difference appears in the following paragraph as well.

69. Marie of Anjou (1404–1463), wife of Charles VII.

70. The chronology here has not been clearly established. Joan was there either from June to September or from August to November 1430.

71. D'Estivet also adds this text. Jeanne de Luxembourg (d. October or November 1430), very old by this time, was a godmother and supporter of Charles VII. Her niece-in-law was Jeanne de Béthune (d. 1459), whose second husband (1418) was Jean de Luxembourg, lord of Beaurevoir.

72. Joan was taken to Arras in late September or November 1430.

73. Brother Richard was a popular Franciscan preacher who had run into trouble for preaching about the Antichrist. He stood near Joan at the sacring at Reims and initially supported her, but they had a falling out over Catherine de la Rochelle. Joan entered Troyes on July 10, 1429.

74. *at Arras*   French text: "at Reims." No portrait survives. On contemporary images of Joan, see Pernoud and Clin, *Joan of Arc*, 240–243.

75. While in Orléans from April 29 to May 8, Joan stayed with the treasurer of the duke of Orléans, Jacques Boucher. His daughter Charlotte shared her bed with Joan.

76. Texts of prayers for Joan have survived. See the references in Tisset, *Procès*, 2:95–96 n. 3.

77. *helped them to bear*   French text and D'Estivet: "helped them as best she could."

78. *does not recall whether he saw*   French text: "does not recall whether she saw him at her entrance."

79. July 10–12, 1429.

80. *five or six days*   French text: "four or five days." (July 16–21, 1429.)

81. Late July 1429. This incident has never been satisfactorily explained.

82. The implication is that Joan was finding lost articles through sorcery. The gift of gloves was traditional ceremonial practice.

83. Gold coins struck in France during the reign of Henry VI. The bishop of Senlis, Jean Fouquerel, was a supporter of the English.

84. *Asked how old the boy*   French text: "Asked how old the child was whom she visited at Lagny." Joan spent several weeks in Lagny in March 1430, before going to Compiègne.

85. *that she had caused*   French text: "that she had brought this about."

86. Catherine de la Rochelle was a visionary of some reputation, attached to Brother Richard. She met Joan in November or December 1429.

87. *She wrote to her king telling him*   French text: "She wrote to her king that she would tell him what should be done about it"; D'Estivet: "She wrote to her king that she would tell him what should be done about Catherine."

88. La Charité, besieged unsuccessfully by Joan in November 1429, was in Burgundian territory rather than in the kingdom of France.

89. The captain was Guichard Bournel, who in May 1430 refused entrance to Joan's army and in July delivered Soissons to the English.

90. Joan left Crépy for Compiègne at midnight on the night of May 22, 1430.

91. That is, May 23 in the early evening.

92. Easter in 1430 was April 16.

93. See further on this episode Pernoud and Clin, *Joan of Arc,* 231–233.

94. Charles VII ennobled Joan and her family in a letter of December 1429, but this letter says nothing about a coat of arms.

95. *Asked what sign*   French text and D'Estivet: "Asked what the sign is that came to her king."

96. The archbishop of Reims, Regnault of Chartres (1380–1445), was present at the interview at Chinon between Joan and Charles VII, and he performed the sacring at Reims. He criticized Joan after her capture for her pride and vanity. Georges de la Trémoille (c. 1385–1446), one of Charles VII's most powerful ministers, opposed Joan vigorously at court. Jean, duke of Alençon (d. 1476) spent much time in Joan's company up to the siege of Paris, and spoke fondly of Joan at the nullification trial.

97. See "Ordinary Trial," the ninth article of March 27–28.

98. One of the Ten Commandments (Exod. 20:12).

99. *Questioned . . . she should tell*   French text: "Questioned whether she had asked her voices to tell her father and mother of her leaving."

100. Easter in 1429 was March 27.

101. D'Estivet also adds this text.

102. D'Estivet also adds this text.

103. D'Estivet also adds this text.

104. Presumably the underlying accusation is that Joan used sorcery to discover things.

105. A town under Burgundian control, at the focus of fighting in May 1430.

106. September 8, 1429.

107. *to Jesus*   French text: "in the name of Jesus." I agree with Tisset that the Latin text appears correct, since the rest of the sentence indicates that the question is *to whom* the town will be surrendered.

108. *that sometimes Saint Catherine answers*   French text: "that Saint Catherine answers at once."

109. Joan's response does not directly answer the question, and text appears to be missing here.

110. In the French text the last two paragraphs appear in reverse order.

111. *whom she had put to death at Lagny*   French text: "who was executed at Lagny." D'Estivet has "who was put to death at Lagny." Franquet d'Arras was a captain of irregular soldiers and a supporter of the Burgundian cause. He was defeated by Joan in May 1430 and put to death.

112. Jacquet Guillaume, executed after taking part in a plot against the Burgundians in April 1430.

113. Joan was taken to Beaulieu-les-Fontaines, a castle of Jean de Luxembourg, shortly after her capture. This was her first attempted escape, before that of Beaurevoir. She squeezed through two planks in the floor of her cell, but she was caught before she could escape.

114. "Aide toy, Dieu te aidera."

115. *Asked again whether she would . . . Mass*   French text and D'Estivet: "Asked to take women's clothing once and for all to go hear Mass."

116. *Asked how she knew they were angels*   French text and D'Estivet: "Asked how she knew it was the speech of angels."

117. That is, the trial register.

118. The Latin and French texts present problems here that have never been satisfactorily explained. But see Tisset, *Procès,* 2:137 n. 2.

119. *son of Charles, king of France, who was*   French text: "son of Charles, king of France, who will be king of France." And yet Joan always referred to Charles as king during the trial. Neither the Latin nor the French text is satisfying. Compare Tisset, *Procès,* 2:138 n. 1.

120. D'Estivet also adds this text.

121. This question refers to the assassination of John the Fearless during a meeting at Montereau with the future Charles VII on September 10, 1419. For details, see Richard Famiglietti, *Royal Intrigue: Crisis at the Court of Charles VI, 1392–1420* (New York, 1986), 191–192.

122. The French text does not supply the answer to this question

123. Literally, "more than the banners of other captains."

124. No request of Joan to hear Mass is mentioned in the testimony of Saturday, March 24.

Ordinary Trial

1. On this term, see the Introduction.

2. The Latin word for "written accusation" is *libellus*—hence the *libellus* d'Estivet, consisting of the preliminary statement, followed by the articles of accusation.

3. For an explanation of this oath, see *Dictionary of the Middle Ages, Supplement 1* (2004), 84–85.

4. Probably books of canon law.

5. *Then, at our command*   French text: "Then, at the command of the reverend judges, Master Thomas de Courcelles began to expound the contents of the book or articles."

6. The lengthy accusation that follows is the so-called *libellus* (register) d'Estivet. While the date given in brackets is not supplied in the manuscripts, it is clear from internal evidence of the text that the first thirty articles were read to Joan on Tuesday and the rest on Wednesday.

7. The article from the creed of the Mass "I believe in one holy catholic and apostolic Church."

8. The closing sentences of this speech include standard formulas found in other trials. See Pierre Tisset, *Procès de condamnation de Jeanne d'Arc* (Paris, 1960–1971), 2:160 n. 1.

9. The summaries in this section take the place of repeated passages in the Latin. In these instances, testimony from preceding days in Joan's trial was introduced verbatim into the record, at Cauchon's request, to supply the basis for each article in Joan's testimony. Readers can refer to the dates in question to read the complete text. It should be observed that some of the accusations in these articles have no clear basis in earlier testimony. Presumably, in those cases the article is based on information gathered about Joan.

10. Joan must have been closer to sixteen at this time (1428).

11. On Joan's clothing, with numerous drawings, see Harmand, *Jeanne d'Arc, ses costumes, son armure: Essai de reconstitution* (Paris, 1929).

12. This statement does not appear in the testimony of February 22.

13. Here the French minute shows four questions. Two of them are included under Article 14, as in the Latin text. The other two appear here in angle brackets.

14. William de la Pole, count of Suffolk (1396–1450), commander of troops at Orléans.

15. John Talbot, earl of Shrewsbury (c. 1373–1453), was considered a model soldier; he was captured at the Battle of Patay, June 18, 1429. Thomas Scales (c. 1399–1460), who led the siege of Orléans with Talbot and Pole, was also imprisoned at Patay.

16. In her testimony in the second session of February 22, Joan said that this should read "to the king."

17. On February 22, Joan also denied including the words "a captain of war" in the original letter.

18. *one and all*   The original French has *corps pour corps*—literally, "body for body"—the last phrase that Joan denied including on February 22.

19. *a greater uproar* French text: *hahay* (a war cry).

20. March 22, 1429.

21. Prov. 24:16.

22. That is, the suggestion of Joan's pride and vanity.

23. Jean d'Estivet must have added the testimony from March 31 and April 18 later.

24. Matt. 7:16.

25. Eccl. 9:1.

26. By "files," they mean tools she could use to escape from prison.

27. "Contingent" here means "able to be or not to be." The notion of "future contingents" was an important topic of theological discussion in the medieval universities. If no future events are contingent, then there is no place for free will in human affairs. Joan's examiners are implying that her claims deny contingency and hence free will.

28. Martin V had died on February 20, 1431, but the news had not yet reached Rouen.

29. These are the prologue and the twelve articles delivered on April 5.

30. Guillaume de Livet, Pierre Carrel, Guérould Poustel, Geoffroi du Crotay, Richard des Saulx, Bureau de Cormeilles, Jean le Doux, Laurent du Busc, Jean Colombel, Raoul Anguy, and Jean le Tavernier.

31. The French text (a much shorter version here) says only that Joan may choose from among those present.

32. Matt. 18:15, 17. The full text of Matthew 18:15–17 reads: "But if your brother offends you, go and rebuke him between you and him alone. If he hears you, you have gained your brother. If he will not hear you, take one or two others along with you, so that every word may stand in the mouth of two or three witnesses. And if he will not hear them, tell the church. And if he will not hear the church, treat him as a gentile and tax collector."

33. Tisset (*Procès*, 2:288 n. 4) remarks on the gravity of this session, where sixty-three persons were assembled, including nine priests of Rouen who appear at no other session.

34. This sentence logically follows the first sentence in this paragraph, describing the homily of Jean de Châtillon.

35. Deut. 22:5.

36. 1 Cor. 11:5–15.

37. Though not a general council, the Council of Gangra (Cankiri) in the

mid-fourth century did publish decrees against cross-dressing that found their way into Gratian's *Decretum*.

38. "By those who joined our party afterward" seems to refer to supporters of Charles VII who had switched allegiance to the Anglo-Burgundian party around the time of Joan's capture.

39. Compare 2 Cor. 11:14: "For Satan himself is transformed into an angel of light."

40. *After the archdeacon* French text: "Then she was told: 'You said earlier that your deeds were seen and cross-examined, as contained in the schedule.' She said her answer is the same now." The French text does not include the admonition of Jean de Châtillon.

41. Jean de la Brosse (d. 1433), marshal of France, led the French army to Orléans.

42. Etienne de Vignolles (d. 1443), or La Hire, was an important military leader and supporter of Charles VII. He entered Orléans with Joan and accompanied Joan and Charles VII to Reims.

43. *three or four clerks* French text: "three or four knights." The Latin text seems preferable.

44. The Council of Basel (1431–1449), which was just convening.

45. May 3, the feast of the Invention of the Cross.

46. The abbot of Mortemer was not Guillaume but Nicolas de Hautmont. On this mistake, see Jean Fraikin, "La date de la rédaction latine du procès de Jeanne d'Arc," *Quaerendo* 3 (1973): 51–53.

47. Lev. 19:18; Matt. 5:43, 19:19, etc.

48. Compare 2 Cor. 11:13–15. The *Lives of the Fathers* is a collection of saints' lives compiled in the sixth century.

49. Luke 10:16.

50. The cemetery was in an enclosure at the south wall of the abbey church. A large cross stood in the middle.

51. The delivery of a sermon at the condemnation of heretics was recommended as standard procedure in the inquisition manuals.

52. Henry Beaufort (d. 1447), cardinal since 1426, chancellor of England, and great-uncle of Henry VI. He crowned Henry VI at Paris in December 1431. Though mentioned only at this session, he followed the trial closely throughout.

53. That is, Mont-Saint-Michel.

54. John 15:4.

55. According to numerous witnesses at the nullification trial, Joan's abjuration was only six to eight lines long, "as long as it takes to say the Our

Father," according to Pierre Miget. The text given here was probably substituted for Joan's actual abjuration, which according to another witness in 1456 contained a promise no longer to carry weapons or wear men's clothing, not to wear her hair cut short, and other things he could not remember. Yet the text probably contains the essential ingredients of Joan's actual abjuration, especially the rejection of her voices and submission to the Church. See the thorough discussion in Tisset, *Procès*, 3.134–143; for the claim by Doncoeur that the Orleans manuscript contains the actual words of Joan, see pp. 134–135 n. 2, and Doncoeur, *Procès en nullité*, 5.112–113.

56. 2 Pet. 2:1.

57. Ps. 16:2.

58. Compare 1 Tim. 1:5.

59. This sentence ("We told her . . . altogether") does not appear in the French text.

TRIAL FOR RELAPSE

1. 1 Cor. 12:26.

2. Prov. 26:11.

3. Delivering the relapsed heretic to the secular arm for punishment was firmly established from at least the early fourteenth century, and appears as standard procedure in the manuals of Bernard Gui and Nicolas Eymeric. See Pierre Tisset, *Procès de condamnation de Jeanne d'Arc* (Paris, 1960–1971), 3:159–162.

4. The first two paragraphs of the abjuration are the same as the abjuration of May 24; these are not reproduced here.

5. Ps. 16:2.

6. The other two manuscripts of the Latin text have 111 and 206 folios here. A "manual sign" was a notary's personal design that in addition to a signature offered a way to authenticate a document. The manual signs can be seen in Tisset, *Procès*, vol. 1, plates 2–4.

7. All three manuscripts bear traces of the original seals of the bishop and the vice-inquisitor.

AFTERMATH

1. A feast celebrating the institution of the Eucharist.

2. Literally, "things" (*res*).

3. Modern French would use *soient* here, where Middle French has the singular verb.

4. Yet the formal sentence pronounced later the same day stated that if Joan showed true signs of repentance, she could receive penance. This problem has not been resolved.

5. The emperor was Sigismund. Henry VI's biographer suggests that this letter and the following were probably composed by John, duke of Bedford. See R. A. Griffiths, *The Reign of King Henry VI* (Stroud, England, 1998), 220. The scriptural references, however, suggest a clerk's involvement.

6. 2 Tim. 4:4.

7. 1 John 4:1.

8. Luke 6:18.

9. See Luke 15:10 for the sinner; compare Gen. 29:7; John 10:11–16, for the sheep brought back to the fold.

10. Compare Prov. 26:11.

11. 1 John 4:1.

12. The copy of this letter that was sent to Philip, duke of Burgundy, was recopied into two chronicles, the *Chronique de Monstrelet* and the chronicle of Eberhard Windecke. See Germain Lefèvre-Pontalis, *Les sources allemandes de l'histoire de Jeanne d'Arc: Eberhard Windecke* (Paris, 1903), 132–134.

APPENDIX

1. The most recent discussion of this text (with translation) is Deborah Fraioli, *Joan of Arc: The Early Debate* (Woodbridge, England, 2000), 45–54. But see the arguments of Roger G. Little, *The Parlement of Poitiers: War, Government and Politics in France, 1418–1436* (London, 1984), 108–113. Little argues that the text is best viewed "not as a *résumé* of the conclusions reached by theologians, but as a form of broad political justification for the Maid's employment at Orléans" (112). The original text is in French, here translated from the edition in Quicherat, *Procès de condamnation et de réhabilitation de Jeanne d'Arc*, 3:391–392; see also 5:471–473.

2. 1 John 4:1.

3. Isa. 7:11.

4. Judg. 6:17 and following.

5. Acts 5:34–39.

Further Reading

The published literature on Joan of Arc is vast. This guide points to some of the recent literature in English. For a more complete bibliography of works published before 1990, see the annotated bibliography by Nadia Margolis, *Joan of Arc in History, Literature, and Film* (New York, 1990).

GENERAL WORKS ON JOAN

There is no standard critical biography of Joan of Arc. A trove of information on many different issues relating to Joan's life and to scholarship on Joan can be found in Régine Pernoud and Marie-Véronique Clin, *Joan of Arc: Her Story*, trans. and rev. Jeremy duQuesnay Adams (New York, 1998). The biographical section is patriotic in tone. The best parts in my view are part 2 (the cast of characters) and part 3, "Issues and Images," which provides a starting point for a variety of topics, scholarly and popular. The bibliographies are also quite useful. Other biographies include those by the novelist Mary Gordon, *Joan of Arc* (New York, 2000), which is short and readable, and Frances Gies, *Joan of Arc: The Legend and the Reality* (New York, 1981), which is thorough, though not scholarly. For a more theoretical approach, see Françoise Meltzer, *For Fear of the Fire: Joan of Arc and the Limits of Subjectivity* (Chicago, 2001). Authors writing in a pious tradition have produced a good deal on Joan. Among the more scholarly of these treatments is George H. Tavard, *The Spiritual Way of St. Jeanne d'Arc* (Collegeville, Minn., 1998). Several collections of essays provide access to recent scholarship on Joan in English, such as Bonnie Wheeler and

Charles T. Wood, eds., *Fresh Verdicts on Joan of Arc* (New York and London, 1996), and Ann W. Astell and Bonnie Wheeler, eds., *Joan of Arc and Spirituality* (New York, 2003).

WORKS ON THE TRIAL OF JOAN

A careful recent study is Karen Sullivan, *The Interrogation of Joan of Arc* (Minneapolis, Minn., 1999). With regard to trial procedure, Henry Ansgar Kelly has argued in several articles that the trial judges failed to try Joan according to canonical procedure. See Kelly, *Inquisitions and Other Trial Procedures in the Medieval West* (Aldershot, England, 2001).

WORKS ON JOAN'S MILITARY CAMPAIGNS

Kelly Devries, *Joan of Arc: A Military Leader* (Stroud, England, 1999), fills a void in the scholarship on this issue and provides bibliography, plates, and maps. See also Jane Marie Pinzino, "Just War, Joan of Arc, and the Politics of Salvation," in *The Hundred Years War: A Wider Focus*, ed. L. J. Andrew Villalon and Donald J. Kagay (Leiden, 2005), 365–396.

WORKS ON THE RECEPTION OF JOAN

The best wide-ranging approach here remains Marina Warner, *Joan of Arc: The Image of Female Heroism* (New York, 1981). A work focusing on treatments of Joan during her lifetime is Deborah Fraioli, *Joan of Arc: The Early Debate* (Woodbridge, England, 2000). Ann W. Astell, *Joan of Arc and Sacrificial Authorship* (Notre Dame, Ind., 2003), treats Joan's reception in modern literature. For a collection of six essays on various aspects of Joan's reception, including modern cinema, see Dominique Goy-Blanquet, ed., *Joan of Arc, a Saint for All Reasons: Studies in Myth and Politics* (Burlington, Vt., 2003). On Joan in cinema, see also Robert Rosenstone, "The Reel Joan of Arc," *Public Historian* 25, no. 3 (2003): 61–77, which clarifies the issues wonderfully; and the relevant chapter in John Aberth, *A Knight at the Movies: Medieval History on Film* (New York, 2003), esp. 313–314, with references to much more bibliography on the films.

Index

Ecrivain, Roland l', 77

Emengart, Erard, 56, 63, 70, 77, 115, 119, 121, 123, 162, 169, 181, 198

English, the (people or army), 61, 72–73, 74, 84, 100, 110–111, 132, 133, 135, 139, 140, 142, 143, 161, 209

Erard, Guillaume, 77, 178, 179, 180, 184, 190, 191, 198

Escape of Joan: from Rouen, 36, 51, 60, 75, 78, 101–102, 105, 116, 139, 151; from Beaulieu castle, 105, 138. *See also* Beaurevoir

Estivet, Jean d', 4, 10, 35, 41, 43, 47, 48, 94–95, 116, 117, 119, 222

Estouteville, Guillaume, 7

Eucharist. *See* Mass

Eude, Jean, 169

Ex officio. See under Legal procedure

Fabrications, Joan's alleged, 135, 163, 174, 184–185, 186

Faculty of canon law, 181, 183, 194

Faculty of theology, 181, 183, 194

Fairies, 62, 110, 114, 126, 127, 157

Fano, Jean de, 63

Fasting, by Joan, 53, 64

Feuillet, Gérard, 43, 44, 45, 46, 51, 57, 63, 70, 77, 86, 91, 93, 94, 99, 102, 104, 108, 111, 114, 115, 116, 118, 119, 122, 123, 155, 162, 166

Fèvre, Jean le, 46, 51, 57, 63, 70, 115, 119, 121, 123, 162, 169, 181, 191, 198

Fiefvet, Thomas, 89, 91, 93

Flosquet, Julien, 196

Fontaine, Jean de la, 4, 35, 42, 43, 44, 47, 52, 57, 63, 70, 86, 91, 93, 94, 99, 102, 104, 108, 111, 115, 116, 118, 119, 120, 123, 222

Fortune-telling, Joan's, 110, 150

Fouchier, Jean, 169, 181, 191

Fountain, 126, 157; Counselors of the, 149, 157

Fouquerel, Jean, 82, 103

Fournier, Jacques, 15, 17

Foville, Nicolas de, 57

French minute. *See under* Trial text

Frique, Thomas, 190

Gabriel, Saint, 73, 78, 112, 145, 147, 151, 157, 161, 179

Gagneux, Richard le, 57

Gastinel, Denis, 47, 52, 57, 63, 70, 119, 122, 123, 164, 169, 179, 180, 181, 198, 199, 200

Gerson, Jean, 3, 230n73

Gilles de Rais, 1–2

Gratian, 14

Graverent, Jean, 3, 33, 44, 46, 90, 222

Great Schism, 29

Grey, John, 51, 73, 95, 111, 139, 155, 196

Grouchet, Richard de, 47, 51, 63, 70, 77, 166, 169, 181, 191, 198

Guérin, Jean, 46, 51, 57, 63, 70, 119, 120, 123, 165, 169, 181, 191, 198

Guesdon, Jacques, 46, 51, 57, 63, 70, 115, 119, 122, 123, 165, 169, 181, 198

Gui, Bernard, 15, 17

Guillaume, Bastard of Vandonne, 37

Guillaume, Jacquet (tavern owner), 237

Hair, Joan's, 129, 130, 159, 173, 183, 185, 192, 195

Haiton, Guillaume, 42, 43, 44, 47, 51, 57, 63, 70, 115, 119, 123, 155, 162, 166, 169, 178, 180, 181, 191, 196, 198, 200

Hampton, John, 119, 123

Hautmont, Nicolas de, 162, 180, 190, 198, 240n46

Henry V (king of England), 3